Philosophy and Art in Southeast Asia

Philosophy and Art in Southeast Asia

A Novel Approach to Aesthetics

Melvin Chen

BLOOMSBURY ACADEMIC
LONDON · NEW YORK · OXFORD · NEW DELHI · SYDNEY

BLOOMSBURY ACADEMIC
Bloomsbury Publishing Plc
50 Bedford Square, London, WC1B 3DP, UK
1385 Broadway, New York, NY 10018, USA
29 Earlsfort Terrace, Dublin 2, Ireland

BLOOMSBURY, BLOOMSBURY ACADEMIC and the Diana logo are trademarks
of Bloomsbury Publishing Plc

First published in Great Britain 2024

A catalogue record for this book is available from the British Library.

A catalog record for this book is available from the Library of Congress.

ISBN: HB: 978-1-3504-1416-7
       PB: 978-1-3504-1417-4
       ePDF: 978-1-3504-1418-1
       eBook: 978-1-3504-1419-8

Typeset by RefineCatch Limited, Bungay, Suffolk
Printed and bound in Great Britain

To find out more about our authors and books visit www.bloomsbury.com
and sign up for our newsletters.

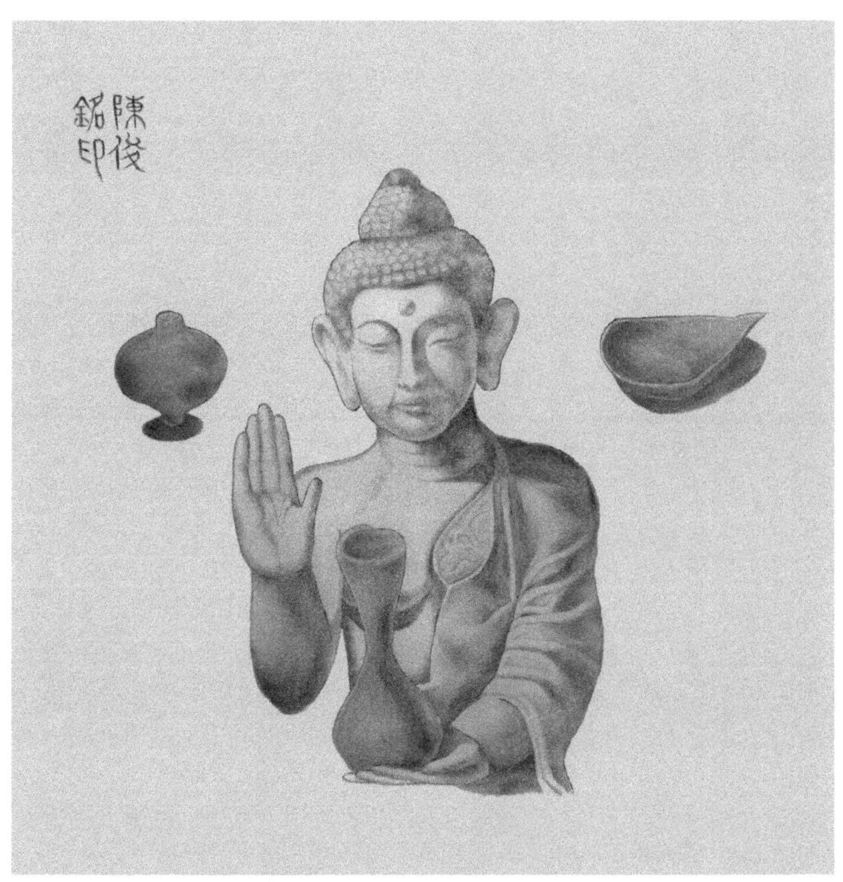

Melvin Chen's (2024) *Samatha*. Tinted charcoal, graphite, and ink on paper. Image courtesy of the author.

Contents

Figures

Tables

Acknowledgements

This textbook on a Southeast Asian philosophical perspective on art would not have been possible without two of the most cherished and important people in my life: Barbora and Henrik. Thank you both for having been a constant source of love, joy, inspiration, encouragement, support and renewal. My gratitude and appreciation naturally extend to my parents, whose patience, wisdom and guidance inform virtually every aspect of this intellectual undertaking and the various decisions over the course of my life that have led me to the path of academia. I recall the very first Superman drawing by my father, whose graphic abilities inspired me in my training as an artist. My artistic background has in turn been an invaluable point of reference for my aesthetic deliberations. I must thank my academic colleagues and fellow philosophers for their professional advice and ever-generous store of good humour and camaraderie. Roger Nelson's (2019) *Modern Art of Southeast Asia* has been a veritable treasure chest of information and I am equally fortunate to count Roger as a colleague. In addition, special acknowledgement must go to Mookie Katigbak-Lacuesta (Philippines), Arahmaiani Feisal (Indonesia), Melati Suryodarmo (Indonesia), Phaptawan Suwannakudt (Thailand), Dinh Q. Lê (Vietnam and the United States), Sonny Liew (Singapore), Edwin Thumboo (Singapore), Yeo Siak Goon (Singapore), Ho Tzu Nyen (Singapore), Hee Suhui (Singapore) and Catherine Coe (University of North Carolina-Chapel Hill, United States) for having generously granted me permission to reproduce their works in full and without payment. Thumboo's 'After the leaving' first appeared in *Focus 1983: 21st Commemorative Issue* (published by the NUS Literary Society), before featuring in Thumboo's (1993) *A Third Map*.

I am equally grateful to Arabelle Zhuang (National Gallery Singapore), Felinda Leow (Epigram Books), Ella Liao (Edouard Malingue Gallery), Taufik Sulaiman (Sulaiman Esa Art Space), Hannah Klakeg (Shoshana Wayne Gallery), John Paul T. Orallo (BSP Museum), Cecille T. Gelicame (BSP Museum), Gretchen J. Flores (BSP Museum) and National Heritage Board, Singapore for having permitted me to reproduce high-resolution versions of various images that have been used in this book. It would also be remiss of me to omit mention of Sarena Abdullah (Universiti Sains Malaysia), Sukontip Nakasem (Warin Lab), Sandra Ross (St Joseph's Church), Adrian Tee (Pixelmusica Pte Ltd), Monica Park (Brooklyn Museum), Ella Zheng (Singapore),Victoria Huang (Christie's Singapore), Elena Assini Thomson (Addicted Art Gallery), Katie Kujala (Harvard Art Museums) and Anne Maxwell (University of Melbourne), all of whom helped to point me in the right direction when seeking permission for reproducing images. Last but not least, I would like to express my indebtedness and profound gratitude to my home country of Singapore, warts and all. Few would have imagined an entire textbook on aesthetics and the philosophy of art emerging from its shores, much less one teeming with delightful examples from the broader Southeast Asian region of which Singapore is an integral part. In some sense, this work functions as both an introduction to aesthetics and the philosophy of art and a celebration of the cultural context within which the very conditions for its possibility are firmly embedded.

Introduction

What is aesthetics? At a first pass, aesthetics is a branch of philosophy that is concerned with the nature of art and aesthetic experience. Given the synonymity between 'aesthetics' and 'art', it may be difficult to escape a sense of definitional circularity. At the same time, it remains debatable whether an authoritative and non-circular definition of aesthetics can ultimately be furnished. At least some philosophers maintain that any attempt to identify the necessary and sufficient conditions for the application of the concept of art will inevitably come to grief, especially given what we understand about the entire enterprise of art (viz. its sense of adventure, boldness, creativity, open-endedness, possibility, etc.). Whatever the case might be, we will still be within our philosophical means to explore the nature of truth, meaning, knowledge, taste, aesthetic merit, aesthetic judgement, the role of perception and conception in art, creativity and the possibility of machine art, and morality and the possibility of immoral art in the context of art.

Would works of art count as valuable in virtue of their satisfying the requisite artistic constraints? In what sense might artworks be considered dangerous? Why might Socrates recommend the banishment of the poets? How might suitably virtuous members of the audience resist artworks that might pose certain moral dangers? What are some plausible modes of aesthetic knowledge? How might our aesthetic preferences be justified with respect to certain established norms and practices of evaluation? What is the nature of aesthetic judgement? What is it in virtue of which certain entities get categorized as works of art? What are the problems and challenges posed by forgery? How might the phenomenon of conceptual art extend our understanding of art? Given the importance of creativity of thought or action in the artistic context, how might we make sense of creativity? In addition, how might examples of machine art lead to interesting philosophical issues about what constitutes real creativity and what implications might they have for our understanding of the nature of art, artworks and the artistic process?

How do we resolve ambiguity when interpreting and making sense of works of art? Where might the locus of authority be located in interpretation? Last but not least, what is the nature of the relationship (or lack thereof) between art and morality? Can there be such a thing as immoral art?

I have offered a sample of the central questions with which this textbook on aesthetics and the philosophy of art, deliberately infused with Southeast Asia-themed examples and references, will be concerned. The textbook has been specifically designed to address a number of issues. In the first instance, aesthetics and the philosophy of art constitute a relatively understudied domain in philosophy. The *Stanford Encyclopedia of Philosophy* or SEP (available at https://plato.stanford.edu/) is the premier reference work in philosophy, covering a comprehensive range of philosophical topics and concerns. Visualizing SEP (available at https://www.visualizingsep.com/ and optimized for Chrome) is a visualization of the SEP that has been created by Joseph DiCastro, a data engineer and developer. Relative to Table 0.1, it may be observed that the total number of domain-specific articles for aesthetics and the philosophy of art pales in comparison to the total number of domain-specific articles for the other philosophical branches of logic, metaphysics, epistemology and ethics.

In the second instance, where philosophical investigation has been conducted in the relatively understudied domain of aesthetics and the philosophy of art, the prevailing tendency has been to invoke examples and references from Western art in support of various claims and assertions. This is no more evident than in certain *loci classici* in aesthetics and the philosophy of art, when works of art from the Western canon offer justificatory support at critical philosophical junctures. Plato (1925) cites Homeric poetry when developing the art-as-inspiration account of art in the Platonic dialogue *Ion*, Walton (1970) uses Pablo Picasso's *Guernica* to construct a thought

Table 0.1 Number of domain-specific articles for each philosophical branch. The figures have been taken from the Visualizing SEP resource and are accurate as of 9 March 2023. © Melvin Chen

Philosophical branch	Number of domain-specific articles
Metaphysics	243
Logic	223
Epistemology	155
Ethics	237
Aesthetics and philosophy of art	64

experiment that allows for a conceptual distinction to be made between standard and variable features relative to categories of art, and Nelson Goodman (1968) relies on Rembrandt's *Lucretia* to construct a thought experiment involving an original painting and its perfect fake. This textbook functions as a timely corrective: its thematization of aesthetic concerns is intended to redirect philosophical attention to an oft-neglected and understudied domain, while its deliberate and regular use of examples and references from Southeast Asian art serves to counteract the prevailing tendency to defer to the Western artistic canon when works of art are cited. Through this unique approach, I hope to raise the level of intellectual curiosity about and interest in both aesthetics and the philosophy of art and Southeast Asian art.

My textbook is influenced by the work of Sally Haslanger (2006, 2012) and her ameliorative approach. According to Haslanger, there are at least three ways to respond to a 'What is X?' question: conceptual, descriptive and ameliorative. According to the conceptual (internalist) approach, we rely on *a priori* methods such as introspection for an answer. According to the descriptive (externalist) approach, we are interested in the objective type (if any) that our usage of the term 'X' tracks. According to the ameliorative approach, the questions we should be asking include: what is the point of having this concept? Which concept would serve these purposes best? Whereas the conceptual and descriptive approaches aim to deliver our ordinary understanding or use of the concept, the ameliorative approach aims to reveal the concept that we should be using, given our purposes and goals in that inquiry (León, 2020). The latter is known as the target concept.

In the context of the question 'What is Taiwanese philosophy?', Liao (2021b) believes that the proper metaphilosophical response involves relying on Haslanger's distinction between conceptual and descriptive approaches (on the one hand) and the ameliorative approach (on the other). Our responses to the metaphilosophical and metaaesthetic questions 'What is Southeast Asian philosophy?' and 'What is Southeast Asian art?' may equally rely on Haslanger's distinction. Whereas the conceptual and descriptive approaches are discovery-oriented and take the concepts (e.g. philosophy, art) as they are, the ameliorative approach is engineering-oriented and makes concepts as we want them to be.

Conceptual engineering, properly construed, is the general process of improving our linguistic or conceptual repertoires. Haslanger's ameliorative approach is widely considered to be a paradigm case of conceptual engineering, given its development of surprising definitions (in terms of hierarchies of privilege and subordination) for 'man', 'woman', 'race', etc., in pursuit of social justice (Pinder, 2022). The general task associated with the ameliorative approach involves developing a suitably inclusive concept of X, thereby allowing us to avoid the inclusion problem (Jenkins, 2016). An ameliorative approach to the concept of woman invites feminists to consider the concept of woman that would be most useful in the fight against gender injustice. By analogy, an ameliorative approach to the concepts of philosophy and art paves the way for a revisionary analysis that is capable of avoiding both Eurocentrism and the marginalization or exclusion of voices and output (both philosophical and artistic) from the Southeast Asian region.

Since I am a Southeast Asian philosopher, residing in Southeast Asia and working in the Western philosophical tradition within which aesthetics and the philosophy of art remain understudied, you could say that I have a dog in both fights. Wherever possible, I have also tried to inflect my analytic aesthetics with certain ideas from philosophers connected to the Southeast Asian region: Pham Van Duc (Vietnamese Academy of Social Sciences), Emerita Quito (De La Salle University), Rolando Gripaldo (De La Salle University), Ferry Hidayat (Universitas Gadjah Mada), Tran van Doan (National Taiwan University), Soraj Hongladarom (Chulalongkorn University), Liao Shen-yi (ex-Nanyang-Technological-University), Bryan Van Norden (ex-Yale-NUS), Ben Blumson (National University of Singapore) and Neil Sinhababu (National University of Singapore). Furthermore, at least some of these philosophers (e.g. Liao, Sinhababu, Blumson) also work in analytic aesthetics. If the regional and tropical flavour is not entirely objectionable to your palate, then I hope that you will enjoy the philosophical odyssey that commences from Chapter 1.

1

Notes on Philosophical Method

1.1 Philosophy as a discipline

Before any odyssey is embarked on, the adventurer must first have a requisite understanding of the general lay of the land and be appropriately equipped with the relevant tools for the adventure. An understanding of the philosophical discipline within which we may locate the understudied domain of aesthetics and the philosophy of art and the standard philosophical method will be vital. The former will provide the general backdrop and the latter will function as a toolkit when we engage with various aesthetic concerns, questions and issues during this odyssey. In Chapter 2, we shall venture into the domain of Southeast Asian art, which will provide us with our supply of examples and references in support of various aesthetic claims and assertions.

What is *philosophy*? It has been famously asserted that philosophy is the attempt to understand how things in the broadest possible sense of the term hang together in the broadest possible sense of the term (Sellars, 1962). As illustrated in Figure 1.1, the four main branches of philosophy are metaphysics, epistemology, axiology and logic.

Logic is concerned with the laws and structure of thought, reasoning, inference and related notions (validity, proof, consistency, completeness, etc.). Metaphysics is concerned with the fundamental nature of reality (being, existence, identity and change, space and time, causality, mind and matter, etc.) and our understanding of it. Epistemology is concerned with the nature, origins, scope, methods and limits of knowledge. Axiology is concerned with the nature of criteria of values and value judgements.

Axiology – also known as value theory – encompasses ethics, moral philosophy, aesthetics, social philosophy, political philosophy, philosophy of

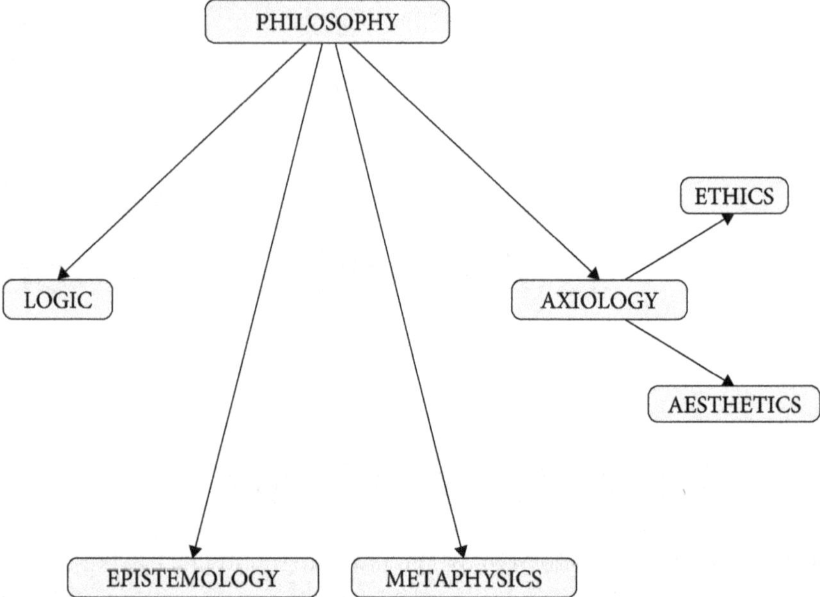

Figure 1.1 The branches of philosophy. © Melvin Chen (L^ATEX)

religion, and any other branch of philosophy that has at least some evaluative aspect. Our concerns about aesthetics are philosophical, insofar as aesthetics constitutes a branch of axiology. At the same time, at least some of these concerns might traverse the other main branches of philosophy such as epistemology (e.g. concerns about truth, knowledge and meaning with respect to works of art) and metaphysics (e.g. concerns about the identity conditions and ontological status of works of art).

1.2 The standard philosophical method

The standard method of philosophy, it is commonly held, involves analysis and delivers understanding. Analysis, in turn, refers (roughly) to the process of breaking up a concept, proposition, linguistic complex, or fact into its simple or ultimate constituents (Audi, 1999). Elements of the standard philosophical method include the use of strict, precise and clear language, a reliance on abstract definitions, rigorous conceptual analysis and the use of precise arguments.[1]

Philosophers typically rely on the medium of natural language to provide a reasoned defence of some position. This position may be constituted by either a claim or a set of claims. As claims are sentences in the declarative mode, asserting or affirming what someone might take to be the case, they may be represented propositionally. A proposition is a primary bearer of truth values (truth, falsity) and propositional attitudes (that which is believed, asserted, affirmed, etc.). Furthermore, arguments are a connected series of propositions, the first part of which (viz. the premise set) is intended to establish the second part (viz. the conclusion set). A philosopher who wishes to provide us with reasons to believe their claim or set of claims could therefore construct arguments that allow us to infer the claim or set of claims in question. Arguments are constructed within particular systems of logic (one of the four main branches of philosophy) and permit the use of formal language and logical analysis. To reiterate, the reliance on argumentation is stock-in-trade for the philosopher and an element of the standard philosophical method. Appendix A may be consulted for more detailed information about the use of formal language and notation in this textbook.

1.3 Scepticism about Asian philosophy

The standard method is traditionally associated with Western analytic philosophy and offers a set of prevailing Eurocentric norms for philosophy in general. These philosophical norms encourage the conception of philosophy as an exclusively Western product. Can Asian philosophy be legitimated according to these prevailing Eurocentric norms? Joseph Prabhu believes that the answer is a resounding 'yes'. If philosophy consists of systematic attempts to address fundamental questions about the nature of reality and the self (metaphysics), the nature and methods of knowledge (epistemology), the basis of moral and aesthetic values and judgements (axiology), etc., then there is much philosophy to be discovered in Indian, Chinese and Islamic thought, notwithstanding their different orientations (Prabhu, 2001, p. 30) The philosopher of science Massimo Pigliucci, on the other hand, begs to differ. In a blog discussion about whether we ought to take Asian philosophy seriously, Pigliucci (2006) first identifies several Zen *kōan* (公案) for consideration:[2]

What is the sound of one hand clapping?

What did your face look like before your ancestors were born?

Pigliucci's response to both *kōan* is that we should refrain from conflating pseudo-profundity with philosophy. The first *kōan* is nonsensical, since clapping requires two hands. The second *kōan* is equally nonsensical, since I must first exist before I can have a face and I did not exist before my ancestors were born. According to Pigliucci, philosophy is an activity of a particular kind: it is a form of inquiry into the nature of the world and the human condition. In addition, this inquiry involves the reasoned defence of a position using logical reasoning and empirical evidence.[3]

Pigliucci concludes that there is no such thing as Asian philosophy. Whatever it is and however useful it might be, Asian thought (e.g. in Buddhism, Taoism, Confucianism, etc.) is ultimately more akin to Jewish and Christian mystical writings than philosophy. If Pigliucci's argument holds and there can be no such thing as Asian philosophy, then it follows *a fortiori* that there cannot be such a thing as Southeast Asian philosophy either. Pigliucci's approach is implicated in what Kristie Dotson (2012) has memorably described as philosophy's culture of justification. This culture of justification privileges legitimation as a vetting process, where legitimation denotes practices and processes aimed at judging whether some belief, practice, or process conforms to accepted standards and patterns (i.e. justifying norms). Whereas questions of the form 'Is X really philosophy?' standardly crop up with non-canonical intellectual traditions, they standardly fail to do so with canonical ones (Liao, 2021b).

Bryan Van Norden responds to Pigliucci-style scepticism about the philosophical status of Asian thought by pointing out the wide-ranging use of arguments by Mohists, Mencius, Han Fei and Zongmi in defence of certain claims and the modern engagement by Mou Zongsan and Liu Shaoqi with Kant and Marxism respectively from the Western philosophical tradition (Cleary, 2016). Van Norden's response is grounded in his specialization in Chinese philosophy, although he cites several works on Indian philosophy (Bhushan & Garfield, 2011; Ganeri, 2014; Gupta, 2021; Perrett, 2016; Phillips, 1997) and Islamic philosophy (Adamson, 2015; Adamson & Taylor, 2004; McGinnis & Reisman, 2007) in support of his broader claim that we ought to take Asian philosophy seriously.

Van Norden's response is a step in the right direction, away from a culture of justification and toward a culture of praxis. According to this alternative culture of praxis, we need to recognize and make room for multiple canons, multiple ways of understanding disciplinary validation and multiple contributions from diverse philosophical projects situated in historical questions, contemporary needs and new or emerging investigations (Dotson, 2012). Whereas a culture of justification seeks legitimation, a culture of praxis strives after validation.[4]

1.4 Scepticism about Southeast Asian philosophy

Although Van Norden's response is a step in the right direction and functions as a useful corrective against Eurocentric assumptions, his characterization of Asian philosophy in terms of Chinese philosophy, Indian philosophy and Islamic philosophy still leaves much to be desired.[5] Pham (2013) distinguishes between three views of Vietnamese thought and this distinction may be adapted for our argumentative purposes here. According to the first view, Western philosophy has a systematic character and functions as the gold standard. Relative to this gold standard, neither Chinese nor Indian thought would count as philosophy, let alone thought from the Southeast Asian region. According to the second view, although Chinese and Indian thought would count as philosophy, thought from the Southeast Asian region may be interpreted as mere fragments, copies, or miniaturized versions of Chinese, Indian and Islamic philosophy. According to the third view, thought from the Southeast Asian region counts as philosophy and is distinct from both Western philosophy and Chinese, Indian and Islamic philosophy.

While Van Norden's response in § 1.3 to Pigliucci-style scepticism about the philosophical status of Asian thought allows us to reject the first view, its curious omission of Southeast Asian philosophy suggests that thought from the Southeast Asian region may be subsumed with minimal fuss under Chinese, Indian and Islamic philosophy. The second view arbitrarily favours major traditions in Asian philosophy (Chinese, Indian, Islamic) over minor ones (Southeast Asian), risks equating minor traditions with non-entities and ignores the distinctive nature of Southeast Asian philosophy.

What is it in virtue of which we can distinguish between Southeast Asian philosophy and Chinese, Indian and Islamic philosophy? Important clues may be found in Gripaldo's (2000, 2003) three possible approaches to classifying Filipino philosophy. The first approach is traditional or enumerative, based on the assumption that philosophy results from an individual's activity of thinking about universal philosophical themes in logic, epistemology, metaphysics and axiology (§ 1.1). An enumeration of the Greek philosophers Thales, Anaximenes, Anaximander, Xenophanes, Parmenides and Zeno and their philosophical activity will be sufficient for us to cover Greek philosophy, just as an enumeration of Indonesian thinkers Ferry Hidayat, Mpu Tantular, Mpu Kanwa, Mpu Panuluh, Syeikh Siti Jenar, and even the world-renowned logician Dharmakīrti and their philosophical activity will be sufficient for us to cover Indonesian philosophy.

The second approach is anthropological or cultural, based on the notion of the spirit of the people or national spirit (*Volksgeist* from German Romanticism or *diwa*, its Filipino equivalent). Given the universal nature of philosophy, the spirit of the people ought not to be sought in philosophical texts but rather the collective folk perspective, as it may be represented in or inferred from myths, folklore, sayings, epithets, etc.[6] The third approach is national or constitutive: Bertrand Russell, Confucian philosophy and Zen may be American, Chinese and Japanese respectively, but the interpretation or analysis of philosophical themes based on Western and Eastern philosophical traditions could be constituted by Filipino if the interpreter is Filipino.

The first approach (traditional or enumerative) will appeal to the historian of philosophy, the second approach (anthropological or cultural) will be attractive to someone who is drawn to a folk or grassroots conception of philosophy, and the third approach (national or constitutive) will be favoured by defenders of a hermeneutic approach. Besides Gripaldo's (2000, 2003) three approaches to Filipino philosophy, Hongladarom's (1996) two senses of cultural philosophy will be helpful. At a first pass, we may distinguish between philosophy (normative) and area studies (empirical). Nonetheless, Hongladarom denies that philosophy has absolutely no role to play for area studies, before identifying certain conditions of possibility for Thai philosophy. According to its first sense, cultural philosophy is a way of doing philosophy and consists of a shared set of problems and methods. It is helpful to think in terms of philosophical traditions (e.g. Western, Chinese, Indian, Islamic, etc.), defined through shared canonical texts, sets of problems and methods. Plato's dialogues, Aristotle's writings and the Vedic corpus would count as canonical works in their respective traditions. Membership in each tradition is not a function of birth but rather a function of subscription to the same set of shared and tradition-defining problems and methods. According to its second sense, cultural philosophy need not rely exclusively on the shared set of texts. What matters is the nationality or cultural identity of the philosopher conducting the interpretation or analysis, rather than the provenance of the problems or shared methods. Therefore, a Thai philosopher working on an interpretation of Confucius, intended primarily for a Thai audience, would be doing Thai philosophy in this sense. Given their intention that their work is of service to the Thai people, they could put their own cultural identity into their philosophical work. It follows that they will actually be doing Thai philosophy.

1.5 The possibility of Southeast Asian philosophy

We began this chapter with a general account of philosophy in terms of its desired aim (understanding how things in the broadest possible sense of the term hang together in the broadest possible sense of the term, providing a reasoned defence of some position), four main branches (metaphysics, epistemology, axiology, logic) and the standard philosophical method (use of language in a certain way, reliance on abstract definitions, conceptual analysis, argumentation) (§§ 1.1–1.2). Philosophy involves the activity of arriving at a reasoned defence of some position through analysis, argumentation, debate, refutation, affirmation. According to the third approach (national or constitutive), transposed to a Singaporean setting, the interpretation and analysis of aesthetic themes based on the tradition of analytic Western philosophy could be constituted as an instance of Singaporean philosophy (and therefore Southeast Asian philosophy) if the interpreter is Singaporean (§ 1.4). According to the second sense of cultural philosophy, a Singaporean philosopher (yours truly) working on a problem in analytic aesthetics, relying on examples from the canon of Southeast Asian art, and writing for an intended audience with an interest in the Southeast Asian region, would be doing Southeast Asian philosophy. As a result, the approach to aesthetic themes in this textbook, though grounded in Western analytic philosophy, may be classified as Southeast Asian.

Philosophy typically involves the reasoned defence of at least some claims. This defence could take the form of rigorous argumentation, the provision of supporting reasons, or an appeal to evidence. Pigliucci is therefore correct in his characterization of philosophy as an activity involving the reasoned defence of a position using logical reasoning and empirical evidence (§1.3). However, Pigliucci's lack of imagination of what might count as an instance of cultural philosophy (e.g. Asian, Southeast Asian, etc.) leads him to draw the incorrect conclusion that Asian philosophy is a non-starter. Van Norden's critique of the Eurocentric assumptions underlying Pigliucci's sceptical conclusion is praiseworthy, but he omits mention of Southeast Asian philosophy in his account of Asian philosophy. We must recognize both the major (Chinese, Indian, Islamic) and minor (Southeast Asian) traditions in any complete account of Asian philosophy.

As pointed out in an important footnote by Tran (2008), one can hardly find any entries on Southeast Asian philosophy in almost all the philosophical dictionaries or encyclopediae edited by scholars (Western or Asian). An exception among Western scholars would be George F. McLean, former Director of the Centre for the Study of Culture and Values at the Catholic University of America, who took steps to overcome this unfortunate omission. As a result of McLean's assistance, the Southeast Asian Philosophical Association (SEAPA) was formed in Bangkok in 2001 by a group of Southeast Asian philosophers. An appeal to the ameliorative approach of Sally Haslanger (2006, 2012) would be salutary in this regard: instead of taking the concept of philosophy as we find it, we make this concept as we want it to be. The target concept of philosophy should be inclusive, non-Eurocentric, and contain a diversity of perspectives (including perspectives hailing from or connected to the Southeast Asian region). My claim that this textbook is an instance of Southeast Asian philosophy is supported by this target concept and ideas from Van Norden, Pham, Gripaldo, Hongladarom, Haslanger and Tran.

More specifically, Gripaldo's three approaches to Filipino philosophy, Hongladarom's distinction between Thai area studies and Thai philosophy and the two senses of cultural philosophy, and Pham's account of the three views of Vietnamese thought all have the potential to inspire philosophers of the other Southeast Asian countries in developing their approaches (Hidayat, 2015). I hope that this textbook will serve as a worthy reflection of the power and strength of their overtures in favour of Southeast Asian philosophy. Furthermore, it must be emphasized that while this textbook counts as an instance of Southeast Asian philosophy, it is no less rigorous than a standard work of analytic aesthetics. An important source of evidence here is the domain of Southeast Asian art from which examples and references will be drawn, in support of various claims and assertions. We are now ready to acquire a keener understanding of the domain of Southeast Asian art.

2

Notes on Southeast Asian Art

2.1 Southeast Asia

Any adequate response to the question of what Southeast Asian art might be must first be able to furnish a proper account of what is meant by the term 'Southeast Asia'.[1] What is it in virtue of which something counts as Southeast Asian? In the first instance, Southeast Asia is a vast tropical territory (*c.* 4,500,000 km^2) of mountains, plains, archipelagos and peninsulas, lying south of China, east of India and north of Australia on any map of Asia (Nelson, 2019). It is a geographically distinct region that is neither fully South Asian (India) nor fully East Asian (China). As a term, 'Southeast Asia' is of relatively recent provenance, intended to designate a specific geographical region as a theatre of operations during the Second World War (Patke, 2012). The orthographic depiction of this geographical region may be found in Figure 2.1.

In the second instance, Southeast Asia is characterized by a shared geopolitics and history. The Southeast Asian region – with the exception of Siam or Thailand – has been a theatre for various nineteenth- and twentieth-century imperialisms: the British in Malaya, Singapore, Myanmar (formerly Burma) and Northern Borneo; the French in Vietnam, Cambodia and Laos; the Dutch in Indonesia; the Spanish and Americans in the Philippines; and the Portuguese in Timor-Leste (formerly East Timor).[2] It should be added that European colonial influence in the Southeast Asian region was historically preceded by a even longer history of maritime relations with and cultural influence from China, India and Islam. In the post-Second World War context, the rise of the modern nation-state model and the emergence of nationalism as a challenge to colonialism are a part of this shared

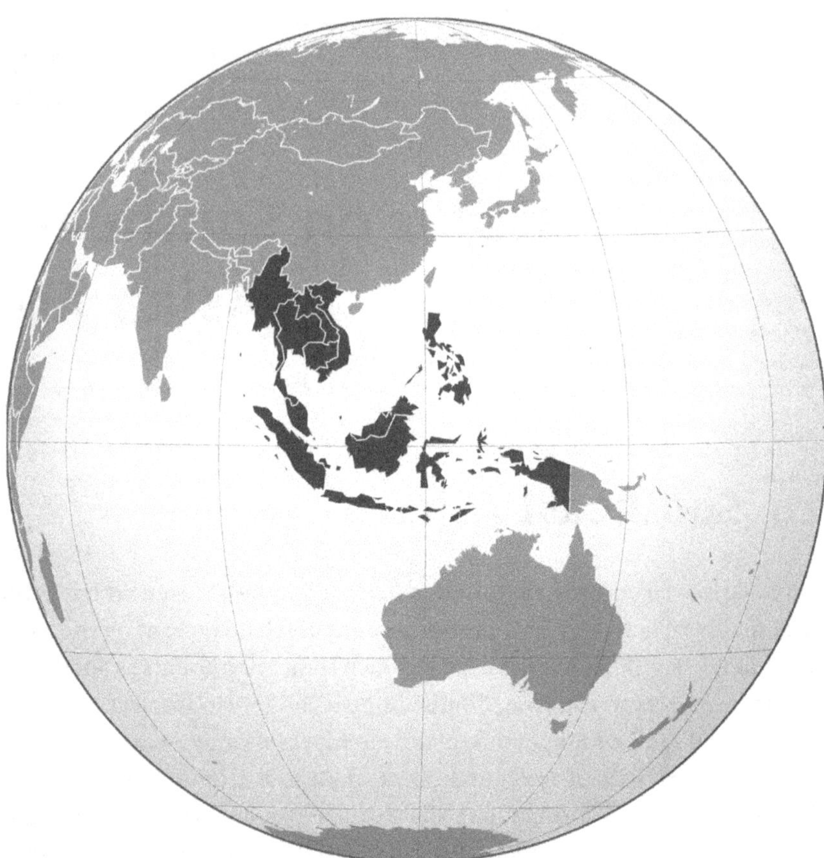

Figure 2.1 Orthographic projection of Southeast Asian region (shaded). Reproduced under the Creative Commons Attribution-ShareAlike 3.0 Unported (CC BY-SA 3.0) licence via Wikimedia Commons.

Southeast Asian geopolitics and history, as is the creation of ASEAN (Association of Southeast Asian Nations) in 1967. Consistent with a model of regionalism and regional cooperation, ASEAN is now a political and economic union of ten member states in the Southeast Asian region: Indonesia, Malaysia, Philippines, Singapore, Thailand, Brunei, Laos, Myanmar, Cambodia and Vietnam. However, given the loose and informal nature of this ASEAN federation, it still makes sense for us to ask the following: what is it in virtue of which the Southeast Asian region is neither fully South Asian (modelled after India) nor fully East Asian (modelled after China) but rather a distinct and coherent identity?

2.2 Scepticism about Southeast Asian art

It by no means follows from the Southeast Asian region being a geographically distinct region, characterized by a shared geopolitics and history, that the art associated with this region will be regarded as distinct and standalone. In American academic circles, for instance, it is conventional to subsume Southeast Asian art under South Asian art (Taylor, 2000).[3] As there has never been a fully satisfactory definition of Southeast Asian art, Thompson (2022) speaks of a certain foundational existential anxiety with respect to the domain itself. Is there even such a thing as Southeast Asian art?[4] Can there be an identity criterion of Southeast Asian art, allowing us to identify Southeast Asian art reliably as Southeast Asian art?

While the Southeast Asian region is characterized by a shared geopolitics and history, it is equally characterized by diversity, plurality, complexity, and the sheer kaleidoscopic nature of the cultures, languages, religions and histories of different parts of this region. This diversity, plurality and complexity is both a source of richness and inspiration and a source of divergences between the ideas, institutions, techniques and histories of art from one Southeast Asian nation to the next. If these divergences are sufficiently significant, then might we not have grounds to infer that the identity criterion of Southeast Asian art will be impossible to satisfy except perhaps in the most trivial of fashions (e.g. works of art counting as Southeast Asian art in virtue of hailing from a geographically distinct region)?[5]

Besides the challenges posed by the diversity, plurality and complexity of the Southeast Asian region to the feasibility of an identity criterion of Southeast Asian art, another challenge concerns the lack of a well-defined canon of Southeast Asian art. In art and culture, a canon is a body of works of art that have generally been recognized as foundationally significant relative to a tradition. The absence of a canon encompassing the entire Southeast Asian region may be contrasted with the presence of strong and well-defined national canons in many Southeast Asian nations. Certain artists (e.g. Cambodia's Nhek Dim and Thailand's Inson Wongsam) may be lionized in the art history of their own nations but remain largely unknown in the region. At the same time, we have reasons to retain hope of better-defined conceptual boundaries for Southeast Asian art in the future, as a universal consensus is being reached about the significance of certain figures in the narrative of Southeast Asia's art history (e.g. Raden Saleh and Redza Piyadasa) (Nelson, 2019).[6]

Yet another challenge concerns the relative absence of Southeast Asian works of art from exhibitions, biennales, museums, collections and university curricula (Wee, 2010). However understudied the domain of aesthetics and the philosophy of art may be (see Chapter 1), there is a clear sense in which the domain of Southeast Asian art is even more understudied and deserving of intellectual attention. In this regard, an encouraging development concerns the attempts by institutions in well-to-do nations such as Japan, Singapore and Australia to collect works of art from across Southeast Asia, organize related exhibitions, biennales, symposia and lectures, and promote extensive research on these works of art. The Fukuoka Asian Art Museum (Japan), National Gallery Singapore (Singapore) and Queensland Art Museum (Australia) are examples of institutions that have contributed in this fashion and their efforts have resulted in a certain stabilizing of the art canon in the Southeast Asian region (Kee, 2011).[7]

Add to these curatorial efforts the growing body of critical discourse on the uncertain identity of Southeast Asian art (e.g. Sabapathy (2018) and Whiteman et al. (2018)) and we are now in a far better position to deny the sceptical claim that there is no such thing as Southeast Asian art.[8] With all the relevant caveats, provisos and nuances in place, we are now ready to embark on our philosophical odyssey and draw on Southeast Asian art as a veritable source for examples and references in support of various aesthetic claims and assertions.

3

Art, Truth, Knowledge and Danger

3.1 Ang ku kueh and a hypothetical tale

Ang ku kueh is an oval-shaped Chinese confectionery that consist of soft, sticky glutinous rice flour wrapped around a sweet filling. Its distinctive design is intended to invoke a tortoise shell ('ang ku kueh' literally means 'red tortoise cakes' in Hokkien), setting it apart from other snacks.[1] This glutinous snack first originated in southern Fujian (Xiamen, Quanzhou and Zhangzhou) in China, before making its way along migration routes across maritime Southeast Asia (Cao, 2021).

In the quest for good fortune and longevity, tortoises were believed to be used as sacrifices to Chinese deities in ancient China. Given the difficulties involved in sourcing live tortoises, tortoise-shaped offerings were eventually developed as convenient alternatives. Ang ku kueh continues to be offered in Singapore, Malaysia, the Philippines and other parts of Southeast Asia on such religious festivals as the Chinese New Year, the Jade Emperor's birthday and the Hungry Ghost Festival month. In addition, ang ku kueh are traditionally bought in sets of twelve, since twelve is considered an auspicious number. While ang ku kueh is typically made of sweet mung bean paste and red in colour, symbolizing joy and happiness, other flavours and colours exist.[2]

Making ang ku kueh requires skill and patience. The filling must first be ground, mixed and divided, before being wrapped in dough skin, with consistency being ensured throughout. Each ang ku kueh is then carefully moulded by hand (Cao, 2021). A wooden mould containing the design of a tortoise may be used: when the filled dough is pressed into this mould and the mould is struck lightly on the kitchen top, the patterned dough will be released from the mould. Each moulded ang ku kueh is then placed on an oiled banana leaf. The leaf adds fragrance to the flavour of the kueh, while simultaneously serving as a lining to prevent the kueh from sticking to the steamer. As the ang ku kueh on the oiled banana leaf is being steamed over low to medium heat, care must be taken to ensure that it does not lose its pattern as a result of expansion due to the heat.

No details have been spared in evoking the provenance, modes of cultural transmission, cultural significance, varieties and mode of preparation of ang ku kueh, not least because the intention is to represent ang ku kueh as a historically nostalgic food. Shen-yi Liao (2021a), a Taiwanese philosopher formerly at Nanyang Technological University, characterizes historically nostalgic food as having the social function of evoking nostalgia.[3] There is a philosophical debate about the artistic status of food (Meskin, 2013). Is food art in the way that literature and painting count as art? Some philosophers have answered in the negative, denying that food can be art (Korsmeyer, 1999). Although Elizabeth Telfer (1996) responds in the affirmative, she believes that food is only a minor art, since it lacks permanence, cannot have meaning, and is unable to evoke significant emotional responses.

Liao (2021a) defends the stronger claim that food can still qualify as a major art, since food can afford aesthetic experiences comparable to the ones afforded by literature and painting. The role of imagination in the aesthetic experience of food is exemplified by historically nostalgic food. Historically nostalgic food, including ang ku kueh from the Southeast Asian region, can stay with us, be meaningful to us and move us. Given the important role that ang ku kueh plays in the construction of individual and cultural identities, there is a strong case to be made in favour of at least some Southeast Asian food counting as art.[4]

Suppose that I decide to write the tale of an ang ku kueh seller in 1980s Singapore. Several passages in this work of historical fiction about the ang ku kueh seller will describe the art of making ang ku kueh: preparing the dough, mixing the glutinous rice flour with salt and sugar, kneading the dough, rolling the mung bean paste filling into a ball, fitting the dough with the mung bean paste filling into a traditional mould to create the ang ku kueh pattern, placing the ang ku kueh on a banana leaf and steaming the ang ku kueh. Given my choice of the literary genre of historical fiction, I will have to strive to capture the details of 1980s Singapore as accurately as possible to ensure a sense of authenticity. If my tale about the ang ku kueh seller satisfies all the artistic constraints satisfied by works of historical fiction, would it count as valuable?

Plato's answer would be an emphatic 'no'. Art (narrative or otherwise) does not necessarily involve knowledge.[5] Our dear ang ku kueh seller in 1980s Singapore would be hypothetical rather than actual and, however vivid and engaging my tale of this hypothetical individual might be, I cannot, as an outsider to the ang ku kueh industry (especially in the context of 1980s Singapore), count as a legitimate source of epistemic authority. Reasoning about knowledge is a central concern of a branch of modal logic known as epistemic logic. According to axiom T in epistemic logic:

$$(T)\ K_s\phi \rightarrow \phi$$

Axiom T informs us that if agent S knows that ϕ, then ϕ is true. Where ϕ denotes any proposition that may be gleaned from a work of narrative art and S denotes the audience:

P1: $\neg\phi$
C1: $\therefore\ \neg K_s\phi$ – (axiom T and *modus tollens*)[6]

It follows that if art does not (necessarily) involve truth, then art does not (necessarily) involve knowledge either. Our discussion about the value of art will therefore engage with joint concerns about knowledge and truth. In many Homeric passages, Homer describes the arts of charioteering, medicine, fishing and prophecy. As the Platonic dialogue *Ion* (Plato, 1925) makes abundantly clear, however, the charioteer, physician, fisherman and prophet will be better judges of Homer's lines about the respective arts of charioteering, medicine, fishing and prophecy than either Homer himself or a rhapsode of Homer (e.g. Ion).[7] If Homer had possessed true knowledge of charioteering, medicine, fishing and prophecy, he would have offered sound advice relative to each of these arts. As he has not done so, we have good reason to doubt that Homer's lines about charioteering, medicine, fishing and prophecy count as a source of knowledge. Likewise, as I am neither a culinary expert at making ang ku kueh nor a historical expert on 1980s Singapore, my lines about how an ang ku kueh seller would have prepared their ang ku kueh in 1980s Singapore would have to be treated with caution.

3.2 Art as imitation

Realist fiction strives to represent its subject matter truthfully. More generally, realist art employs the principle of verisimilitude to ensure a certain likeness to truth. More generally, realism is generally thought to refer to any kind of representation in art in which a true-to-life depiction is offered of people, places, objects and events that, even if they might never have existed or occurred, could have existed or occurred. In Southeast Asian visual art, the transfer of various European techniques of drawing and painting from life helped artists to produce verisimilitudinous or true-to-life representations of people, places, objects and events (Nelson, 2019).

These techniques included the use of linear perspective to create an illusion of depth on a flat surface and the use of chiaroscuro to represent light and shade as they define three-dimensional objects. Simon Flores' (1875) *Portrait of Cirilo & Severina Quiason & Their Two Children* is a prime example of realist Southeast Asian art (Figure 3.1). The real-life subjects of this oil painting were Cirilo Quiason y Cunanan of Pampanga, his wife Ceferina Henson y David, and their two boys. Quiason and his family members were part of the nineteenth-century Filipino upper class and Flores followed the conventions of the genre of realist portraiture to capture the likeness of the sitters, their ornaments, the architectural space (including the elegant living room within which the sitters are posing and its capiz windows), American Victorian gasoliers, and the lived sense of the nineteenth-century Filipino upper class and how they might wish to be depicted.

Notwithstanding that Flores was one of the most celebrated realist painters of his period, we still cannot escape the sense that his commissioned Quiason family portrait remains at the level of appearance rather than reality. Given the flat surface of the painting, our sense of the three-dimensionality of the depicted figures and spatial depth is an illusion generated by Flores' use of linear perspective and chiaroscuro. As Nelson (2019) has pointed out, no family would actually gather in the configuration seen in the Quiason family portrait. Last but not least, the older of the two Quiason boys is regularly mistaken for a girl, underscoring the ultimately deceptive nature of appearances.

In the *Republic*, Plato (*c.* 375 BCE/1935) places *mimêsis* at the heart of theories about poetry and other forms of art and offers a radical critique of mimetic art in Book 10. According to the Platonic account of art as *mimêsis* or imitation, mimetic poetry imitates or produces appearances alone and not the truth of things. Flores' Quiason family portrait counts as an instance of mimetic art: it relies on the principle of verisimilitude and imitates or produces appearances. Suppose that my work of historical fiction about an ang ku kueh seller in 1980s Singapore is a realist artwork that relies on the principle of verisimilitude. By analogy, this hypothetical tale may be

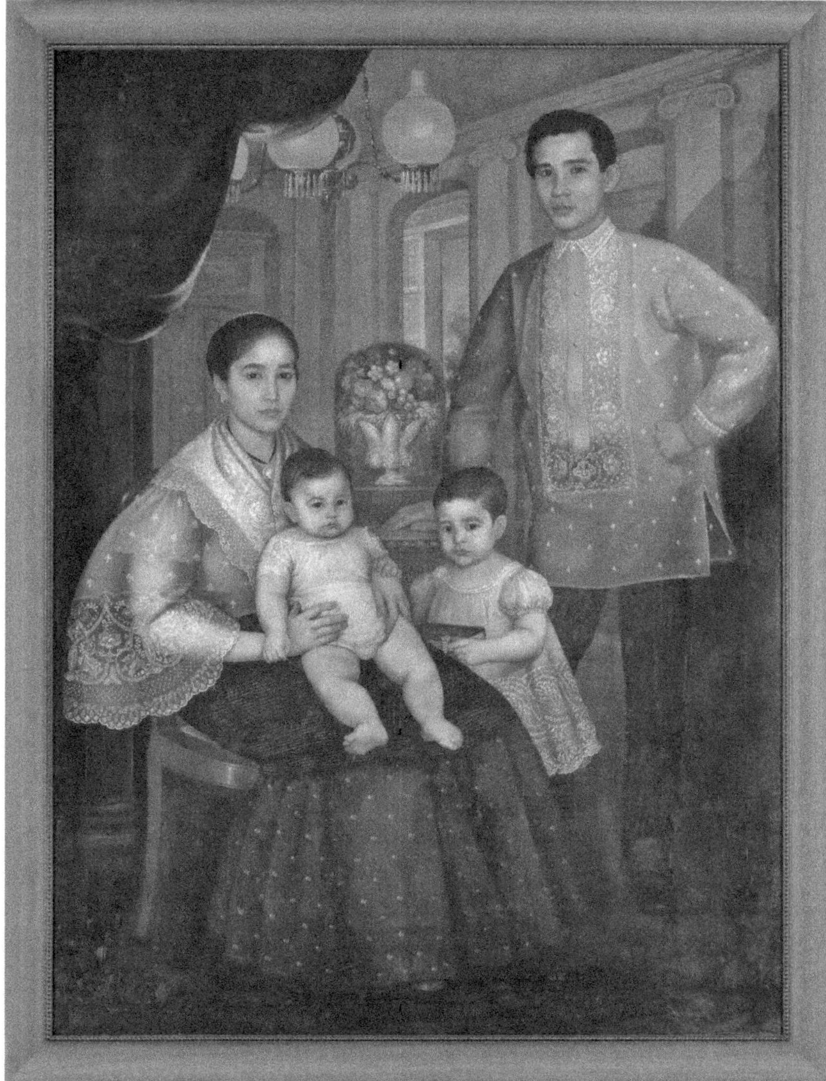

Figure 3.1 Simon Flores' (1875) *Portrait of Cirilo & Severina Quiason & Their Two Children*. Oil on canvas. Reproduced with permission of Bangko Sentral ng Pilipinas.

characterized in terms of *mimêsis* (imitation and representation): it is neither lived reality itself nor a documentary account of lived experience but rather an imagined or fictional account that imitates appearances.

The gulf between truth and appearance is expressed by Plato in terms of two tripartitions (see Table 3.1).

Table 3.1 Two Platonic tripartitions. © Melvin Chen

	1st tripartition	**2nd tripartition**
Highest rank	The form of the table made by God	Using the flute with knowledge
Intermediate rank	The table made by the carpenter	Making the flute based on correct opinion
Lowest rank	The image of the table made by the mimetic artist	Imitating the flute in ignorance

The first tripartition is concerned with the relative reality of three objects: one made by God, another by the carpenter, and yet another by the mimetic artist. The second tripartition is concerned with the different ways of experiencing an object (viz. the flute). Not only do these two tripartitions fail to showcase art as *mimêsis* or imitation in the best possible light, but they also intimate that there is something defective about art precisely in virtue of its being mimetic.

3.3 The dangers of bovarysme

When art imitates or produces appearances and not the truth of things, there will be certain epistemic dangers concerning the nature of its reception: the audience may well end up confusing appearance with reality. This phenomenon has been termed bovarysme, after Emma Bovary, the titular protagonist of Gustave Flaubert's *Madame Bovary*.[8] An example of Asian bovarysme would be Sugawara no Takasue no musume, also known as Takasue's Daughter or Lady Sarashina. In her *Sarashina Diary*, one of the Japanese court women's memoirs (nikki) from the Heian period (794–1185 CE), Lady Sarashina writes about how her younger self, infatuated with romantic illusions that are fuelled and shaped by her reading of fiction, ends up disillusioned with reality as she grows older.[9]

Is there an example of bovarysme in the Southeast Asian canon? The answer may surprise you. Joseph Conrad (1912) describes, in his autobiographical *A Personal Record*, writing his first novel *Almayer's Folly* (1895) while land-locked in Rouen (France) aboard the Adowa. Chapter 10 of this novel was written in plain sight of the Rouen café visited by Emma Bovary and her husband Charles after their night at the opera. Furthermore,

Conrad imagines being visited by the shade of Gustave Flaubert. Despite Conrad being a Polish-British novelist with limited acquaintance with the people of Southeast Asia, the Southeast Asian region looms large in his early novels (including *Almayer's Folly*). The contested nature of Southeast Asian art and its identity criterion has already been discussed in § 2.2. Suppose that our identity criterion is sufficiently broad to embrace art in Southeast Asia (written by local and non-local residents in Southeast Asia), art from Southeast Asia (written by local residents in Southeast Asia and the Southeast Asian diaspora), or art for and about Southeast Asia. While a novel written by a Polish-British novelist based outside of Southeast Asia might not count as Southeast art relative to the first two disjunctive conditions, it could still count as a work of Southeast Asian art insofar as it satisfies the third disjunctive condition (viz. as art for and about Southeast Asia). After all, Conrad's *Almayer's Folly* is set in Indonesia and meditates on the excesses of colonialism.

The case for acknowledging the bovaryste similarities between Conrad's titular protagonist Kaspar Almayer (a Dutch businessman based in the Borneo jungle) and Flaubert's titular protagonist Emma Bovary is a strong one (Hampson, 1992). While Emma dreams of romance and fame in an exotic setting, Almayer, located in precisely the sort of exotic environment that Emma desires, harbours similarly unrealistic dreams of success (viz. finding a hidden gold mine and becoming wealthy). Both Emma and Almayer lose sight of reality in their infatuation with their dreams, resort to self-deception, and are ultimately doomed to failure. Bovarysme, whenever it might be present in fictional characters such as Conrad's Almayer or even the real-life audience of works of art, is associated with the dangers of conflating dreams, imaginings, and fictions with reality. Mimetic art, insofar as it encourages make-believe, fiction, and the imagination, can lead to bovarysme and delusion. Book 10 of the *Republic* refers to *kêlêsis* (or charm) in mimetic works and Socrates readily concedes that we are *kêloumenois* (or bewitched) by mimetic works. There is no doubt that we will need a medicine (whatever that might ultimately be) that will work as a counter-charm against mimetic art and the bewitchment and bovarysme that are induced by it.

3.4 The no-expertise argument

If one is planning to learn something about the art of ang ku kueh making, one would presumably be better off checking in with an ang ku kueh expert.

If one is planning to learn something about the history of Singapore in the 1980s, one would similarly be better off consulting a historian such as Tan Tai Yong at the Singapore University of Social Sciences. The experts – whether in ang ku kueh-making or Singaporean history – ought to be consulted rather than the narrative artist on those subject areas that they have already mastered.[10] By contrast, the narrative artist has no claim to special expertise in any branch of knowledge, save that of the artform of the narrative, its medium, and the medium-relevant techniques (e.g. style, plot, perspective, themes, characters, etc.). These conclusions are supported by what has been famously termed by Carroll (2007) as the 'no-expertise' argument. The no-expertise argument may be represented as follows:

> P1: If anyone lacks the relevant expertise relative to what they describe, then they cannot be relied on (epistemically speaking).
> P2: Narrative artists lack the relevant expertise relative to what they describe.
> C: ∴ Narrative artists cannot be relied on (epistemically speaking).[11]

3.5 Incorrect information

Suppose that I would like my protagonist, the ang ku kueh seller, to feature in Kueh Appreciation Day. Kueh Appreciation Day was started in 2015 by Slow Food (Singapore) to get food lovers acquainted with the humble kueh. Suppose further that I am unaware of the year in which Kueh Appreciation Day first began. Its inclusion in the narrative of my work of historical fiction (set in 1980s Singapore) would constitute an anachronism, although I would be ignorant of this fact. My situation would be analogous to that of Charles Dickens's anachronism in *Barnaby Rudge*. Dickens's historical novel, published in 1841, was largely set around the time of the Gordon Riots of 1780. However, an anachronistic claim is made in an early version of the novel that someone is hanged for passing bad one-pound notes, even though notes under five pounds were not issued in reality until 1797. Both Dickens's and my anachronisms count as inaccurate information. This inaccurate information could interfere with pre-existing knowledge, get mistakenly integrated into the knowledge bases of readers of our literary artworks, give rise to deductive inferences that are improperly grounded, and adversely influence our readers' beliefs.[12]

To revive the Conradian thread, Joseph Conrad's (1899) *Heart of Darkness*, a novella set in nineteenth-century Congo, served as the inspiration for Francis Ford Coppola's (1979) *Apocalypse Now*, an anti-war film about the Vietnam War. In 2000, *Apocalypse Now* was recognized for its cultural, historical, or aesthetic significance and selected for preservation in the National Film Registry by the US Library of Congress. The broader version of the identity criterion, as discussed in § 2.2, could allow us in principle to recognize Coppola's *Apocalypse Now* alongside Conrad's *Almayer's Folly* as art for and about Southeast Asia and therefore as Southeast Asian art.

At the same time, Coppola's *Apocalypse Now* is rife with mistakes and inaccuracies. Historical errors include the misidentification of the colour of tracer bullets: Viet Congs used green tracer bullets and the Americans used red tracer bullets, although Coppola's film mistakenly depicts an American patrol boat being attacked with red bullets in a scene. A continuity error refers to a lapse in the self-consistency of the scene or story being depicted. Continuity errors in Coppola's film include three huts with communist flags on top of them exploding and then reappearing intact, before being destroyed again in Lieutenant Colonel Bill Kilgore's raid of the Viet Cong at the coastal mouth.

Most problematically and as pointed out by the Vietnamese academic and novelist Viet Thanh Nguyen, Coppola's film, despite being an anti-war film about the Vietnam War that is regularly feted by cinephiles and film critics alike, ends up being about Americans, with the Vietnamese being either silenced or erased (Streitfeld, 2016). Nguyen's Pulitzer-winning debut novel *The Sympathizer* (2015) attempts to redress this error: its anonymous narrator (a Vietnamese spy) plays the role of a consultant for *The Hamlet*, a Hollywood film on the Vietnam War. The intended reference here is unmistakably to Coppola's mistake-ridden *Apocalypse Now*. Nguyen's film-within-the-novel is shot in the Philippines, uses Vietnamese-looking actors for the main roles, and has crowd scenes peopled by Vietnamese refugees (whom the narrator has to manage). Nguyen's rage against Coppola about how the Vietnamese are represented in a film about the Vietnam War is latent in his novel (Prabhu, 2018).

3.6 The poetic licence argument

Dickens was sufficiently concerned about the anachronism in *Barnaby Rudge* when informed about it by a correspondent that he altered the text of his historical novel and thanked the correspondent for having identified the error. However, even if I am informed about the anachronism in my work of historical fiction, I may have artistic grounds (e.g. a desire to show, through the adventures of the main character, the development of episodes important to the history and values of a nation) for including Kueh Appreciation Day in my narrative. This can be compared with the dramatic grounds that Shakespeare may have had for moving around the dates of the battle and victory of his eponymous protagonist Julius Caesar. The inclusion of incorrect information in literary artworks may be motivated by what I term the poetic licence argument:

> P1: If a deviation from fact produces a desired artistic effect, then a narrative artist has *pro tanto* reasons to deviate from fact.
> P2: A deviation from fact produces a desired artistic effect in at least some instances.
> C: ∴ A narrative artist has *pro tanto* reasons to deviate from fact in at least some instances.

Some version of the poetic licence argument may be at work in Sonny Liew's (2015) *The Art of Charlie Chan Hock Chye* (see Figure 3.2). A graphic novel by the Malaysia-born and Singapore-based Liew about the titular character and fictional cartoonist Charlie Chan Hock Chye during the formative years of the history of modern Singapore, *The Art of Charlie Chan Hock Chye* interweaves historical fact and fiction. Ample nods are made to historical events and personages in Singapore such as Lee Kuan Yew (the first Prime Minister of Singapore and its founding father), Lim Chin Siong (trade union leader and opposition politician), and the 1987 Marxist Conspiracy (or Operation Spectrum).[13] Liew's success at attaining various desired artistic effects is reflected in the multiple awards that have been conferred to his graphic novel, including the 2016 Singapore Literature Prize and several 2017 Eisner Awards.[14] The success and industry-wide recognition of aesthetic merit of Liew's graphic novel provide justification for the view that Liew had *pro tanto* reasons to deviate from fact in at least some instances.

At the same time, some sense of the power or dangers of art – especially when an artist wields poetic licence in pursuit of certain artistic ends – may be inferred from the withdrawal of a publishing grant by the National Arts Council (NAC) for *The Art of Charlie Chan Hock Chye* on the eve of its Singapore launch.[15] Last but not least, we may consider the following question: given the success enjoyed by both Francis Ford Coppola (§ 3.5)

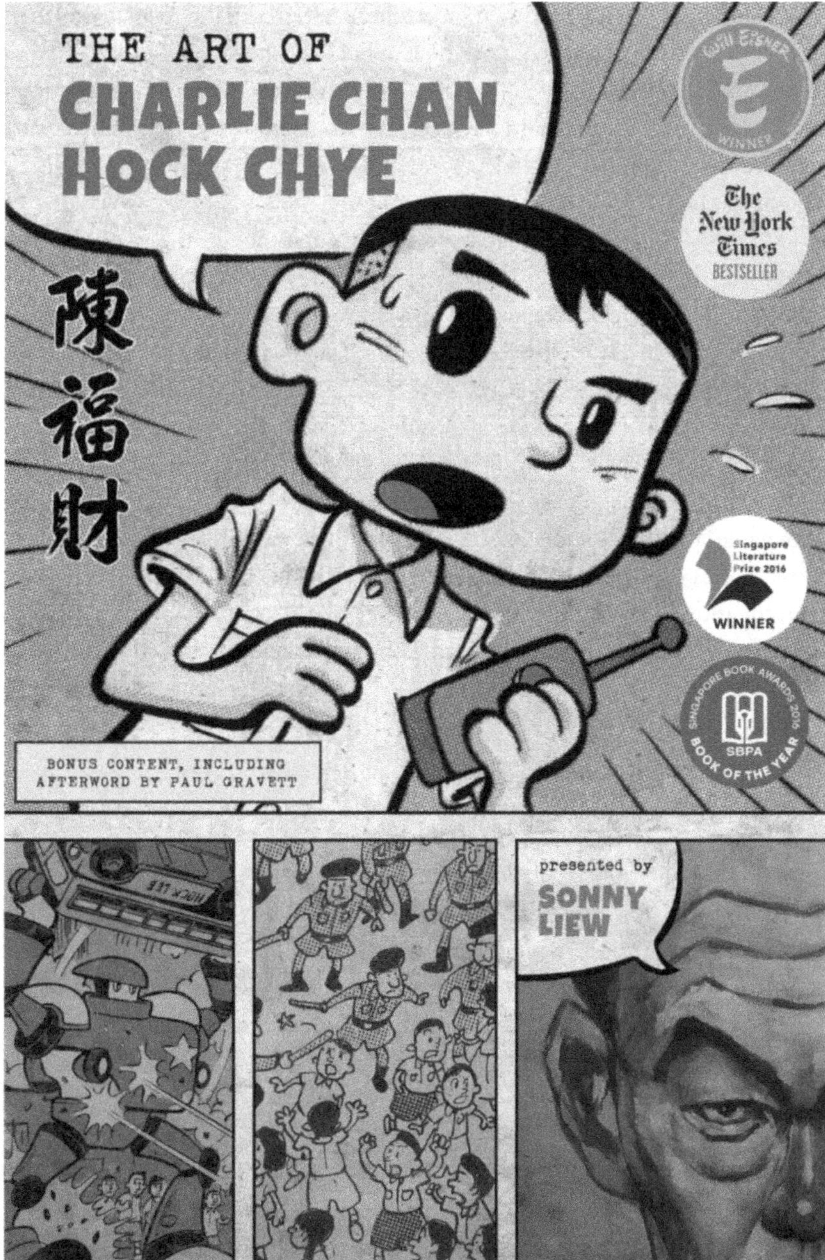

Figure 3.2 Cover of Sonny Liew's (2015) *The Art of Charlie Chan Hock Chye*. Reproduced with permission of Epigram Books and the artist.

and Sonny Liew in producing certain desired artistic effects in their respective works of art, why might Coppola not have the same degree of freedom to deviate from fact as Liew? Alternatively, what is it in virtue of which Nguyen's rage against Coppola about how the Vietnamese are represented might be justified, whereas the NAC's reservations against Liew might not be?

Pro tanto reasons to deviate from fact, as identified in the poetic licence argument, do not appear to cover the liberties taken by Coppola in his representation of the Vietnamese in a film about the Vietnam War. Given Coppola's choice of the epic war film genre, certain genre-based expectations about historical accuracy and authenticity will function as necessary constraints on poetic licence. By contrast, Liew's *The Art of Charlie Chan Hock Chye* is commonly thought to be a genre-bending fictional biography of a fictional artist, specifically designed to present alternative histories alongside the hegemonic historical narrative, celebrate the redemptive possibilities of narrative, and pose questions about the agency of the artist and the individual in a postcolonial society (Holden, 2016). The imaginative interweaving of historical fact and fiction is therefore entirely consistent with the expectations that arise with the genre-busting nature of this graphic novel.[16]

3.7 The institutional argument

The poetic licence argument (about what a narrative artist or poet has *pro tanto* reasons to do) is distinct from the institutional argument (about what the set of conventions governing literary studies as an institutional practice might imply). According to this institutional argument (Gaut, 2003a):

P1: At least some branches of literary studies are concerned with the study of narrative techniques and motifs.

P2: No branch of literary studies is concerned with the study of the truth or falsity of claims advanced by literary works.

P3: Literature is not indifferent to a topic if and only if (hereafter: iff) at least some branches of literary studies are concerned with the study of that topic.

C1: ∴ Literature is not indifferent to narrative techniques and motifs.

C2: ∴ Literature is indifferent to the truth or falsity of claims advanced by literary works.

The institutional argument supports the no-truth theory of literary value (Lamarque & Olsen, 1994), according to which the truth of any claim in a literary work is never relevant to its aesthetic value and literature in general is indifferent to matters of truth or falsity (C2 of the institutional argument).

3.8 Art as inspiration

The Platonic claim that art does not necessarily involve knowledge may be substantiated in another manner. According to an alternative Platonic account of art as *enthousiasmos* or inspiration, the Muses take over the minds of poets, who then write in an *enthousiazôn* (possessed or inspired state). This account of art as inspiration is distinct from the Platonic account of art as *mimêsis* or imitation. Whereas the former denies that art results from *technê* (skill or knowledge), the latter affirms that it is indeed the case that art is the product of the skill or knowledge of the artist.[17]

The alternative Platonic account of art as *enthousiasmos* or inspiration is supported by an argument by analogy that may be traced to Plato's *Ion*. According to the source of the analogy, a magnet (described as the stone of Heraclea) attracts iron rings and gives them the power to attract other iron rings. All iron rings in turn derive their power from the original magnet. According to the target of this analogy, the Muses first inspire certain individuals like Homer. From these divinely inspired individuals, a chain of other individuals like Ion (a rhapsode who performs Homeric epics) is suspended who take inspiration derivatively.

3.9 Two constructive dilemmas

In the exchange between Socrates and Ion, Socrates remarks that Ion has failed to explain the nature of the art of the rhapsode. Either Ion possesses the art of the rhapsode or he does not. If Ion possesses the art of the rhapsode, then he has been dishonest in not having disclosed this art to Socrates. If Ion does not possess the art of the rhapsode, then he can perform Homer's lines simply because he is divinely inspired. The implication here is that Ion is either dishonest or inspired and the argument takes the form of a constructive dilemma:[18]

P1: $p \veebar \neg p$
P2: $p \rightarrow q$

P3: $\neg p \rightarrow r$
C: $\therefore q \veebar r$

Between the charge of dishonesty and the (milder) charge of being divinely inspired, Ion appears to be more content with the latter charge. However, when an individual speaks from inspiration and under the influence of the Muses, that individual cannot be said to be epistemically reliable. After all, might the Muses not be Cartesian evil demons who deceive poets and lead them astray at each and every turn? In the final analysis, whether the artist is dishonest or inspired, in neither instance would the artist be considered as epistemically reliable. In addition, the existence of gods and muses may imply that artists are hostages of fortune and not in fact self-sufficient.

In the context of Singaporean dragon kiln pottery, various kiln gods are worshipped and offered food and incense by potters before the kiln is fired (Chin, 2022; Lim, 2015). The Thow Kwang dragon kiln in Singapore, built in 1940 by a group of Hokkien and Teochew immigrants, is 27 metres long, less than 1 metre wide in the front chambers and about 2 metres wide at the back. Alongside the kiln are seventeen pairs of stoke holes, where wood is added. Wood-firing is long and tedious: it may last for up to three days. In addition, the potters take turns to monitor the temperature, which may rise up to 1,300 degrees celsius. To wake the dragon up, the potters pray to the kiln gods with incense and food offerings for a smooth procedure. Might not the existence of gods and muses and the need for prayers, incense and offerings imply that artists (e.g. of kiln-fired clayware) are hostages of fortune and therefore not in fact self-sufficient?

There is a constructive dilemma relative to the audience that is an analogue of the constructive dilemma relative to the artist. Either the audience is epistemically inferior or it is not epistemically inferior (P1). According to the first horn of this dilemma, if the audience is epistemically inferior, then it cannot judge whether an artist is epistemically reliable (P2). When an artist is divinely inspired and epistemically unreliable, the audience will be at the mercy of the whims of the Muses. When the artist is epistemically reliable, the audience will only have its good luck rather than its sound judgement to thank. According to the second horn of this dilemma, if the audience is not epistemically inferior, then it will not learn anything new from the artwork (P3). By implication, the artwork will be banal, trivial, or limited in cognitive value. It follows that the audience will either be unable to judge whether an artist is epistemically reliable (if the audience is epistemically inferior) or be forced to concede the banality of the artwork (if it is not) (C). The second constructive dilemma is formally identical to the first constructive dilemma and differs only in terms of argumentative content:

P1: $p \veebar \neg p$
P2: $p \rightarrow q$
P3: $\neg p \rightarrow r$
C: $\therefore q \veebar r$

3.10 The tripartite theory of the soul

According to the first constructive dilemma relative to the artist, the artist is either dishonest or divinely inspired. According to the second constructive dilemma relative to the audience, the cognitive value of the artwork is either uncertain (if the audience is epistemically inferior) or limited (if the audience is not epistemically inferior). Quite apart from divine inspiration being unable to ground knowledge, art that is divinely inspired will tend to trigger our emotions. According to Plato's tripartite theory of the soul, our emotions are associated with the baser part of our soul. Each soul consists of reason (over which logic holds court), appetite (governed by physical urges) and spirit (characterized by emotions). According to the chariot analogy employed in *Phaedrus* (Plato, 1914), reason is the charioteer who must guide the soul toward truth, while controlling the horses representing appetite and spirit.

In Ganson's (2009) interpretation of Plato's tripartite theory of the soul, there is a broad division between reason and the inferior and non-rational part of the soul. Furthermore, the inferior and non-rational part of the soul can be further subdivided into spirit and appetite. My tale of the ang ku kueh seller in 1980s Singapore is grounded in the inferior and non-rational part of the soul in two senses: it appeals to sense perception (e.g. by evoking certain sense experiences) and emotion rather than reason. Worse yet, my work of historical fiction has a negative influence on us: it arouses, appeals to and strengthens the inferior and non-rational part of the soul. If my hypothetical work of historical fiction succeeds in its artistic intentions, then the reader of my tale ought to feel empathy for my protagonist and folk hero, the ang ku kueh seller. However, my reliance on empathy to produce certain desired artistic effects could undermine the authority of reason and make it difficult for reason to guide the soul toward truth.

3.11 Banishing the poets

Let us return to the original question with which we had begun this chapter: if my tale about the ang ku kueh seller satisfies all the relevant artistic constraints that are satisfied by works of historical fiction, would it count as valuable? A Platonic response to this question would comprise a set of the following claims:

Claim 1: Art does not necessarily involve knowledge.
Claim 2: Art does not necessarily involve truth.

The modalities of knowledge and truth in Claims 1 and 2 are related by axiom T in epistemic logic (viz. $K_s\phi \rightarrow \phi$). Claim 1 is supported by the two Platonic tripartitions for expressing the gulf between truth and appearance, the poetic licence argument and the institutional argument. Claim 2 is additionally supported by the no-expertise argument, the constructive dilemma in favour of the epistemic unreliability of the artist, and the constructive dilemma in favour of the uncertain or limited cognitive value of an artwork.

Considered on their own, Claims 1 and 2 do not yet allow us to conclude in favour of art being dangerous. There is a further claim that Plato appears to accept in conjunction with Claims 1 and 2:

Claim 3: Art is powerful.

According to the tripartite theory of the soul, reason is the natural ruler, whereas the non-rational part of the soul – including the imagination (pre-rational) and the emotions (irrational) – is inferior. Art arouses, appeals to and strengthens the inferior and non-rational part of the soul (viz. the imagination and the emotions). Furthermore, the most successful art is in principle capable of portraying even the most vicious characters in a sympathetic light. Claims 1, 2 and 3 constitute premises in an argument in favour of the dangers of art:

P1: Art does not necessarily involve knowledge.
P2: Art does not necessarily involve truth.

P3: Art is powerful.

P4: Whatever is powerful and involves neither knowledge nor truth necessarily is dangerous.

C: ∴ Art is dangerous.

The argument in favour of the dangers of art motivates Socrates to banish the poets from his conception of the ideal and just city-state in Book 10 of the *Republic*. After all, the dangers of poetry are intrinsic to its nature: poetry and other forms of narrative art typically enjoin us to engage with them with our imagination and emotions (i.e. the inferior and non-rational part of the soul). Where artists succeed in their artistic intentions, the audience might even be altered and shaped by the artworks in potentially dangerous ways. A sense of precisely how dangerous art might be perceived to be may be gleaned from the 1993 installation *Etalase* by the Indonesian artist Arahmaiani (see Figure 3.3) and its reception. Arahmaiani's installation presents a Qur'an and a statue of the Buddha – sacred symbols of spiritual devotion, especially in a Southeast Asian region where religion and spirituality are profoundly important to many individuals – in a vitrine, alongside a box of soil, a packet of condoms and a bottle of Coca-Cola. *Etalase* was designed to question the relationship between religion and

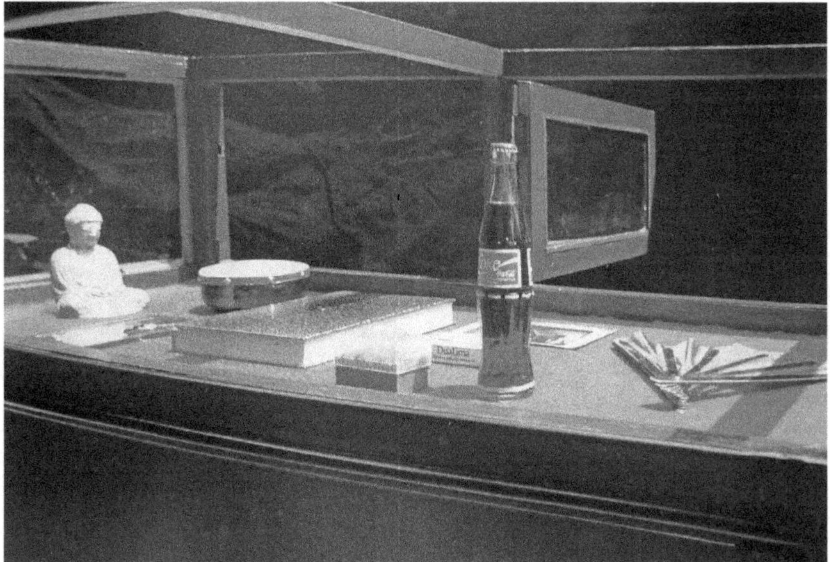

Figure 3.3 Arahmaiani's (1993) *Etalase*. Installation with found objects. Collection of the artist. Reproduced with permission of the artist.

commercialism and between Islam and other religions, although this work of art resulted in Arahmaiani receiving death threats and feeling sufficiently compelled to flee Indonesia in fear for her own life (Nelson, 2019).

At the same time, Socrates expresses some degree of regret in having to banish the poets and concedes that he will be happy to allow the poets back into the city-state if anyone can present an argument in their defence. In the final analysis, we must agree with Dorter (1990) that Plato's decision to banish the poets is a political rather than a cognitive one. The character of art is such that it can undermine rationality and virtue and leave its audience in error. Do you agree with Plato's decision? If you do, then what might your reasons be? If not, then how can we resist the Platonic verdict and on what grounds might we be able to lift the ban and welcome the banished poets back to the fold?

4

Modes of Aesthetic Knowledge

4.1 Revisiting the argument in favour of the dangers of art

In Chapter 3, an argument in favour of the dangers of art was formulated on the basis of Claims 1, 2 and 3. To recapitulate, this is what the argument (let us call it Argument 1) that supports the banishment of the poets looks like:

P1: Art does not necessarily involve knowledge.
P2: Art does not necessarily involve truth.
P3: Art is powerful.
P4: Whatever is powerful and involves neither knowledge nor truth necessarily is dangerous.
C: ∴ Art is dangerous.

Let us first introduce some formal notation to determine the argumentative form instantiated by Argument 1. Where $P, Q, \cdots$ represent n-place predicates, x, y and z represent individual variables, a, b and c represent individual constants, $\forall$ represents the universal quantifier ('for all'), $\neg$, $\wedge$ and $\rightarrow$ represent logical connectives (respectively: 'not', 'and' and 'if … then') and $\square$ represents the alethic modal operator for necessity, Argument 1 may be represented as follows:

P1: $\neg\square Ka$
P2: $\neg\square Ta$
P3: Pa
P4: $\forall x((Px \wedge \neg\square Kx \wedge \neg\square Tx) \rightarrow Dx)$
C: ∴ Da

Here are some axioms and rules of inference that we will accept for our system of logic:

$[R_1]\ p \rightarrow q, p \vdash q - \rightarrow_{E1}$ (see Appendix A)
$[R_7]\ p, q \vdash p \wedge q - \wedge_I$ (see Appendix A)
$[R_{15}]\ \forall x \phi \vdash \mathrm{Subst}(\{x/a\}, \phi) - \forall_E$ (see endnote 11 in § 3.4)

Proof of Argument 1:

1. $\neg \Box Ka$ – P1
2. $\neg \Box Ta$ – P2
3. Pa – P3
4. $\forall x((Px \wedge \neg \Box Kx \wedge \neg \Box Tx) \rightarrow Dx)$ – P4
5. $\therefore \neg \Box Ka \wedge \neg \Box Ta$ – R_7 or $\wedge_I$ (from 1 & 2)
6. $\therefore \neg \Box Ka \wedge \neg \Box Ta \wedge Pa$ – R_7 or $\wedge_I$ (from 3 & 5)
7. $\therefore (Pa \wedge \neg \Box Ka \wedge \neg \Box Ta) \rightarrow Da$ – R_{15} or $\forall_E$ (from 4)
8. $\therefore Da$ – R_1 or $\rightarrow_{E1}$ (from 6 & 7)

This proof allows us to conclude in favour of the proof-theoretic validity of Argument 1 relative to a system of logic that accepts R_1, R_7 and R_{15} among its axioms and rules of inference. In other words, assuming the truth of P1–P4 of Argument 1, the truth of the conclusion in favour of the dangers of art follows as a matter of logical necessity. More generally, an argument is valid iff, assuming the truth of all its premises, its conclusion cannot be false. An argument is sound iff it is valid and all its premises are true. Therefore, if we are to resist the Platonic verdict in favour of the banishment of the poets, then we must show that Argument 1, though proof-theoretically valid, is unsound. We can demonstrate the unsoundness of Argument 1 by denying the truth of at least one of its premises and furnishing reasons for this denial.

4.2 Denying P3

One possible strategy might involve denying P3 (i.e. that art is powerful). According to defenders of this strategy, Plato is paying art the perverse compliment of thinking it is powerful enough to be dangerous. This compliment is however ultimately unjustified, since it is rather the case that art has too little power to move us in precisely those instances where it might be dangerous (e.g. morally speaking). According to David Hume (1757), if an artwork deviates from certain moral standards and fails – as it were – to track the moral truth, then the moral defect would count as an aesthetic defect. Furthermore, if the artwork is immoral in the relevant sense, then it will be unable to move a suitably virtuous audience (i.e. it will be impotent rather than powerful). The virtuous audience exhibits a response known as imaginative resistance (Moran, 1994).[1]

4.3 Imaginative resistance

When we engage in make-believe, we believe that we are largely unconstrained by what we take to be factual. However, when an author invites us to imagine a fictional scenario, they seem to have much less freedom in what they can make fictionally true. For instance, when the artwork is immoral in the relevant sense, the audience may fail to follow the author's lead in make-believing. Walton's (1994) Giselda scenario runs as follows: 'In killing her baby, Giselda did the right thing; after all, it was a girl.' The audience (rather unsurprisingly) imaginatively resists the fictional scenario in which female infanticide is morally acceptable. In Moran's (1994) Macbeth example, when it is prescribed that Duncan's murder was unfortunate only for having interfered with Macbeth's sleep or that the audience is relieved at these events, then imaginative resistance is evoked. In Gendler's (2000) Mice story, we are informed that the white mice are hardworking and industrious. Conversely, the black mice are slothful and shiftless, with a large number of them addicted to drugs and eating watermelon. The white mice tended to be better off than the black mice. While the white mice were generous to the black mice, the black mice kept to their old ways. Since it is nigh impossible for us to read it as anything but an extremely crude allegory for race relations, we imaginatively resist the Mice story.

The Humean move of denying P3 (i.e. that art is powerful) can be justified by an appeal to the phenomenon of imaginative resistance: when art might pose certain moral dangers, it will have too little power to arouse, appeal to and engage with the imagination and emotions of a suitably virtuous audience. Where we can trust a suitably virtuous audience to imaginatively resist morally dangerous artworks, there will be no need to banish the poets. At the same time, imaginative resistance might arise whenever artists seek to critically engage with and interrogate taboos. When people are asked to trade their sacred values for secular values, they tend to exhibit moral outrage, anger and disgust, become increasingly inflexible in negotiations, and demonstrate an insensitivity to strict cost-benefit analysis. Psychologists have referred to this as the taboo trade-off phenomenon (Fiske & Tetlock, 1997; Tetlock et al., 2000; Waytz, 2010). Taboo trade-off violates normative intuitions about the integrity and sanctity of certain relationships (e.g. between the dead and the living, between ourselves and our own bodily waste products, etc.).

It is considered taboo to be in the presence of dead bodies in several Southeast Asian cultures, since corpses are regarded as unclean and reminders of mortality. Araya Rasdjarmrearnsook, a Thai contemporary artist, interrogates precisely this taboo by sitting alongside corpses veiled in white sheets and humming, chanting and talking to them in *Conversations I* (2005). Rasdjarmrearnsook's taboo-challenging *Conversations I* is (paradoxically) informed by the Thai Buddhist tradition of sitting and conversing with the deceased for several days, to help them on their way toward the next spiritual realm. Her intention is to shift taboos and cultural attitudes and treat dead bodies as if they are on an equal footing with living ones. At the same time and given the taboo trade-off phenomenon, it is likely that such art will invoke imaginative resistance.

With respect to the relationship between ourselves and our own bodily waste products, it is considered taboo for us to ingest our own urine and faeces. An *enfant terrible* of the Singaporean art scene, Vincent Leow challenged this taboo by drinking his own urine in a 1992 performance, before offering bottles of his own urine for sale as artworks soon afterward.[2] The anarchic and rebellious nature of Leow's performance resulted in him gaining public notoriety and garnering headlines from Singaporean newspapers such as 'Drink Urine? Urgh! But …' and 'But Is This Really Art?' (Nelson, 2019).[3] Again, given the taboo trade-off phenomenon, we have good reason to believe that Leow's performance is likely to invoke imaginative resistance.

4.4 Denying P1

Another possible strategy might involve denying P1 (i.e. that art does not necessarily involve knowledge). Aesthetic cognitivists are a certain group of philosophers for whom art gives its audience knowledge and the capacity of art to give its audience knowledge enhances its aesthetic value.[4] We have good reason to expect justification for the denial of P1 from the aesthetic cognitivists.

Knowledge is traditionally interpreted in terms of propositional knowledge or the knowledge of propositions. A proposition is a sentence in the declarative mode and it is a bearer of truth values: it can be either true or false. Where ϕ denotes a proposition, the modal operators K (for knowledge) and B (for belief) can take scope over ϕ. We have already encountered axiom T in epistemic logic (see § 3.1):

$$\text{(T) } K_s\phi \to \phi$$

Here are a few other axioms in epistemic logic (Hintikka, 1962):

$$\text{(KB1) } K_s\phi \to B_s\phi$$
$$\text{(KB2) } B_s\phi \to K_sB_s\phi$$
$$\text{(D) } B_s\phi \to \neg B_s\neg\phi$$

According to axiom KB1, if agent S knows that ϕ, then they believe that ϕ. According to axiom KB2, if S believes that ϕ, then they know that they believe that ϕ. According to axiom D, if S believes that ϕ, then it is not the case that they believe that not-ϕ. Certain propositions about human nature, human society and the human condition might count as sources of knowledge, even if they are propositions that have been asserted or implied by fictional characters in fictional works. For example, consider the following propositions:

S1: A certain kind of straight talk could very well get you in trouble.
S2: There is no curse more terrible than to give birth to a pretty female in a world of men as nasty as dogs in heat.

S1 is asserted by the grandson character in Kuo Pao Kun's *The Coffin is Too Big for the Hole*, a Kafkaesque play about an individual's efforts to bury his grandfather's traditional, grand, oversized coffin in a standard-sized plot. S1 makes sense relative to a context in which a grandson, responsible for the funeral rites of his grandfather, has to reckon with the ideology of state regulation. S2 is asserted by the prostitute-protagonist Dewi Ayu in Eka Kurniawan's *Beauty is a Wound*, a novel that spans the dying days of Dutch colonialism, the Japanese occupation and the era of independence in Indonesia. S2 acquires its meaning from the context of a history of violence wrought against Indonesian women by Dutch colonizers, Japanese invaders and occupiers and Suharto's brutal dictatorship. The possibility of acquiring propositional knowledge from literary artworks weakens the force of the Platonic charge in Chapter 3 that art never engages with reason and only arouses, appeals to and strengthens the inferior and non-rational part of the soul.

In equal measure, we can acquire propositional knowledge from propositions that have been asserted in the context of visual works of art. There is a wealth of knowledge to be gleaned from propositions about modern and contemporary Southeast Asian art in T. K. Sabapathy's *Writing the Modern*, a non-fictional and art-historical work. Sabapathy is a Singaporean art historian and *Writing the Modern* contains selected texts from newspaper columns, exhibition catalogues, artist monographs, symposium proceedings, etc. written by Sabapathy. Furthermore, consider the following proposition:

S3: The term 'Mooi indie' ('Beautiful Indies'), used to describe paintings depicting Indonesian natural landscape, does not reflect the reality of the situation for the colonial subjects of the Dutch East Indies.

S3 is one of several assertions made by Sindudarsono Sudjojono (1939) in a diatribe against the mooi indie genre. Instead of merely depicting mountains, hills, forests, rice fields, idyllic huts and villages, Sudjojono wanted Indonesian artists to paint sugar factories, emaciated peasants, the automobiles of the wealthy and the gabardine trousers and shirts of tourists. Sudjojono's article in October 1939 may be regarded as an artistic manifesto, declaring the intentions, motivations and views of the artist. Furthermore, Sudjojono is widely regarded as having played a key role in leading his fellow Indonesian artists away from the mooi indie genre and toward realism and (later) abstraction.

Fredericus Jacobus van Rossum du Chattel's (n.d.) *Indonesian Landscape* and Jumaldi Alfi's (2014) *Rereading Landscape Mooi Indies #08* are two paintings that may be evaluated in the light of Sudjojono's striking remarks about the mooi indie genre. The use of the term 'Mooi indie' can be traced to du Chattel (1930) and its genre constraints in favour of volcanoes, mountains, river valleys and villages bathed in golden sunshine are carefully observed in du Chattel's *Indonesian Landscape*. Paintings in this romantic colonial genre, designed to both evoke a nostalgia for the East Indies and cater specifically to European tastes, are unlikely to be viewed in an entirely positive light if we incorporate the propositional knowledge from S3 into our evaluative procedure. On the other hand, Alfi's *Rereading Landscape Mooi Indies #08* is a painting that may be regarded as part of a reclamation project: it reclaims the mooi indie component of Indonesian art history and culture, re-appropriates the mooi indie genre first identified by du Chattel, and rewrites Indonesian art history in a manner that is sensitive to the critical insight afforded by Sudjojono in S3. However, we are under no strict obligations to confine our understanding of knowledge in art to mere propositional knowledge, as might be contained in assertions in non-fictional works (e.g. art-historical works, art manifestoes) or fictional works (e.g. assertions by fictional characters about human nature, human society and the human condition).

4.5 Modes of aesthetic knowledge

A denial of P1 could be substantiated by an appeal to the non-propositional modes of aesthetic knowledge. Apart from propositional knowledge, artworks could help us to gain practical knowledge: we could learn how to feel appropriately, improve our practical reasoning abilities, develop our imaginative capacities and attend to the world in a more focused fashion.[5] This practical knowledge (or knowledge-how) is distinct from propositional knowledge (or knowledge-that).

Art could also help us to attain conceptual knowledge.[6] Whereas a proposition may be characterized in terms of a combination of or connection between ideas, a concept is an idea that may or may not be connected to other ideas in propositional form. Artworks might present us with problems that put the very terms of our thought in question. Art might lead to conceptual revision, affecting the future thought, speech and behaviour of its audience.

Art might even be said to be capable of granting conceptual knowledge of art itself. *Towards a Mystical Reality* was an exhibition staged by Redza Piyadasa and Sulaiman Esa in Kuala Lumpur in 1974 (see Figure 4.1). This event caused quite a stir, not least because Piyadasa and Esa chose to exhibit an assortment of found objects and detritus (e.g. opened and half-drunk Coca Cola bottles, a store-bought birdcage, a discarded silkscreen, a discarded raincoat, a randomly collected sample of human hair, used mosquito coils, an empty chair, etc.). *Towards a Mystical Reality* is also the title of a book co-written by Piyadasa and Esa in conjunction with the exhibition (its namesake). In their book manifesto, Piyadasa and Esa (1974) identify their primary concern to be the direction of Malaysian art in the 1970s and the concept of modern Malaysian art.

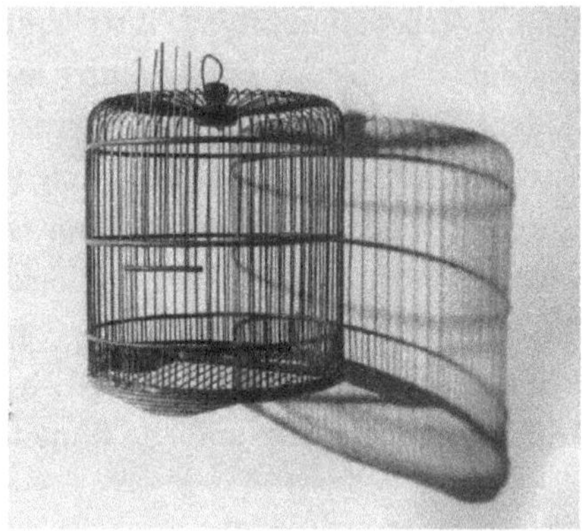

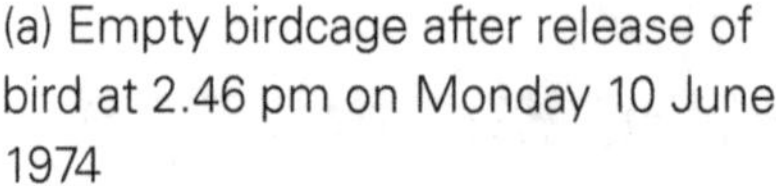

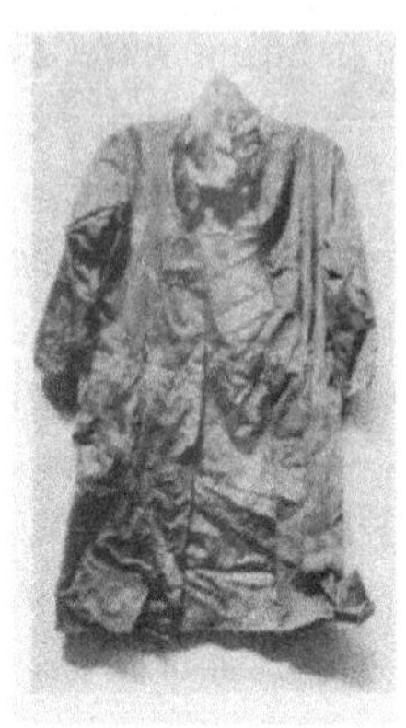

(a) Empty birdcage after release of bird at 2.46 pm on Monday 10 June 1974

(b) Discarded raincoat found at a Klang rubbish dump at 4.23 pm on Sunday 13 January 1974 that must have belonged to someone

Figure 4.1 Redza Piyadasa and Sulaiman Esa's (1974) *Towards a Mystical Reality*. Exhibition held at Dewan Bahasa dan Pustaka, Kuala Lumpur Image sources: Abdullah and Chung (2014) and Sabapathy (1994). Reproduced with permission of Sulaiman Esa Art Space.

According to Piyadasa and Esa, there are alternate ways of approaching reality besides the Western empirical viewpoint and these alternative approaches do not necessitate the dependence on and emulation of forms and idioms that have their origins in the West. Rather, art is about heightening the audience's perception and experience of reality and the artist can dictate that process of perception. Piyadasa and Esa envision modern Malaysian art as a conceptual and dialectical activity, untethered from illusionistic devices and grounded instead on the real, the concrete and the daily happenings of everyday life that are taken for granted. Piyadasa and Esa's 1974 exhibition provides us with insight into their concept of modern Malaysian art, while their 31-page book manifesto offers this knowledge in the form of propositions.

Plato's desire to banish the poets from the ideal and just city-state stems from a sense of how art might be dangerous (e.g. morally speaking). After all, art typically engages with, arouses and appeals to our imagination and emotions (i.e. the inferior and non-rational part of the soul). In contrast with this Platonic reservation, aesthetic cognitivists have argued that artworks might provide us with knowledge about moral values and the moral requirements of concrete situations. In addition, this moral knowledge need not be propositional in nature. According to Nussbaum (1990), moral attention and moral vision find their most appropriate articulation in the novels of Henry James and we have good grounds to include inside moral philosophy certain artworks (e.g. Henry James's novels). The possibility of acquiring moral knowledge from artworks may even constitute part of the argument in defence of poets that eventually allows poets back into the city-state.

Furthermore, artworks can provide us with phenomenal knowledge (or knowledge-what-it-is-like) (Walsh, 1969). Knowledge-what-it-is-like is experiential and phenomenal in nature and has cognitive value. For example, my work of historical fiction might be able to provide us with knowledge of what it is like to be an ang ku kueh seller trying to make ends meet in 1980s Singapore. On a far darker though no less important note, art often bears witness to the worst horrors of the city-state.[7] Genocide refers to the deliberate and mass extermination of a particular group of people and it is (unfortunately) an indelible part of Southeast Asian history.[8] The Khmer Rouge genocide led to the deaths of 1.5–2 million people in Cambodia in the 1970s. Vann Nath was a Cambodian painter who survived and depicted the horrors of the Khmer Rouge's S-21 prison. Vann Nath's paintings, painted by the artist to ensure that history will not repeat itself, are now exhibited at the Tuol Sleng Genocide Museum (formerly the S-21 prison). These paintings provide graphic and sobering knowledge-what-it-is-like-to-live-in-a-genocide-ridden-state from the perspective of a survivor, document the worst aspects of human nature, bear witness to the horrors of the Khmer Rouge genocide (including the horrendous torture at S-21) and were used as evidence to convict prison chief Kaing Guek Eav (or Comrade Duch).

Against the worst horrors that may be experienced (e.g. torture, genocide, etc.) must be balanced the more typical and traditional rituals and rhythms of the experience of Southeast Asian people (e.g. love, work, courtship, marriage, moral development, etc.). Nothing precludes this phenomenal knowledge from being transmitted through songs. The *dikir barat* is a style of Malay group choral singing, popular in both Malaysia and Singapore. The *dikir barat* is traditionally Kelantanese and may have been derived from a form of religious chanting known as *zikir*, in which groups of men gather to sing praises to the Prophet of Islam (Matusky, 1985).[9] Nonetheless, the *dikir barat* is generally considered to be a secular art form. The *dikir barat* is thought to have spread to Singapore and other parts of Malaysia from Kelantan (Osman, 1998). Its lyrics are witty and relevant to the daily lives of people, covering themes such as village life, changes due to modernization and work, advice about how to be a good person and what to look for in a partner (Brennan, 2001). Given the sheer range and diversity of themes encompassed by the *dikir barat*, it may be regarded as a veritable source of knowledge-what-it-is-like-to-live-and-love-and-learn. Banishing poets from the city-state could stymie the opportunity to acquire this brand of phenomenal knowledge and deprive us of a potential source of cultural and epistemic value.

The format of the *dikir barat* renders it a convenient means through which information and new values can be disseminated and promulgated. In 1996, certain groups had already used their *dikir barat* performance to thematize important issues such as AIDS and corruption. This led the Chief Minister Datuk Nik Abdul Aziz bin Nik Mat to observe that the *dikir barat* could satisfy the Horatian platitude (normally reserved for poetry) of instructing and delighting. At the same time, the *dikir barat* was subject to a temporary proscription or ban in May 1998, when that same Chief Minister accused certain organizers of having turned their *dikir barat* performances into a form of entertainment incorporating immoral elements and contradicting Islamic teachings. The ban was lifted in July 1998, after new guidelines were put in place to specify how the *dikir barat* could be performed in the future.

The epistemic and moral dangers or powers of art compelled Plato to banish the poets from the ideal and just city-state (§ 3.11). The epistemic and moral dangers or powers of the *dikir barat* resulted in a curious Southeast Asian analogue to this Platonic move: the short-lived proscription on the *dikir barat* between May–July 1998. Nonetheless, the *dikir barat* remains a lively and key tradition in Kelantan, with the popularity of *dikir barat* performances remaining undimmed and no further proscriptions being introduced (Brennan, 2001). Perhaps this decisive upturn in the fortunes of the *dikir barat* may be attributed to its ability to satisfy the Horatian platitude of instructing and delighting in a manner consistent with contemporary notions of Islamic cultural identity in Kelantan.

4.6 Aesthetic anti-cognitivism

To recapitulate, a denial of P1 (i.e. that art does not necessarily involve knowledge) will give us grounds for maintaining that Argument 1 (or the argument in favour of the banishment of poets), though valid, is unsound.[10] We may rely on the appeal that aesthetic cognitivists make to various modes of aesthetic knowledge, including (though not limited to) practical knowledge, conceptual knowledge, moral knowledge and phenomenal knowledge. To the extent that one narrowly defines knowledge in terms of propositional knowledge, one will fail to encompass these other non-propositional modes of aesthetic knowledge.

On the other hand, aesthetic anti-cognitivists may deny either that art gives its audience knowledge or that the capacity of art to give its audience knowledge enhances its aesthetic value (Diffey, 1995; Lamarque & Olsen, 1994; Stolnitz, 1992). Recall the constructive dilemma relative to the audience that was first introduced in Chapter 3: either the audience is epistemically inferior or it is not epistemically inferior (P1). According to the first horn of this dilemma, if the audience is epistemically inferior, then it cannot judge whether an artist is epistemically reliable (P2). According to the second horn of this dilemma, if the audience is not epistemically inferior, then it will not learn anything new from the artwork (P3). By implication, the artwork will be banal, trivial, or limited in cognitive value. The first horn of the dilemma may be blunted, once we recognize that each audience member can overcome their epistemic inferiority by learning about the rules of art and related conventions that govern artistic creation and the context of creation and background beliefs common to the community to which the artist belonged. However, the second horn and the related problem of banality or triviality remain.

4.7 Argument in favour of aesthetic anti-cognitivism

This problem of banality or triviality could be incorporated into a more general argument (let us call it Argument 2) in support of aesthetic anti-cognitivism. Here is what Argument 2 looks like:

P1: Either we learn something from art or we do not learn anything from it.
P2: If we do not learn anything from art (e.g. we merely have the illusion of knowledge), then aesthetic anti-cognitivism is correct.
P3: If we learn at least something from art, then this aesthetic knowledge is either trivial or non-trivial.
P4: If this aesthetic knowledge is trivial or banal, then aesthetic anti-cognitivism is correct.

P5: If this aesthetic knowledge is non-trivial, then either it is difficult to articulate this knowledge precisely or it is not difficult to do so.

P6: If it is difficult to articulate this aesthetic knowledge precisely, then aesthetic anti-cognitivism is correct.

P7: Even if it is not difficult to articulate this aesthetic knowledge precisely, this knowledge does not contribute to the aesthetic value of the artwork.

P8: If this aesthetic knowledge (though it may be articulated precisely) does not contribute to the aesthetic value of the artwork, then aesthetic anti-cognitivism is correct.

C: ∴ Aesthetic anti-cognitivism is correct.

Formally:

P1: $p \veebar \neg p$

P2: $\neg p \rightarrow t$

P3: $p \rightarrow (q \veebar \neg q)$

P4: $q \rightarrow t$

P5: $\neg q \rightarrow (r \veebar \neg r)$

P6: $r \rightarrow t$

P7: $\neg r \rightarrow s$

P8: $s \rightarrow t$

C: ∴ t

Argument 2 is proof-theoretically valid in the same way that Argument 1 is proof-theoretically valid.[11] If P1–P8 are all true, then it must be true that aesthetic anti-cognitivism is correct. The implication would be that it is neither true that art gives its audience knowledge nor true that the capacity of art to give its audience knowledge enhances its aesthetic value. Argument 2 provides justification for P1 in Argument 1 and aesthetic anti-cognitivism may be invoked in support of the banishment of the poets.

In summary, Argument 1 supports the conclusion in favour of art being dangerous and the Platonic verdict of banishing the poets. Assuming the truth of all its premises, the conclusion of Argument 1 cannot be false. Notwithstanding the validity of Argument 1, however, we may have reasons to deny its soundness. If P3 (i.e. that art is powerful) is denied, then we might invoke the phenomenon of imaginative resistance and point out how art has too little power to move us in certain instances. Alternatively, if P1 (i.e. that art does not necessarily involve knowledge) is denied, then we might appeal

– as aesthetic cognitivists have already done – to such non-propositional modes of aesthetic knowledge as practical knowledge, conceptual knowledge, moral knowledge and phenomenal knowledge (§§ 4.4–4.5). However, Argument 2 is an argument that may be wielded on behalf of aesthetic anti-cognitivism to diminish the strength of any appeal to aesthetic cognitivism. What do you think? Is the matter already settled in the debate between aesthetic cognitivism and aesthetic anti-cognitivism? Where might your sympathies lie in this particular debate and how might you go about justifying your position?

5

Art, Merit and Taste

5.1 Aesthetic merit

In the debate between aesthetic cognitivism and aesthetic anti-cognitivism that we encountered in the previous chapter, here are the central questions:

Q1: Can art confer knowledge to its audience?
Q2: If art has the capacity to confer knowledge, does this knowledge-conferring capacity enhance its aesthetic value?

Let us call Q1 the epistemic question and Q2 the aesthetic question. Aesthetic cognitivism, as we have already seen, is constituted by the conjunction of responses in the affirmative to the epistemic (Q1) and aesthetic questions (Q2). Aesthetic anti-cognitivists, on the other hand, will respond in the negative to at least one of either the epistemic question (Q1) or the aesthetic question (Q2). Aesthetic cognitivists typically appeal to such non-propositional modes of aesthetic knowledge as practical knowledge, conceptual knowledge, moral knowledge and phenomenal knowledge. A healthy sense of scepticism toward aesthetic cognitivism may however be fostered by Argument 2 in favour of aesthetic anti-cognitivism. Whether one responds in the affirmative or negative to the aesthetic question (Q2), one must first be able to provide a non-question-begging account of aesthetic value or merit. What is the concept of aesthetic merit, how might it be distinguished conceptually from other concepts, and are there any criteria according to which we might be able to determine the degree of aesthetic merit of an object? Our philosophical attention will now be devoted to these considerations.

5.2 **The century of taste**

The eighteenth century has been characterized as the century of taste (Dickie, 1996). Eighteenth-century theories of taste foregrounded their concern with judgements of aesthetic merit or aesthetic value and eighteenth-century philosophers who devoted their attention to questions about aesthetic merit or aesthetic value include Francis Hutcheson, Alexander Gerard, Archibald Allison, David Hume and Immanuel Kant.

The following claims have been defended by eighteenth-century theories of taste:

>   Claim 1: The concept of aesthetic value or merit is related to the concept of aesthetic taste.
>   Claim 2: There is a disanalogy between aesthetic taste and gustatory taste.
>   Claim 3: The degree of aesthetic merit of an object is determined relative to certain standards (i.e. established norms and practices of evaluation).

A key development in the century of taste involved the use of taste as a metaphor for judgements of aesthetic merit or aesthetic value (Claim 1). At the same time, theorists of taste were keen to distinguish between judgements of aesthetic merit (reflecting aesthetic taste) and gustatory judgements (Claim 2). Last but not least, these theorists were interested in identifying certain established norms and practices of evaluation (viz. standards of taste) that might permit the determination of the degree of aesthetic merit in an object (Claim 3).

5.3 **The paradox of taste**

The paradox of taste is a paradox that arises in virtue of two seemingly quite plausible assumptions (Mothersill, 1989):

>   Assumption 1: Tastes are diverse and subjective character;
>   Assumption 2: Tastes are better or worse.

Assumption 1 in favour of the diversity and subjective character of tastes is reflected in such saws and proverbs as *'chacun à son goût'* (French), *'de gustibus non disputandum est*' (Latin) and '蓼食う虫も好き好き' (Japanese).[1] From Assumption 1, it appears to follow that disputation about judgements is impossible because of the subjective character of taste. From Assumption 2, on the other hand, it appears to follow that disputation about judgements is possible because of the existence of various evaluative norms. It cannot be the case that disputation about judgements is both impossible (in line with Assumption 1) and possible (in line with Assumption 2), hence the paradox.

5.4 Resolving the paradox

One way of resolving the paradox could involve disambiguating between two senses of taste. Whereas Assumption 1 holds with respect to gustatory taste (or $Taste_1$), Assumption 2 holds with respect to aesthetic taste (or $Taste_2$):

Assumption 1: $Tastes_1$ are diverse and subjective character;
Assumption 2: $Tastes_2$ are better or worse.

When speaker S utters 'This Canary wine is agreeable', the logical form p of the utterance is 'This Canary wine is agreeable relative to the gustatory taste of S'. When speaker T utters 'This Canary wine is not agreeable', the logical form q of the utterance is 'This Canary wine is not agreeable relative to the gustatory taste of T'. There is no contradiction between the utterances of speakers S and T, since $\diamond(p \wedge q)$: we may simply conclude in favour of Canary wine being agreeable to S and not agreeable to T. Assumption 1 about the diversity and subjective character of gustatory tastes can be upheld.

Conversely, when S utters 'This tale of the ang ku kueh seller has some aesthetic merit' and T utters 'This tale of the ang ku kueh seller does not have any aesthetic merit', the former is affirming (whereas the latter is denying) that the tale has some aesthetic merit relative to certain established norms, practices of evaluation, or standards of aesthetic taste. Insofar as these standards are held in common between S and T, there is the possibility of critical argument about aesthetic taste and Assumption 2 about the superiority or inferiority of aesthetic taste can equally be upheld.

One possible explanation for the disanalogy between gustatory and aesthetic judgements of taste may be found in the differing degrees of complexity between the former and the latter. In a statement by Wittgenstein (as reported in G. E. Moore's notes on Wittgenstein's lectures), you can say more in discussing whether an arrangement of flowers in a bed is beautiful than in discussing whether the smell of lilac is beautiful. Whereas gustatory judgements (e.g. the smell of lilac, the taste of Canary wine) might not be sufficiently complex to allow for the possibility of critical argument, the same cannot be said about aesthetic judgements (e.g. the beauty of a flower-bed arrangement, the aesthetic merit of the tale of an ang ku kueh seller).[2] In other words, while both gustatory taste ($Taste_1$) and aesthetic taste ($Taste_2$) allow for judgements of taste to be made, only aesthetic judgements of taste are sufficiently complex to allow for the possibility of critical argument.

The diversity of tastes, as described in Assumption 1, is keenly felt in the Southeast Asian context: to the long history of cultural influence from China, India and Islam must be added the court tradition and the royal patronage of the arts by kings and princes, European colonial influence, and even American neo-colonial influence. At the same time, normative motivations and considerations may give rise to a contestation over the forms that Southeast Asian art should take and lend force to Assumption 2. Recall Sudjojono's (1939) diatribe against the mooi indie genre that was first described in § 4.4. According to Sudjojono, paintings and photographs in the mooi indie genre were overly romanticized depictions of Indonesian natural landscape, designed to make the Dutch East Indies look exotic, evoke a nostalgia for the colonial way of life and cater to foreign tastes.

In a similar vein, Fabián de la Rosa was a Filipino master of genre painting, whose skilled and classicist draughtsmanship was complemented by a balanced and austere palette. De la Rosa was the uncle and mentor to Fernando Amorsolo and both de la Rosa and Amorsolo offered idealized bucolic depictions of landscapes, women and peasant life in the Philippines (see Figure 5.1).

However, Victorio Edades' (1928) *The Builders* constitutes a powerful modern reaction to the prevalence of picturesque scenes and genre paintings. The heavy brush strokes and sheer contortion of human bodies engaged in labour in *The Builders*, in stark contrast with pastoral scenes of farmers planting rice and local beauties bathing by the river, are designed to shock viewers who had become used to the picturesque aesthetic of de la Rosa and Amorsolo.

It may be argued that the antiquated taste for the picturesque, against which both Sudjojono and Edades inveighed, is simpler than the more modern tastes that Sudjojono and Edades sought to cultivate. It by no means follows that this taste for the picturesque, reflected in the mooi indie genre of Indonesia and the genre paintings of the Philippines, is a gustatory taste

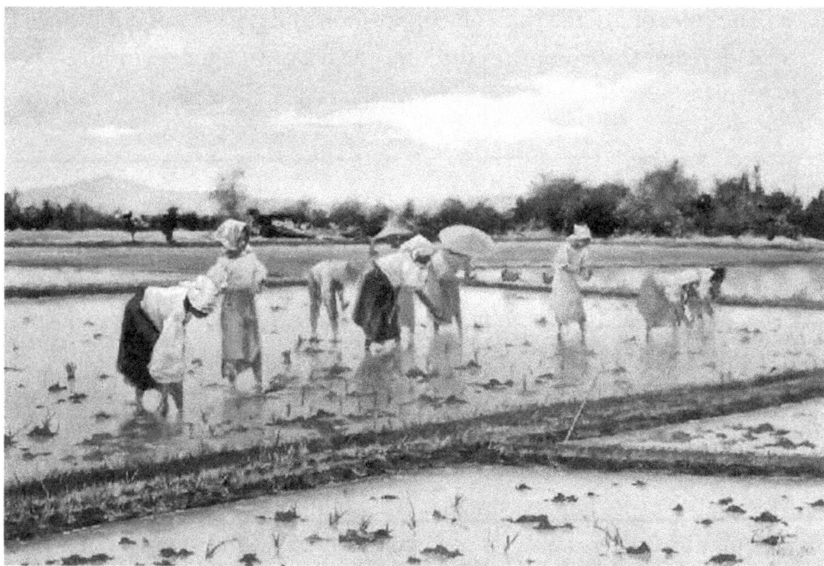

Figure 5.1 Fabián de la Rosa's (1902) *Women Working in a Rice Field.* Oil on canvas. Public domain. Art Collection 2/Alamy Stock Photo.

(Taste$_1$) rather than an aesthetic one (Taste$_2$). Instead, when we declare that a taste for the modern is better than or superior to a taste for the picturesque, much of the heavy lifting appears to be done by various norms, practices of evaluation and standards of aesthetic taste relative to which judgements of taste are made. A better approach to resolving the paradox of taste will focus on these norms, practices of evaluation, or standards of aesthetic taste.

5.5 The Ogilby-Milton phenomenon

According to David Hume's (1757) approach to the paradox of taste, we have good normative grounds for maintaining that tastes are better or worse (Assumption 2). These normative grounds yield standards, norms and practices of evaluation that help us to achieve consistency and coherence in our aesthetic preferences. Let S denote a set of standards, established norms and practices of evaluation and may be defined as follows: $S := \{s_1, s_2, \cdots, s_n\}$.

Here are some examples of standards, established norms and practices of evaluation (Hume, 1757):

s_1: The rules of art, the rules of composition and the laws of criticism;
s_2: A decision that comprises the joint verdict of true judges or ideal critics;
s_3: A canon.

$(s_1 \wedge s_2)$ comprise Hume's double standard of taste and have been referred to as his official doctrine (Shelley, 1994). s_3, on the other hand, forms Hume's unofficial doctrine (Levinson, 2002). The rules of art, the joint verdicts of true judges and artistic canons recognize the existence of certain formal constraints on aesthetic preferences. According to the principle of verisimilitude ($P1$), we have *pro tanto* normative reasons to favour artworks that have a truthlikeness or semblance of reality. The more verisimilitudinous an artwork is, the more believable certain things are in the context of the world-according-to-the-artwork. According to the principle of realism ($P2$), on the other hand, we have *pro tanto* normative reasons to favour artworks that offer an accurate and unembellished depiction of the nature of reality (as opposed to an idealized and imaginative one).

Let $\geq_s$ stand for a complete aesthetic preference order relation indexed to S and ranging over objects a, b, c, etc. in the sample space Ω. Certain principles (e.g. $P1, P2$, etc.) ensure that $\geq_s$ will satisfy the following conditions:

(Completeness) $a \geq_s b$ or $b \geq_s a$
(Reflexivity) $a \geq_s a$
(Transitivity) $((a \geq_s b) \wedge (b \geq_s c)) \rightarrow (a \geq_s c)$

In general, $a \geq_s b$ iff $v_a \geq_s v_b$: I aesthetically prefer object a to object b if a is at least as aesthetically valuable as object b. According to the completeness condition, either a is at least as good as b (aesthetically speaking) or b is at least as good as a (aesthetically speaking). According to the reflexivity condition, a is at least as good as itself (aesthetically speaking). According to the transitivity condition, if a is at least as good as b and b is at least as good as c (aesthetically speaking), then a is at least as good as c (aesthetically speaking).

Hume's (1757) approach to the paradox of taste involves a particular observation:

Whoever would assert an equality of genius and elegance between Ogilby and Milton, or Bunyan and Addison, would be thought to defend no less an extravagance, than if he maintained a mole-hill to be as high as Teneriffe [sic], or a pond as extensive as the ocean. Though there may be found persons, who give preference to the former authors; no one pays attention to such a taste; and we pronounce without scruple the sentiment of these pretended critics to be absurd and ridiculous. The principle of the natural equality of tastes is then totally forgot.

Hume (1757, pp. 209–10)

Here is how we might represent the Ogilby-Milton phenomenon: $m >_s o$. Relative to a set of standards, norms and practices of evaluation collectively denoted by S and their associated principles (e.g. $P1, P2$, etc.), we have good normative grounds for favouring John Milton the poet over John Ogilby the poet. In the context of Southeast Asian art, we have at least some *pro tanto* reasons to favour the mooi indie genre photographs of (say) Thilly Weissenborn and the picturesque genre paintings of Fabián de la Rosa and Fernando Amorsolo (§ 5.4). After all, these artworks have a certain truthlikeness or quality of verisimilitude that may be attributed to the skill and technical ability of the artists. Weissenborn's unique style of studio-based, commercial photography is evident in her *View of the High Plateau of Garut & the Tikoeraj, on the Way to Kamodan*, in which her subject is as much the light and its luminous effects as the flooded paddy fields of Tjisoeroepan (Maxwell, 2020). Given Weissenborn's obsession and special skill with light, it is little wonder that she has been described as a calligrapher with light (Drissen & Landell, 1983).

At the same time, the reasons for favouring Weissenborn's mooi indie photograph (generated by the principle of verisimilitude or $P1$) must be balanced with the reasons against favouring it (generated by the principle of realism or $P2$). As an overly idealized or romanticized depiction, it is minimally grounded in the actual nature of Southeast Asian reality. Weissenborn's photograph, given its romantic effects and idealization of the landscape in the Preanger province, is consistent with the desire of colonial authorities to represent Indonesia as a desirable tourist destination, evokes a nostalgia for the colonial way of life, and is complicit with Dutch colonialism. Like the rest of the mooi indie genre of which it is a part, Weissenborn's photograph is out of touch with the true nature of the colonial regime, the outbreaks of rebellion and the gritty reality of agricultural life in Southeast Asia. More generally, picturesque genre photographs and paintings like Weissenborn's photograph add impetus to Plato's worry that art leads us away from truth and knowledge (§ 3.11). The realist impulses of Sindudarsono Sudjojono and Victorio Edades would count as a useful corrective in this regard. All things considered and on the balance of reasons, we have good normative grounds for aesthetically preferring the modern and realist artworks of Sudjojono and Edades over their picturesque counterparts.

5.6 The joint verdict of true judges

Who are these true judges or ideal critics whose joint verdict constitutes s_2 or one of the standards of aesthetic taste? They are individuals who happen to possess the following characteristics in conjunction: freedom from prejudice and an ability to enter an artwork on its own terms; delicacy of taste; strong and sound sense; sufficient practice; and sufficient comparative appreciation of artworks. Xenophilia refers to the love of and attraction to all things unknown and foreign and it is associated with the tendency for modern artists – including Southeast Asian ones – to seek approval abroad and especially in the West. As has been pointed out by Nelson (2019), there has been a tendency, dating from the nineteenth century, for Southeast Asian artists to seek artistic education and esteem in Europe. Many of these Southeast Asian artists (e.g. Raden Saleh, Juan Luna, et al.) mastered European styles and techniques, won prizes in competitions when pitted against their European peers and even (in certain instances) adopted European manners. The xenophilic acclaim reserved for Southeast Asian artists who achieved recognition abroad appears to imply that these true judges or ideal critics reside outside of Southeast Asia. At the same time, these artists will still have had to prove their worth to local audiences upon their eventual return to Southeast Asia. In recent years, regional institutions such as the Fukuoka Asian Art Museum (Japan), National Gallery Singapore (Singapore) and Queensland Art Museum (Australia) have played an important role in curating Southeast Asian art (§ 2.2). All things considered, the geographical base of true judges or ideal critics matters less than the reliability of their verdicts and the breadth of appeal enjoyed by artistically significant works of art.

Are these true judges real or ideal? If we concede from the outset that no judge or critic is beyond making mistakes, the judges are real, and the joint verdict of judges or critics may be fallible, then s_2 will be accessible though epistemically unreliable (Horn 1). Nonetheless, these real judges might afford us a real basis for deriving the rules of art (s_1). Conversely, if these judges are ideal, then they can never be wrong and we may require the joint verdict of all true judges, near or far, living, dead, or yet unborn, actual or possible. This would make s_2 epistemically reliable though inaccessible (Horn 2). Horns 1 and 2 jointly constitute the Humean dilemma with respect to the judges and critics identified in s_2.

If we take the financial value of artworks to be defeasible indicators of their artistic and art-historic worth, then Redza Piyadasa's (1978) *Art*

Proposition is effectively a challenge to true judges and ideal critics to determine or justify the mutable nature of this financial value. In the text that has been stencilled over the image, Piyadasa reveals that he bought an oil painting from Anuar Rashid for 130 Malaysian dollars, before blacking out most of this painting and offering it for sale at 500 Malaysian dollars. One implication of *Art Proposition* is that Piyadasa's artwork could command a higher price than the original artwork of his student Anuar Rashid in virtue of Piyadasa's superior reputation. As the market value of *Art Proposition* has since likely increased beyond 500 Malaysian dollars, even Piyadasa is not the best judge of the actual financial value of his own artwork.

5.7 The canon and the real problem of taste

Inclusion in the canon is associated with higher financial, artistic and art-historical value. While the lack of a well-defined canon of Southeast Asian art was one of the challenges identified in § 2.2, the fact that Piyadasa's blacked-out version of Anuar Rashid's painting (plus a few simple interventions) justifiably commands more than thrice the asking price of Rashid's original painting suggests that a canon, especially one in which Piyadasa has a prominent role, is already taking shape (Nelson, 2019). s_3 or the canon comprises great artworks or masterpieces that stand the test of time. It may even be argued that s_3 could be used to identify the true judges of s_2 and weaken Horn 1 of the Humean dilemma, since s_3 could help us to identify true judges who might be able to serve as measuring rods of aesthetic merit.

The canon contains masterpieces or great artworks whose aesthetic value or merit is durable across temporal barriers, wide across cultural barriers, and broadly appreciated at some level by almost all who engage in these artworks. Here, an inference to the best explanation would be that the aesthetic merit of these masterpieces is responsible for their passing the test of time. In line with an ameliorative approach and a culture of praxis, we need to minimize Eurocentric bias in the construction of this canon, make room for multiple canons, and recognize Southeast Asian works of art alongside their Western counterparts.[3]

Let Rashid's original painting be denoted by r and let Piyadasa's original painting be denoted by p. v_i' and v_i denote (respectively) the financial and aesthetic values of any object i. Here is the argumentative support for the inferences we have made about Rashid and Piyadasa's artworks:

P1: $v'_p > v'_r \rightarrow v_p >_{s3} v_r$
P2: $v'_r = 130$ – in Malaysian dollars (as asserted by Piyadasa)
P3: $v_p' = 500$ – in Malaysian dollars (as asserted by Piyadasa)
C1/P4: $\therefore v_p' > v_r'$ – P2–P3
P5: $p >_{s3} r \leftrightarrow v_p >_{s3} v_r$ – from § 5.5
C2: $\therefore v_p >_{s3} v_r$ – P1 & P4 (*modus ponens* or R_1)
C3: $\therefore v_p >_{s3} v_r \rightarrow p >_{s3} r$ – P5 ($\leftrightarrow_E$ or R_{14})
C4: $\therefore p >_{s3} r$ – C2 & C3 (*modus ponens* or R_1)

Let an izeal critic be a critic who is introverted, zany, left-handed, arrogant, etc. On what grounds in particular should one defer to the tastes of the ideal critic, as opposed to (say) the tastes of an izeal critic? Levinson (2002) has termed this the real problem of taste. In response to the real problem of taste, one might argue that true judges or ideal critics have a special relationship to the masterpieces or great artworks in the canon (s_3). If a is a great artwork and therefore a member of the canon, it follows that the true judge will appreciate a as such. We may conclude that the true judges or ideal critics identified in s_2 have a criterial connection to masterpieces in the canon (s_3). These true judges or ideal critics are the individuals to whom we look to explain why Piyadasa's (1978) *Art Proposition* can command a much higher price than Rashid's original oil painting and how Piyadasa has come to enjoy his position of prominence in the emerging Southeast Asian artistic canon. We will equally look to true judges or ideal critics to provide an account of how a blacked-out version of Rashid's painting might be more valuable than the original painting itself.

6

Kant's Response to Hume

6.1 Kant's critical project

Hume's approach to philosophical aesthetics, as we have already discovered in § 5.5, is grounded in the existence of certain standards of taste (viz. standards, established norms and practices of evaluation). Elsewhere, Hume's attack on metaphysics in general and the concept of cause and effect in particular is what prompts Immanuel Kant to construct his critical philosophy as a response to Hume. What is the nature of Hume's attack on metaphysics?

According to Hume (1739), knowledge is probabilistic rather than apodictic in nature and probabilistic knowledge rests on causal reasoning about causes (C) and their effects (E). Furthermore, causal reasoning rests on a uniformity of nature assumption (A1), according to which nature is sufficiently uniform that unobserved instances of Cs and Es in the future will resemble observed instances of Cs and Es in the past. Hume then provides an argument in support of the conclusion that we should maintain a mitigated scepticism about probabilistic knowledge:

P1: If A1 is to count as a principle of inductive reasoning, then it needs to be justified.
P2: A1 may be justified either deductively or inductively.
P3: A1 cannot be justified deductively.
P4: A1 cannot be justified inductively.
C: ∴ A1 cannot count as a principle of inductive reasoning.

Formally:

P1: $p \rightarrow q$
P2: $q \leftrightarrow (r \veebar s)$

P3: $\neg r$

P4: $\neg s$

C: $\therefore \neg p$

This will not do for Kant, whose approach to philosophical aesthetics is grounded on human autonomy and human understanding as the source of the general laws of nature that structure all our experience (including our aesthetic experience). Hume's attack on the concept of cause and effect, arguably the most important concept in metaphysics, awakens Kant from his dogmatic slumber (Kant, 1783). Kant's critical philosophy or critical project involves his constitution of experience by certain *a priori* concepts and principles of the understanding. This critical project comprises three parts: the *Critique of Pure Reason*, whose concern is with the limit and scope of metaphysics and whose analysis addresses the principles that define the concepts whereby we can experience and understand the world around us; the *Critique of Practical Reason*, whose concern is with moral philosophy and whose analysis addresses the principles that define the concepts of moral obligation and moral duty; and the *Critique of Judgment*, whose concern is with judgement and its relationship with reason (freedom) and understanding (necessity). Kant's *Critique of Aesthetic Judgment* (Kant, 1952), the first part of the *Critique of Judgment*, may be regarded as a response to Hume's 'Of the Standard of Taste' (Hume, 1757).

6.2 The analogy between logical judgement and aesthetic judgement

As far as philosophical aesthetics goes, both Kant and Hume take for granted the following: gustatory taste serves as a plausible model for aesthetic judgement, we often disagree about our judgements of taste, and the determining ground of an aesthetic judgement cannot be other than subjective (i.e. one's feelings of pleasure and displeasure).[1] However, whereas Hume asserts the existence of certain standards of taste, established norms and practices of evaluation (viz. s_1, s_2 and s_3), Kant denies their existence.[2] Instead, Kant characterizes aesthetic experience in general and aesthetic judgement in particular in terms of a set of moments: universality, disinterestedness, purposiveness and necessity. This characterization of aesthetic judgement in terms of its moments is of a piece with Kant's attempt to constitute experience by certain *a priori* concepts and principles of the understanding in response to Hume's attack on metaphysics. As Kant's denial of the existence of certain standards of taste depends on his characterization of aesthetic judgement in terms of its moments, it will be fruitful for us to outline Kant's account of aesthetic judgement.

From the outset, Kant's account of aesthetic judgement relies on an analogy between logical judgement and aesthetic judgement. Logical judgement has four aspects:

Quantity – $\forall$ (universal), $\exists$ (particular), $\varnothing$ (nullity);
Quality – p (affirmation), $\neg p$ (negation);
Relation – $p \rightarrow q$ (hypothetical), $p \vee q$ (disjunctive);
Modality – $\square p$ (necessity), $\diamond p$ (possibility)[3]

Analogously, aesthetic judgement has four moments:

Moment 1 (Quantity) – universality;
Moment 2 (Quality) – disinterestedness;
Moment 3 (Relation) – purposiveness;
Moment 4 (Modality) – necessity.

6.3 Aesthetic judgement and its moments

By the universality (or Moment 1) of an aesthetic judgement is meant the following: the aesthetic judgement does not rest on the concepts of objects. One must refer the object immediately to one's feelings of pleasure and pain and not by means of concepts. The Angkor Wat is a Hindu temple complex that was originally dedicated to Vishnu and built for Suryavarman II, a Khmer king, during his reign in the twelfth century (1113–49 CE) (Cœdès, 1920, 1940).

Helen Churchill Candee, a feminist writer, survivor of the sinking passenger liner RMS *Titanic*, and explorer of Southeast Asia, wrote the first major English-language study of the ruins of the Angkor Wat (see Figure 6.1). Candee (1924, p. 82) describes how the bas-relief carved decorations in the portico of the outer enceinte (enclosure) of the Angkor Wat humanize the entire temple and are infinite in variety and rich in grace and originality, evoking an art that is altogether 'strange and compelling'.

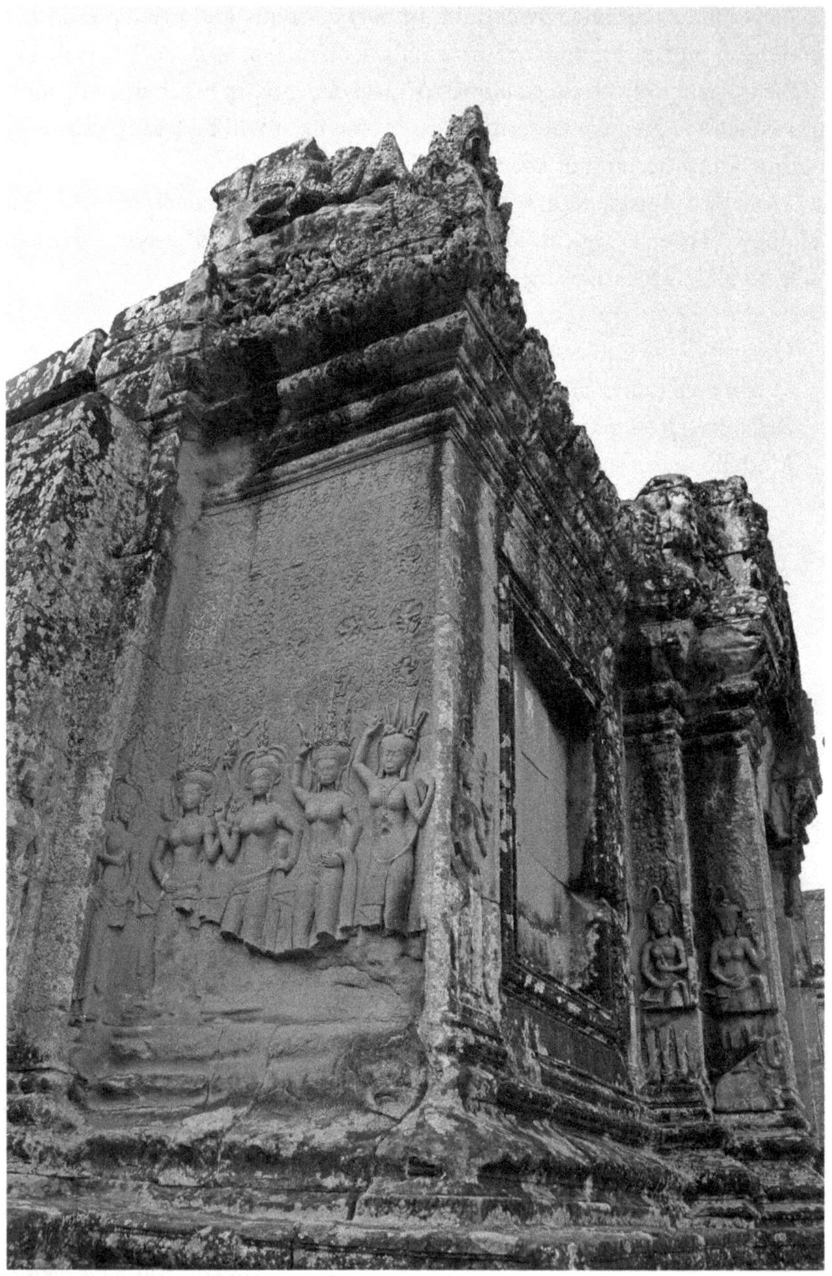

Figure 6.1 Angkor Wat. © Mig Gilbert, 2018. Reproduced under the Creative Commons Attribution-ShareAlike 2.0 Generic licence via Wikimedia Commons.

Candee asserts elsewhere that there is only cause for wonder (rather than cause for study) with respect to the moat of the Angkor Wat. If one claims – as Candee has done – that the Angkor Wat has aesthetic merit, then it is Kant's belief that this judgement must, as an aesthetic judgement, claim validity for everyone. At the same time, this universality must not depend on the concept of the Angkor Wat. Rather, one must refer the object of one's aesthetic judgement (viz. the temple complex itself) immediately to one's feeling of pleasure.

According to Moment 2 of an aesthetic judgement, an object of aesthetic merit is said to be the object of disinterested satisfaction. Disinterested satisfaction in turn implies in a person's aesthetic judgement a ground of satisfaction for everyone. One cannot find the ground of this satisfaction in any private conditions connected to one's own subject. Rather, the satisfaction must be grounded on what one can presuppose in every other person. Certain culture-specific artistic conventions have been imposed on the Khmers responsible for the art, iconography and architecture of the Angkor Wat and Candee recognizes how these conventions are not shared by the West. At the same time, Candee implies that the ground of satisfaction may be found in both the Khmer and non-Khmer people, since our sense of beauty, splendour, wonder and allure at the temple remains undimmed by our knowledge of the cultural specificity of these Khmer artistic conventions.

According to Moment 3 of an aesthetic judgement, its determining ground is the mere form of purposiveness in the representation by which an object is given to us. Aesthetic judgements have at their basis a merely formal purposiveness (i.e. a purposiveness without a purpose) and this is quite independent of the concept of the good. The formal purposiveness of an artwork is the mere formal structure of an integrated whole from a manifold of parts. To perceive the aesthetic value or merit of an artwork is to see that and how the manifold of parts fit together into an integrated whole. Whereas the concept of the good presupposes an objective purposiveness (i.e. the reference of the object to a definite purpose), the purposiveness without purpose of the artwork is a subjective rather than an objective purposiveness. The layout of the Angkor Wat – a pyramid surrounded by a moat – has a celestial significance: it is supposed to evoke Mount Meru (the home of the gods in Hindu mythology) and the surrounding Sea of Milk from which ambrosia was churned by the gods and demons (Glaize, 1944). At the same, there is no need to be either a Hindu or someone with a sense of the celestial significance of the layout of the temple for Hindus to appreciate how the different parts (viz. the pyramid, moat, quincunx of towers, walls, moats, bas-reliefs, decorations, etc.) integrate into a whole that collectively evokes beauty, splendour, wonder and allure.

According to Moment 4 of an aesthetic judgement, a meritorious artwork has a necessary reference to satisfaction. This necessity is neither a theoretical objective necessity nor a practical necessity. Rather, it is an exemplary necessity: it is the necessity of the assent of all comers to a judgement that is regarded as the example of a universal rule that we cannot state. At the same time, this exemplary necessity cannot be derived from definite concepts and it cannot therefore be apodictic. It is only under the presupposition of a common sense that aesthetic judgements can be laid down. At the same time, we place at the basis of aesthetic judgements a communal rather than a private feeling. Candee's evaluation of the aesthetic merit of the Angkor Wat is grounded in a communal rather than a private feeling and there is an equally clear sense of the necessity of all parties assenting to a judgement in favour of the magnificence and wonder of the Angkor Wat.

Kant's account of aesthetic judgement in terms of Moments 1–4 of universality, disinterestedness, purposiveness and necessity provides support for the following claims:

Claim 1: A judgement of taste is not objective (cognitive or logical) but subjective (aesthetic);
Claim 2: An aesthetic judgement is singular.

Consider the following utterances:

S1: The sandstone used in the Angkor Wat monument is either grey, yellow-brown, red, or green in colour.
S2: The grey, yellow-brown, red, or green colour of the sandstone is pleasant.
S3: All structures built of sandstone have aesthetic value.

S1 constitutes an objective (cognitive) judgement.[4] Conversely, S2 constitutes a subjective (aesthetic) judgement: its determining ground is subjective (i.e. the feeling of pleasure or pain). The contrast between S1 and S2 is helpful in the context of Claim 1 about the subjective (aesthetic) character of judgements of taste. Even when we are justified in concluding from a particular instance that the Angkor Wat monument (a structure built of sandstone) has aesthetic merit, we cannot make an inductive generalization from this instance to derive a rule of aesthetic taste concerning all structures built of sandstone. Strictly speaking, therefore, S3 is a logical rather than an aesthetic judgement: it is the conclusion of an inference that is based on an aesthetic judgement. We have here our basis for Claim 2 about the singularity of aesthetic judgements.

6.4 The Kantian denial

The stage is set for Kant's denial of the existence of standards of taste, established norms and practices of evaluation. According to Kant, there can be no objective rule of taste to determine, by means of concepts, whether something has aesthetic merit or value. The first reason for this denial concerns how each aesthetic judgement is subjective: its determining ground is the feeling of pleasure or pain of the subject and not the concept of an object (see Claim 1). Therefore, one will be labouring in vain when one seeks the standards of taste that shall furnish, by means of definite concepts, a universal criterion for the beautiful or aesthetically valuable. The second reason for this denial concerns how aesthetic judgements rely on the weaker empirical empirical criterion of the universal communicability of sensation (satisfaction or dissatisfaction), without the aid of concepts.

It might be countered that Kant's account of aesthetic judgement ends up constituting (*malgré lui*) a standard of taste. However, the following thought experiment by Kulenkampff (1990) will suffice to put paid to this idea: ask someone to pick out all the beautiful or aesthetically pleasing objects in the world. Tell this person that beauty consists in something's being an integrated whole despite having a manifold of parts (see Moment 3 (Relation) or purposiveness). Even with a proper understanding of Kant's *Critique of Aesthetic Judgment*, this person would not really know what to look for. Therefore, such an individual would not be able to fulfil their original task on the mere basis of Kant's account of aesthetic judgement. This implies that Kant's account of the moments of aesthetic judgement, though informative, stops short of counting as a reliable set of criteria for us to distinguish between those works that possess beauty and those that do not.

6.5 Two further Kantian claims

Recall Claims 1 and 2, supported by Kant's account of aesthetic judgement in terms of Moments 1–4 of universality, disinterestedness, purposiveness and necessity:

> Claim 1: A judgement of taste is not objective (cognitive or logical) but subjective (aesthetic);
> Claim 2: An aesthetic judgement is singular.

These further two claims are consistent with both Claims 1 and 2 and Kant's account of aesthetic judgement:

> Claim 3: An aesthetic judgement involves a free play of imagination and understanding;
> Claim 4: The beautiful is a symbol of the morally good.

Claim 3 is supported by the Kantian notion that reflection on aesthetic qualities and aesthetic judgement is not guided by concepts. Instead, what we have is a free play of imagination and understanding. We have a finite, two-step procedure in Kant's psychology of cognition. At the first step, imagination apprehends the manifold and collects and presents this manifold to the understanding.[5] At the second step, understanding reduces to conceptual unity the non-conceptualized manifold of parts.[6]

Claim 4 suggests that there is at best only a kind of analogy between moral judgement and aesthetic judgement. According to Kant, moral judgements are intersubjectively valid. Analogously, aesthetic judgements, though subjective (Claim 1), are universal and shareable by everyone with common sense (as discussed in Moment 4 (Modality) or necessity). Kant's account gestures toward a community of common sense ungoverned by concepts. Among the concepts that might influence our aesthetic evaluations or judgements is our concept of art (i.e. what art is or should be). As discussed in the Angkor Wat example, although this monument is governed by certain culture-specific Khmer artistic conventions that we may neither fully appreciate nor understand, our concept of what art is or should be (governed by alternative artistic conventions) fails to dim our sense of beauty, splendour, wonder and allure. Our aesthetic judgements are therefore grounded in a communal feeling rather than a private one. Satisfaction or pleasure in the beautiful and sublime is associated with our delight in the cognitive faculties of imagination and aesthetic judgement being freed from subservience to reason and understanding. Although the art, iconography and architecture of the Angkor Wat are governed by Hindu cosmology, our inability to fully understand how these cosmological constraints work to influence the artistic choices of the Khmer artists and architects should not fatally undermine our

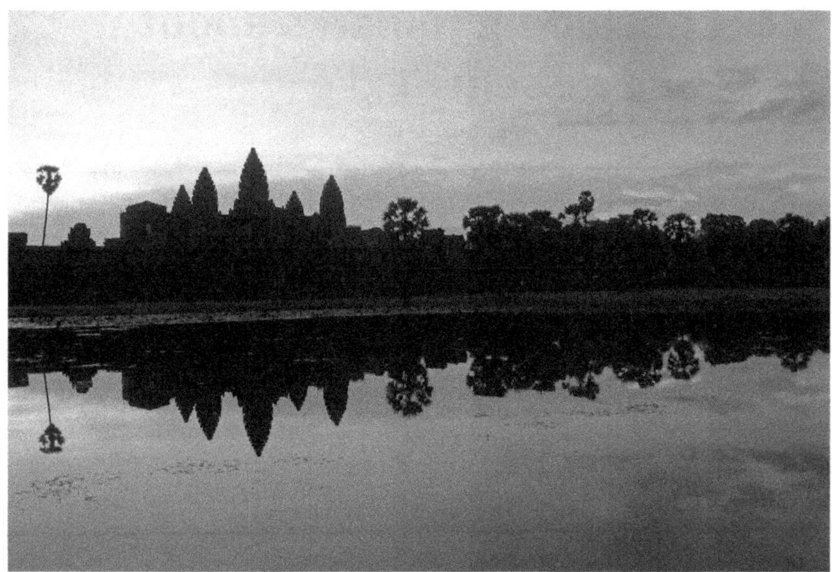

Figure 6.2 Angkor Wat at sunrise. Image source: Catherine Coe (2019, p. 8).

experience of pleasure in the presence of the temple complex. In aesthetic cognition, we are freed from the constraints of propositional discourse. Recall Candee's point in § 6.3 about how the moat of the Angkor Wat is a cause for wonder rather than a cause for study (see Figure 6.2). Nonetheless, while art is unique and autonomous under Kant's account, the price is that art cannot offer morality.

The influence of Kantian aesthetic theory – as represented by Claim 4 – led to the late eighteenth-century view of the aesthetic realm and the ethical realm being autonomous from each other. The view according to which art and ethics are autonomous and independent realms of value is called autonomism and it entails that moral flaws are irrelevant to the aesthetic value of an artwork. Kant-inspired autonomism is distinct from both Humean moralism, which maintains that art will have too little power precisely when it might pose certain moral dangers, and Platonic moralism, which pays art the perverse compliment of thinking it is powerful enough to be morally dangerous.[7] Both Humean and Platonic moralists agree that at least some moral flaws can also count as aesthetic flaws and equally deny that art and ethics are autonomous realms.

6.6 Concluding remarks about Kant and dissent

Recall that the eighteenth century has been described as the century of taste (§ 5.2). Dickie's (1996) theses about the century of taste may be summarized as follows: Francis Hutcheson laid down the basic – limited but promising – theory of taste; David Hume, following Hutcheson's lead, all but perfected the theory of taste; Immanuel Kant led the theorists of taste into a blind alley; and philosophers who came after Hume failed to follow his promising leads, resulting in theories of taste dying out.

Someone who is critically appraising Kantian aesthetic theory may be swift to point out the following: while Kant claims that aesthetic judgements attribute to their object value that is universal and shareable by everyone with common sense, he does not ultimately succeed in producing a convincing idea of what this value is. Kant does however propose that the determining ground of our aesthetic judgements is pain or pleasure. Worse yet, Kant attempts to distinguish between interested pleasure and disinterpreted pleasure (see Moment 2 (Quality) or disinterestedness). In the final analysis, this distinction is invalid. After all, there is an absence of reliable criteria for distinguishing between interested pleasure and disinterested pleasure. More pertinently, there cannot be any such criteria, since there is no such thing as disinterested pleasure (Kulenkampff, 1990).

A final note of dissent may be raised. As was first identified in § 6.2, both Kant and Hume support the claim that the determining ground of an aesthetic judgement cannot be other than subjective (i.e. one's feelings of pleasure and displeasure). It may be countered that this claim offers an incorrect causal aetiology of aesthetic judgement. Neil Sinhababu (2017), a philosopher at the National University of Singapore, defends a desire-based account of aesthetic experience that can be put to good use here. According to this account, vivid representations of desired features in works of art (e.g. melodic structures in music, relationships between fictional characters in drama) cause pleasure. Although introspecting the content of these desires is not easy and the desired features may resist precise characterization, good art critics find ways to provide illuminating descriptions of these features, and good artists create works that have them.

Sinhababu (2017) observes that a desire not to be naked in public could motivate me to put my clothes on before going outside, although I do not usually feel pleasure when I dress myself. Conversely, if I vividly represent myself as being naked in public, then I will feel considerable displeasure. These considerations allow Sinhababu to conclude that desire is the cause of both pleasure and motivation. It is desire that both causes us to direct our attention to features of artworks and causes the pleasure arising from the presence of those features that we desire artworks to instantiate. A desire-based account, grounded in a desire for artworks to instantiate particular features, makes it clear that feelings of aesthetic pleasure and displeasure arise from desires that can also motivate action. Where does our critique of Kant's aesthetic theory – including Sinhababu's (2017) desire-based account of aesthetic experience – leave Kant? Do you find yourself to be more in agreement with Hume's affirmation of the existence of standards of taste or Kant's denial of their existence? If so, what reasons might you adduce in support of your position?

7

The Ontology of Artworks

7.1 Ontological questions

You may recall from Chapter 1 how at least some of our aesthetic concerns might traverse the philosophical branch of metaphysics (e.g. concerns about the identity conditions and ontological status of works of art). Ontology is the branch of metaphysics that is concerned with the nature of being and related notions (becoming, existence, reality, etc.).

Thomasson (2004) has provided us with a useful sample of ontological questions about works of art: what sorts of entities count as works of art? Are works of art physical objects, imaginary entities, or something else? Under what conditions do works of art come into existence, survive, or even cease to exist? More questions may be added to this sample of ontological questions. For instance, what is it in virtue of which certain entities get grouped into the category reserved for works of art? Are there any other ontological distinctions that ought to be observed within the category of artworks? How does a lump of bronze or marble get categorized as a work of sculpture? On what grounds would a pigment-covered canvas get classified as a painting? What is it in virtue of which a sequence of sound waves gets categorized as music as opposed to mere noise? How might a sequence of marks on pages get identified as a work of literary art? A completely successful ontology of artworks should be able to tell us what entities are artworks and what entities are not. Even if complete success is unattainable, a partially successful ontology of artworks should still be able to tell us the identity conditions for artworks (i.e. the conditions under which this work and that are the same work of art).

7.2 The simple physical object hypothesis

According to the simple physical object hypothesis, the artwork is simply a physical object (Davies, 2003; Rohrbaugh, 2013). In other words, the bronze sculpture of Stamford Raffles – nicknamed *orang besi* for iron man – by the sculptor-poet Thomas Woolner is nothing over and above an 8-foot-tall lump of bronze and Liu Kang's portrait of Sun Yee or Shen Yan, the principal of the Singapore Academy of Arts, is a mere arrangement of pastel on paper measuring 64 × 48 cm (see Figure 7.1).

The balitaw, a Visayan folk song-and-dance debate for courtship and dialogue, is constituted by sequences of sound waves and bodily movements.[1] By the same token, Paz Márquez-Benítez's 'Dead Stars', the first Filipino modern English-language short story and an allegory to American imperialism, may be identified with linguistic marks on pages (Igloria, 2007, pp. 1249–50).[2] The simple physical object hypothesis implies that an artwork and its replica should be regarded as numerically distinct if there are fundamental differences in their respective physical bases. The original Mandalay Palace, built as a Burmese royal palace by King Mindon Min in 1857, was razed to the ground as a result of bombings during the Second World War. A modern replica of the palace was rebuilt in the 1990s. However, while the original Mandalay Palace was made of gilded teak wood, the modern replica of this palace relies extensively on concrete and gold paint as building materials. If the simple physical object hypothesis is correct, then plausible grounds exist for us to regard the original palace and its modern replica as numerically distinct works of architecture.

In a related vein, Roman Ingarden (1986, pp. 20–1) has argued that certain works of art are distinct from their numerous performances. Every work of music is absolutely unique, in contrast to the multiplicity of its possible performances. This rules out our identifying a musical work with its multiple performances: while the work is unique and individual ($n = 1$), any number of performances of that work ($n \in N$) is possible. The song 'Mai Phen Rai (Never Mind)' was first composed by Ken Low in 1997 as part of the Singaporean musical theatre production *Chang & Eng* about the famous and eponymous pair of Siamese-American conjoined twins. Since its debut in 1997, Ekachai Uekrongtham's *Chang & Eng* has undergone multiple stagings. If Ingarden (1986) is to be believed, however, then the 'Mai Phen Rai (Never Mind)' song is distinct from its multiple performances at various musical stagings.

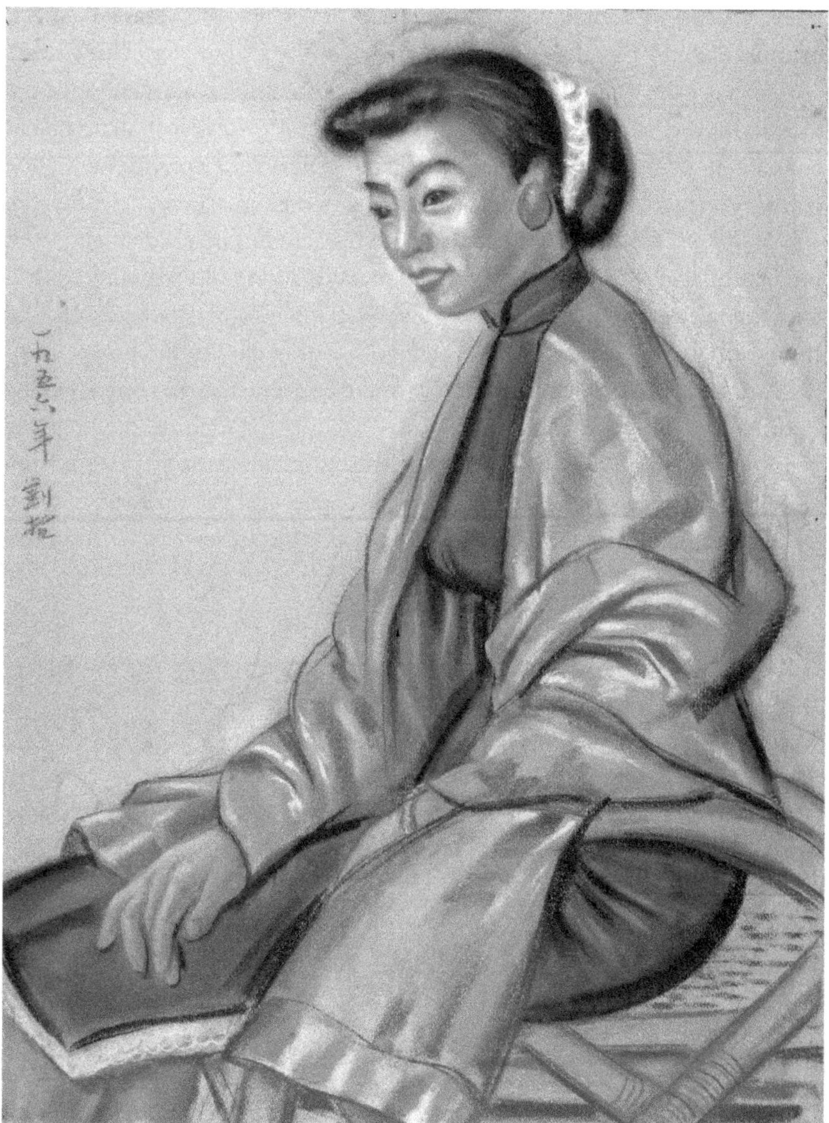

Figure 7.1 Liu Kang's (1956) *Lady in Blue Dress (Artist – Shen Yan)*. Pastel on paper, 64 × 48 cm. Gift of the artist's family. Collection of National Gallery Singapore. Image courtesy of National Heritage Board, Singapore.

While the simple physical object hypothesis might first appear plausible, it is beset with several problems. For starters, it may be sufficient in certain instances for an artwork to be an imaginary entity. After all, a composer like Ken Low could create a work of music in his head merely by imagining the relevant tune, without having to write the score or play the notes. This work of music would therefore be an imaginary entity in the composer's head, rather than a physically instantiated sequence of sound waves (Collingwood, 1938). In the second instance, artworks and the physical matter that constitutes them have different identity or persistence conditions. In the context of Western art, a famous example would be works of ancient Greek and Roman sculpture, which can survive the loss of polychrome and even the loss of arms (as in the case of the Venus de Milo) and remain identical with themselves. At the same time, however, the physical matter constituting these works cannot survive these changes, putting paid to the prospects of the simple physical object hypothesis. In the Southeast Asian context, many Buddha statues of the Angkor Wat (§ 6.3) are missing their heads. Since the heads are the most valued part of Buddha statues, many of them have been knocked off, stolen and sold on antiques markets. At the same time, these Buddha statues can survive the loss of their heads, just as the bodiless

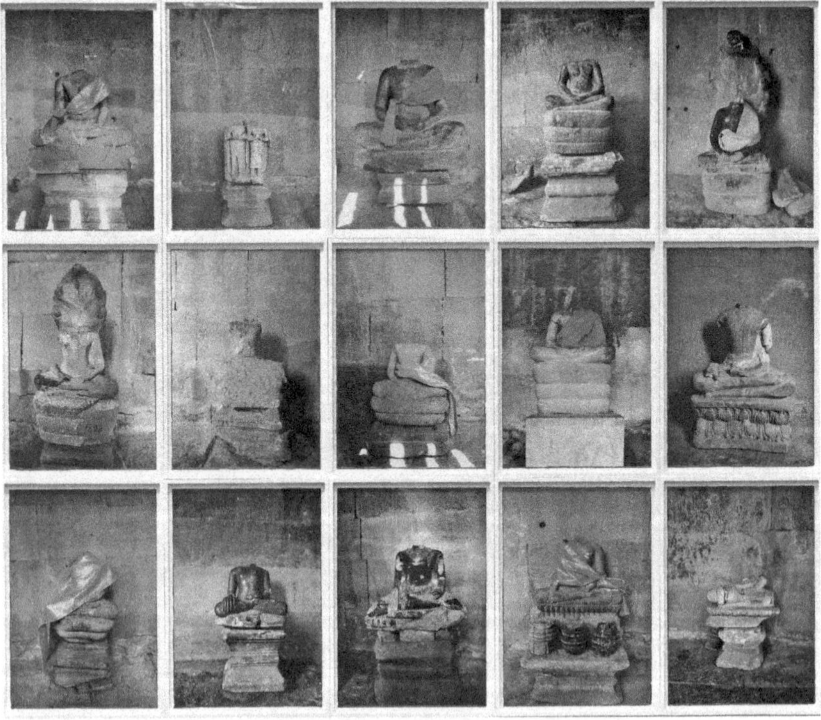

Figure 7.2 Dinh Q. Lê's (2012) *The Headless Buddhas of Angkor.* 15 digital prints. Courtesy of Shoshana Wayne Gallery, Los Angeles and the artist.

Buddha heads that have been sold on antiques markets and made their way into musea and private collections can survive the loss of their bodies. Headless Buddha statues, a powerful symbol of the looting of Southeast Asia's cultural and artistic heritage, have even become the subject of several photographic series by Dinh Q. Lê, a Vietnamese-American multimedia artist (see Figure 7.2).

7.3 The imaginary entity hypothesis

The imaginary entity hypothesis is a rival of the simple physical object hypothesis (§ 7.2). According to the former hypothesis, artworks are just imaginary entities (Collingwood, 1938; Sartre, 1966). Recall how a work of music could be completely entertained, rehearsed, or imagined in the composer's head, without a single note being played or written down. According to Sartre (1966), artworks are imaginary entities, created and sustained by acts of imaginative consciousness, and existing as long as they are objects of these acts of imaginative consciousness.

Tan Teng Kee's (1979) *The Picnic* was an outdoor exhibition, held near Teng Kee's Normanton Estate home in Singapore in 1979. At this exhibition, a 100-metre-long painting was cut up and burnt in a fire sculpture supported by 6-metre-high poles. This outdoor exhibition is often regarded as the first instance of a happening or performance art in Singapore. While information about this exhibition is still preserved in photographic footage, not all the physical matter constituting the artwork-as-a-happening has survived. According to the simple physical object hypothesis (§ 7.2), *The Picnic* survives as an artwork in virtue of its associated physical object, the photographic footage. However, the imaginary entity hypothesis allows us to defend the claim that *The Picnic* will continue to exist as an artwork even if the footage gets lost, as long as this work can be entertained, imagined, created and sustained by acts of imaginative consciousness.

The imaginary entity hypothesis is no less plagued with problems than its rival. In the first instance, how can one and the same imaginary work of art be experienced and evaluated by many different people? Will each of these individuals not appear to be engaged in their own imaginative activities in the absence of any appropriate physical constraints? In the event that the footage of *The Picnic* gets lost, might there not be as many imagined versions of Teng Kee's outdoor exhibition, created and sustained by acts of imaginative consciousness, as there will be people doing the imagining? In the second instance, if artworks exist only in the minds of artists and their audience, then they cannot truly be destroyed. However, given how seriously we take attempts to destroy painted canvases and literary manuscripts, deface statues, or disrupt musical performances, the imaginary entity hypothesis cannot be telling the whole story about art. In the third instance, would we have to allow that an artist has created an artwork of the relevant sort if they have simply created something in their head? If so, then we run the grave risk of overextending our inventory of artworks and trivializing the concept of an artwork.

7.4 The abstract entity hypothesis

The abstract entity hypothesis offers an alternative to both the simple physical object hypothesis (§ 7.2) and the imaginary entity hypothesis (§ 7.3). According to the abstract entity hypothesis, artworks are abstract entities and exist eternally, independently from all human activities (Currie, 1989; Wollheim, 1980; Wolterstorff, 1980). In addition, these artworks cannot genuinely be created by artists. Instead, they are only selected or discovered from the range of available types or kinds.

According to the moderate version of the abstract entity hypothesis, some (though not all) works of art (e.g. painting, sculpture) may be associated with physical objects (Wollheim, 1980; Wolterstorff, 1980). However, works of literature and music are not physical objects and should instead be regarded as abstract entities. According to the strong version of the abstract entity hypothesis, all works of art are abstract entities (Currie, 1989). The action-type hypothesis is a hypothesis according to which we discover a certain structure (e.g. of sounds, colours, etc.) via a specific heuristic path (i.e. the path used by the artist to discover the structure).

Both the abstract entity hypothesis and the imaginary entity hypothesis face similar problems. Much to the chagrin of their staunchest proponents, it is clear that works of art are mind-external public entities: they can be exhibited and they continue to exist once they have been created, even if they are not being perceived, imagined, or reconstructed. Furthermore, at least some works of art are perceptual: they are materially constituted by certain physical objects and may be destroyed if their constituting physical base is destroyed. The Cham people were an Austronesian group who forged

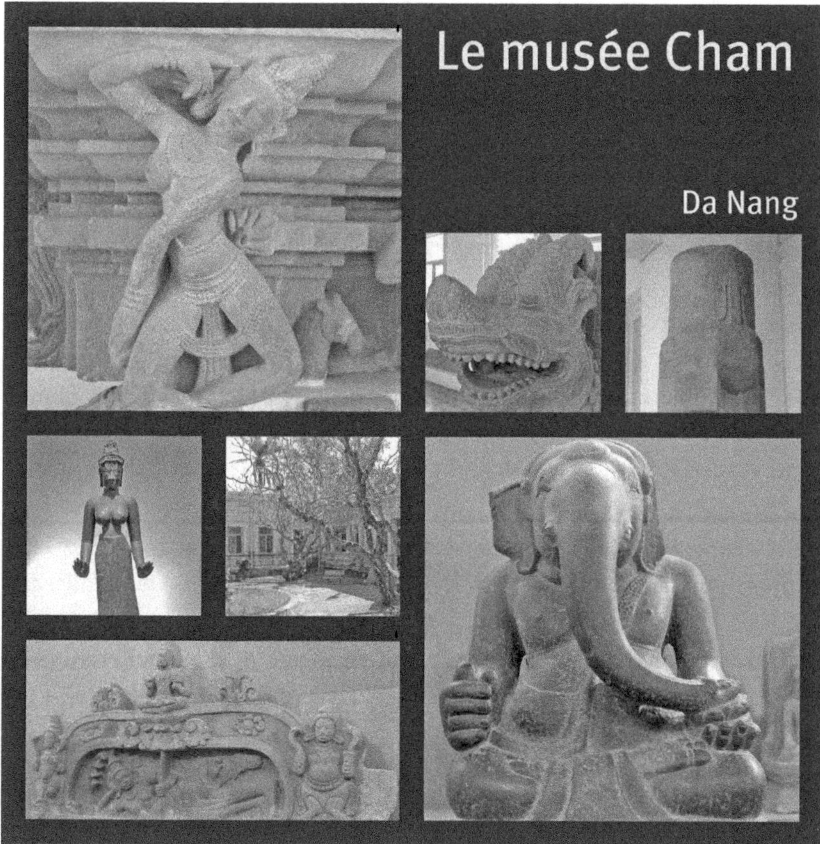

Figure 7.3 Catalogue for the Museum of Cham Sculpture (located in Hải Châu District, Đà Nẵng, central Vietnam). © Jean-Pierre Dalbéra. Reproduced under the Creative Commons Attribution-ShareAlike 2.0 Generic licence via Wikimedia Commons.

a civilization along central Vietnam and flourished between the third and fifteenth centuries (Phuong & Lockhart, 2011, p. 461) (see Figure 7.3). However, much classical Cham art has been lost to looting, vandalism, the devastating impact of the Vietnam War and the ravages of time. In a more contemporary context, more than a thousand works of art by the Singaporean artist couple Anthony Chua Say Hụa and Hong Sek Chern, representing thirty years of artistic labour, were destroyed in a studio blaze in 2013, and there is a sense in which these artworks were destroyed when their constituting physical base was razed by fire. As many of these artworks have no surviving copies, we appear to have good grounds to say of these works that they are now irrecoverably lost or destroyed.

7.5 Goodman's ontology of artworks

Given the naive and generally inadequate nature of the simple physical object hypothesis (§ 7.2), the imaginary entity hypothesis (§ 7.3) and the abstract entity hypothesis (§ 7.4), we have good grounds to look elsewhere for a more sophisticated ontology. Enter Nelson Goodman, whose ontology represents the aesthetic in terms of a set of symptoms relative to symbol systems.

In order to understand Goodman's (1968) ontology, we must first understand his use of terminology. A symbol scheme is a set of characters employed in a system, together with principles by which they are combined into complex characters (Goodman, 1968, p. 131). This symbol scheme is the pure syntactic level of a system, detached from meaning or reference. A symbol system is a symbol scheme correlated with a field of reference: it is a set of characters correlated with a set of extensions (Goodman, 1968, p. 143). Propositional logic L_0 (as described in Appendix A), Arabic numerals, and natural languages all constitute distinct symbol systems. The extension of the character or symbol 'T' is truth, the extension of the character or numeral '1' is the number 1, and the extension of the string of characters 'cat' is the carnivorous mammal (*Felis catus*).[3]

A symbol system is syntactically dense iff it has an infinite number of characters so ordered that between each two there is a third character (Goodman, 1968, p. 136).[4] Otherwise, it is syntactically articulate or differentiated. The distinction between syntactic density and syntactic articulateness is equivalent to the distinction between analogue (continuous) and digital (discrete). An analogue clock is syntactically dense: each position of its minute hand is a character of the clock's symbol system and between two positions of the hand (say at 45 and 46) there is a third intermediate position (45). A painting is syntactically dense, since it is either difficult or impossible to assign line and colour in an unambiguous fashion to definite characters in an articulate schema (e.g. an alphabet). By contrast, the musical notation on which works of music rely is syntactically articulate: there is no third intermediate character between C♯ from C. The first necessary condition for a symbol system to be depictive is syntactic density. A symbol system is semantically dense iff it has an infinite number of extensions so ordered that between each two there is a third extension. The symbol system of an analogue clock is semantically dense: between every pair of times (say four o'clock and half past four), there is a third intermediate time (a quarter past four). The second necessary condition for depiction is syntactic density.

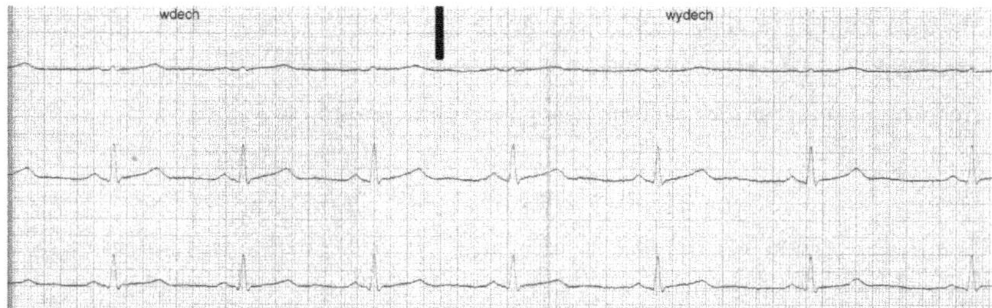

Figure 7.4 Electrocardiogram (ECG). Reproduced under the Creative Commons Attribution-ShareAlike 3.0 Unported (CC BY-SA 3.0) licence via Wikimedia Commons.

Relative repleteness is the third necessary condition for a symbol system to be depictive. One symbol system is less replete relative to another if the character-constitutive aspects under the first system are properly included among the character-constitutive aspects of the second system (Goodman, 1968, p. 230).

Consider the image of an electrocardiogram (ECG) shown in Figure 7.4. Like the ECG, Fua Haribhitak's (*c.* 1956) *Face*, an oil on canvas painting, relies on the use of lines.[5] However, only the relative distances from the originating point of the line are relevant in ECGs. In Haribhitak's *Face*, on the other hand, the colour, thickness, intensity and contrast of the lines are relevant as they are expertly used by Haribhitak in a semi-abstract depiction of part of a person. We may therefore conclude that Haribhitak's cubist-inspired portrait is more relatively replete than the ECG diagram. More generally, pictorial symbol systems are more relatively replete than diagrammatic symbol systems.[6]

7.6 Symptoms of the aesthetic

Following our discussion about the syntax, semantics and relative repleteness of symbol systems, we are now ready to identify the symptoms of the aesthetic. Density (syntactic and semantic) and repleteness allow us to depict (show) rather than describe (tell) and are characteristic symptoms of the aesthetic. According to Goodman, syntactic density, semantic density and repleteness are necessary and jointly sufficient for a symbol system to be depictive. Paintings are typically syntactically dense, semantically dense and more relatively replete than diagrammatic symbol systems. Songs with lyrics, though syntactically articulate and semantically articulate, are more relatively replete than the lyrics when they are merely spoken. Goodman's ontology of artworks should be subsumed under Goodman's nominalist conception of the world, according to which the world is what we create through scientific theories or works of art. We do not cognize the real world beyond scientific theories and works of art. Rather, the real world is only present in these theories and works and accessible to us through them. Through cognizing and understanding works of art, we come to understand our world.

Goodman's ontology of artworks has provided the inspiration for Harvard Project Zero. The principal research tasks of Harvard Project Zero include the following: analysing and classifying different types of symbol systems characteristic of different art forms, identifying and studying the skills and abilities required for understanding and manipulating art symbols, and investigating the methods of nurturing and training those abilities generally and as they bear upon particular art forms.[7]

7.7 The allographic–autographic distinction

Besides allowing us to distinguish between depiction and description (§ 7.6), Goodman's ontology of artworks, grounded in the symptoms of the aesthetic (viz. syntactic density, semantic density, relative repleteness), allows us to distinguish between autographic and allographic art. In autographic artworks, aspects of the work's history of production are essential to the identity of the work and there is a reliance on dense pictorial systems (analogue). Examples of autographic artworks include painting and sculpture. In allographic artworks, on the other hand, instantiations of the work of art are independent of the work's history of production. Allographic works of art rely on pure and articulate notational schemes (digital) that permit the perfect preservation of identity between replicas or performances of the same work.[8] Examples of allographic artworks include music, dance, theatre and literature.

Goodman's ontological distinction between allographic and autographic works of art has several important implications. The history of production is integral to an autographic work of art: only the actual canvas painted by Chua Mia Tee in 1955 counts as the *Epic Poem of Malaya* painting. Anything else, however perceptually indistinguishable from the original, counts as a copy. In addition, we can have multiple instantiations of allographic artworks such as Ken Low's 'Mai Phen Rai (Never Mind)' song from *Chang & Eng* that are independent of the work's history of production. Furthermore, while certain art forms (e.g. painting, sculpture, other autographic works) do not allow for performances, others (e.g. music, dance, other allographic works) might. Last but not least, there is the possibility of forgery in autographic art forms (absence of notation). However, there is no possibility of forgery in allographic art forms (presence of notation).[9]

7.8 Critical evaluation of Goodman

Goodman's influential ontology of artworks has resulted in his *Languages of Art* being lauded for its epoch-making status and powerful new vision of aesthetics grounded in analytic philosophy of language (Ernst et al., 2009; Robinson, 2000) (cited in Guczalski, 2021). At the same time, important objections have been raised against his ontology. As observed by Ben Blumson (2011), a philosopher at the National University of Singapore, syntactic density is not a necessary condition for depiction. Chess diagrams are not syntactically dense, since the number of possible diagrams is limited by the fact that there is a maximum of 32 chess pieces that may occupy only 64 squares. Neither is semantic density a necessary condition for depiction, since the extensions of chess diagrams are essentially the positions of the pieces on the board, of which there is only a finite number. The general notion of density (semantic or syntactic) has been critiqued by Guczalski (2022): if every dense symbol scheme is linear (in accordance with Goodman's ontology), then those symbol schemes that cannot be naturally ordered in a linear way (including the symbol scheme for painting) cannot be dense.

Some philosophers have questioned Goodman's reliance on the analogue/digital distinction in the context of his distinction between syntactic density and syntactic articulateness. For example, Lewis (1971) points out that we could have analogue computers that receive their input in the form of settings of variable resistors (e.g. a setting of m ohms would represent the number m). Therefore, differentiated or articulate analogue representation remains possible. Other philosophers have questioned the validity of the autographic/allographic distinction within Goodman's ontology (Zeimbekis, 2012, 2015). Yet other philosophers have tried to replace Goodman's necessary and jointly sufficient conditions (viz. syntactic density, semantic density, relative repleteness) with other sophisticated alternatives (e.g. semantic richness, syntactic sensitivity and relative repleteness, as proposed by Kulvicki, 2006), although it remains debatable whether more sophisticated accounts of depictive symbol systems are less susceptible to similar counterexamples as Goodman's account (Blumson, 2011).

For the purposes of this textbook, it is important to remember that Goodman's ontology of artworks does not constitute the final word. Furthermore, Goodman's account of the allographic–autographic distinction is grounded in the use of musical notation, betraying its own Eurocentric reliance on the European classical tradition of music as a point of reference. One important Southeast Asian counterexample to Goodman's account would be the gamelan, a traditional ensemble music from Indonesia that consists mainly of the use of percussion instruments. Musical notation is generally not used by Javanese musicians, who learn and memorize each piece by hearing it played and practising it themselves. Rather, kepatihan (a type of cipher musical notation) may be used by ethnomusicologists and foreign students learning gamelan. What are your final thoughts about Goodman's ontology of artworks? Do you think that Goodman provides adequate philosophical support for the claims that he makes about the symptoms of the aesthetic? How does this influential though controversial ontology of artworks fare in the Southeast Asian context?

8

Forgery

8.1 Case study: Chen Wen Hsi

In 1952, Chen Wen Hsi, a Chinese-born Singaporean artist, embarked on a painting trip to Indonesia with Cheong Soo Pieng, Chen Chong Swee and Liu Kang. Their travels took them to Jakarta, Surabaya, Bandung, Yogyakarta and Bali and would provide the inspiration for the Nanyang style of painting. The birth of the Nanyang style itself may be traced to a 1953 group exhibition by Chen Wen Hsi and his travelling companions, showcasing works from their 1952 trip to Indonesia. The Nanyang style is characterized by a depiction of Southeast Asian subject matter (e.g. tropical fruit, *kampung* or traditional village scenes, *batik* fabric, etc.) and a synthesis of techniques from Western traditions (e.g. Impressionism, Fauvism) and the Chinese ink tradition.[1] While Chen's art has evolved through the years from his expressive use of Chinese ink in the 1950s to a tendency toward the abstract in the 1990s, his ink paintings of animals (e.g. cranes, ducks, fish, etc.) are the most recognizable. His *Two Gibbons Amidst Vines* (undated) appears on the reverse side of the Singapore SGD 50 banknote. Chen Wen Hsi is an interesting case study in the context of forgery for a number of reasons. In the first instance, he declared in an interview with *The Straits Times* in 1988 (3 years before his death) that forgeries of his art were rife in the local art market. In the second instance, the National Gallery Singapore, home to the world's largest public collection of Southeast Asian art, was forced to stop displaying a painting entitled *Net Drying* by Chen on its website, after doubts were raised about its authenticity. Patrick Goh, a private art collector, has claimed authenticity for a version of Chen's *Net Drying* that he owns. Despite a further investigation by a team of experts assembled by the National Gallery, the results have been inconclusive.

8.2 What is a forgery?

The case study of Chen Wen Hsi's *Net Drying* is instructive. Unless the same artist makes multiple (possibly perceptually indistinguishable) copies of the same artwork, it cannot be the case that both the painting owned by the National Gallery and the painting owned by the private art collector are authentic. Suppose that Patrick Goh's claims are correct: this would imply that the National Gallery has a forged copy of *Net Drying*. Even if this forgery is a high-quality painting by one of Chen's disciples, it would still be a fake. Recall from Chapter 7 that there is the possibility of forgery with respect to paintings and other autographic works of art under Goodman's influential though contested ontology of artworks. In addition, each forgery poses certain challenges to the identity conditions of works of art, as it can lead individuals (including art experts) to misidentify the forged work as an original work of art.

At a first pass, a forgery refers to the phenomenon according to which something is presented as a work of art with a history it does not actually have. The forged copy of Chen's *Net Drying* cannot be integrated into the history of production of the original copy in a straightforward fashion (e.g. the actual canvas used by Chen when painting the original, the historical context of the painting, Wen Hsi's 1952 painting trip to Indonesia, the Nanyang style of painting that this trip inspired, the larger body of work that may be attributed to Chen, etc.). Instead, the forgery is parasitic on the existence of the original and typically involves a false claim about the identity of the artist. If, as we have supposed, the forged copy was produced by one of Chen's disciples, then the high-quality forgery is apt to mislead individuals to misattribute the work to Chen instead of his disciple.

8.3 Perceptual indistinguishability and aesthetic formalism

Suppose that an original painting by Chen is perceptually indistinguishable from its forged copy by his disciple. There is a school of thought according to which something's being a forgery should be irrelevant to one's considerations about aesthetic value. This school of thought is known as aesthetic formalism and its central tenet is that aesthetic value is a function of appearance or formal features (i.e. what may be perceived by means of the five senses) alone. Whatever false beliefs about the history of the work may be induced by the forged copy of Chen's *Net Drying*, these false beliefs should not affect our judgement of the aesthetic value of the copy.

A range of state-of-the-art scientific tools could help us to determine the truth of a work's provenance: mass spectrometry allows us to identify the pigments used in a painting and detect the presence of pigments not yet created at the time of production of the artwork, X-rays may be used to determine whether a reused canvas has been used for a forgery, infrared reflectography permits the investigation of underdrawings and sketches below the surface of the painting, and microscopes facilitate the examination of craquelure or cracks that appear in older paintings. Combined with good old-fashioned detective research (e.g. combing through archives and art catalogues, examining sales receipts, etc.), these scientific tools may eventually allow us to tell apart the forgery from the original. The aesthetic formalist will maintain that the truth of a work's provenance is a purely academic matter, independent of our aesthetic judgement of the work. Their opponent asserts, rather, that judgements about the work's authenticity are relevant to the appreciation and evaluation of works of art. However, it would appear that this opponent has to unhappily concede that aesthetic judgements are somehow constrained by what mass spectrometry, X-rays, infrared reflectography, microscopes and detective work can tell us about a work's provenance.

8.4 Caveats about forgery

At the same time, since it is universal practice in the world of art to condemn forgery, aesthetic formalism seems to misfire somehow in its normative predictions. Even then, it may not be that easy to identify what is problematic about forgery. Some have asserted that forgery is problematic because it involves deception. However, if by forgery is meant the passing off of an inferior artwork as a superior one, then we could in principle have deception without forgery. An attempt to pass off a work by Chen's disciple as a work by Chen himself constitutes both deception and forgery. An attempt to pass off a work by Chen's disciple as a work by Liu Kang (another pioneer of the Nanyang style of painting) would equally constitute both deception and forgery. However, if we take the works of Liu Kang and Chen to be aesthetically on a par, then an attempt to pass off a work by Liu Kang as a work by Chen, though deceptive, would not count as forgery in the ordinary sense.[2]

To make things even more complicated, forgery need not always involve the breaking of a legal or moral code.[3] Last but not least, we must avoid the fallacy of question-begging or *petitio principii* and refrain from assuming from the outset that there exists a difference between genuine works of art and forgeries. Even forgeries can have strikingly original aspects and the most interesting cases of forgeries are rarely slavish copies of the original. We need to be more precise about what we mean when we define a forgery in relation to the original. Both the forgery and the original are unique in the sense of being non-identical with other objects. A sense of individuality and even imaginative novelty or spontaneity may be present in the more interesting cases of forgery, while several original works of art may lack either imaginative novelty or a sense of great artistic achievement. However, what all original artworks possess that forgeries (however interesting they might be) do not is this sense of an artistic novelty and achievement of the totality of artistic productions of a person or a school (Lessing, 1965).

8.5 What is wrong about forgery?

With all the relevant caveats in place, we are ready to provide an explanation of the universal condemnation of forgery. According to Dutton (1979), the significant opposition is not between a forgery and the original, but rather correctly represented and misrepresented artistic performance. Construed as performances, works of art represent the ways in which artists solve problems, overcome obstacles and make do with available materials. Forgeries harm by misrepresenting artistic achievement, which is key to aesthetic evaluation. Dutton relies on an analogy between an athlete who secretly takes performance-enhancing drugs (source) and a forger who cheats (target). As part of aesthetic understanding involves grasping what sorts of achievement an artwork represents, a forgery thwarts our attempts at aesthetic understanding and evaluation.

Irvin (2007) presses the case further by observing from the outset that aesthetic understanding is a fragile matter. The aesthetic terrain is complex and uncertain, aesthetic understanding lacks foundational axioms and clear test criteria, and the appropriate strategies for development of aesthetic understanding fall within a bootstrapping framework. In this bootstrapping procedure, trust is placed (defeasibly) in art experts (viz. critics, historians and artists), although experts trying to make aesthetic judgements in novel cases are recognizably in the same situation of aesthetic struggle as the rest of us. In the face of this complexity and uncertainty, the pernicious ability of forgeries (especially undetected ones) to undermine our bootstrapping strategy, misdirect our trust, create artificial and spurious associations and contaminate our aesthetic understanding cannot be overemphasized. As forgeries call into question the soundness of the knowledge that we take to ground aesthetic judgements, the damage inflicted by forgeries may be more severe and pervasive than most philosophers realize. Indeed, we may infer that much of what is wrong about forgery has to do with the violation of certain epistemic norms surrounding the correct representation of artistic performance and the facilitation of aesthetic understanding.

8.6 Gunarsa's trial and dealing with the perfect fake

Nyoman Gunarsa (affectionately known as the 'maestro') is a contemporary Indonesian artist whose artworks depict versions of Balinese and Hindu folklore using modern expressionism. His art is characterized by expressive and minimal brushstrokes and a sense of dynamism, freedom, and spontaneity. Gunarsa got embroiled in a legal battle against a group of individuals (including a gallery owner named Sinyo) who had allegedly produced and distributed forged Gunarsa paintings. Gunarsa's legal battle has even been memorialized in Jenkins's (2010) *Rua Bineda in Bali: Counterfeit Justice in the Trial of Nyoman Gunarsa*. This book uses Gunarsa's legal battle over the forgery of his paintings as a pretext for investigating *ruabineda*, an influential concept concerning the contradictory forces of good and evil, truth and falsity, and darkness and light in Balinese art and culture (Goodlander, 2012).

The perfect fake is a perfect and indistinguishable forgery or copy of a work of art. At least some of the counterfeit Gunarsa paintings are clearly not perfect fakes. For example, certain inconsistencies may be observed between Gunarsa's brushstrokes and the brushstrokes on display in the counterfeit paintings. Indrawati, Gunarsa's wife, first observed these inconsistencies in several paintings ostensibly bearing her husband's signature at a Balinese gallery.[4] In addition, the Balinese dancers depicted in at least some of the counterfeit Gunarsa paintings were holding impossible positions.[5]

The judges eventually acknowledged the forgery of Gunarsa's paintings, while absolving the perpetrators from any punishment. This verdict was much to the chagrin of Gunarsa, a pioneering post-war Balinese modernist artist held in high national esteem. In the aftermath of this verdict, Gunarsa declared that the trial was not merely about his paintings but concerned the upholding of copyright laws in Indonesia and the need for Indonesia to shed its image as a 'nation of pirates' ('Negeri Pembajak'). Both the Lawyers for the Indonesian Anti-Corruption Movement (GerRAK) and the Bali Corruption Watch have since labelled the trial an instance of 'mafia justice' and it has been widely speculated that organized crime figures may have manipulated the verdict (Jenkins, 2010). Given the universal condemnation of forgery, the consensus on the epistemic risks posed by forgery, and the valuable lessons that may be drawn about the weaknesses of copyright law and jurisprudence in the Southeast Asian context, we need to know how to go about dealing with counterfeit paintings and their limiting case: the perfect fake.

Suppose that at least some perfect fake of an original Gunarsa painting, *Penari*, exists. There are neither any discernible inconsistencies in the brushstrokes nor dead giveaways concerning the counterfeit nature of the perfect fake (e.g. impossible positions in Balinese dance being held).[6] Suppose that we have Gunarsa's original *Penari* on the left and the perfect fake on the right. Suppose further that while there may be differences between the two (e.g. in authorship, age, physical and chemical characteristics, market value, etc. we cannot see any difference between the two paintings merely by looking. While we may at present be unable to tell the difference between Gunarsa's original *Penari* and an apparently indiscernible copy of that original (i.e. its perfect fake), it by no means follows that we will never be able to discern a difference between them. After all, we can exercise, train, hone and develop our powers of discrimination with respect to paintings (including Gunarsa and their superlative imitations). The aesthetic properties of an artwork include both properties that are found by looking at a painting and properties that determine how a painting is to be looked at.

For instance, learning how to see a painting as a painting rather than a mere arrangement of pastel or oil on paper (recall the simple physical object hypothesis in § 7.2) requires training the perceptual and cognitive faculties to such a degree that we can engage with the painting in the appropriate fashion. This training may involve developing our perceptual ability to attend to, distinguish between and evaluate certain formal elements in the visual presentation of the painting (e.g. color, shape, form, texture, composition, perspective), cultivating our aesthetic sensibilities (e.g.

knowledge of style, genre, period, convention), developing our awareness of the context of production (e.g. history, culture, artist's biography) and becoming familiar with art theories that could help us make sense of that painting. With the requisite practice, training and development, we may learn to see a difference between Gunarsa's original *Penari* and its perfect fake. The reliance on mass spectrometry, X-rays, infrared reflectography and microscopes when determining the truth of a work's provenance can only help rather than hinder us in this regard: with better-quality information at our disposal, we will be able to distinguish scientifically between an original and its perfect fake. In time, once our powers of discrimination have played catch-up, they should be sufficiently developed to draw the relevant aesthetic distinctions.

9

Conceptual Art

9.1 Perceptual art

Traditional theories of art – whether in the guise of Platonic moralism and its recommendation that poets are banished from the city-state (§ 3.11), Humean moralism and its evocation of the phenomenon of imaginative resistance (§§ 4.2–4.3), or Kant-inspired autonomism and its central thesis that art and ethics are autonomous and independent realms of value (§ 6.5) – tend to take for granted that the aesthetic appreciation (or appreciation of the aesthetic merit or value) of an artwork is exhausted by its perceptible features. Furthermore, we understand perception in terms of its five sensory modalities: hearing, vision, touch, taste and olfaction.

At the same time, it is not easy to determine precisely how aesthetic judgement and aesthetic appreciation proceed from the perceptible features of artworks. For example, consider Georgette Chen's (1963) *Singapore Waterfront* (Figure 9.1). Georgette Chen's landscape painting is an aesthetically significant artwork in the post-impressionist Nanyang style of art (§ 8.1). Why however do we not merely see it as the inanimate physical object that it simultaneously is: a 50 × 61 cm canvas covered in oil pigment and hanging on a wall at the National Gallery Singapore? On what grounds are we able to see it as a work of art rather than an inanimate physical object? On what grounds do we distinguish aesthetically between two objects that have similar or even the same perceptible features?

In the extreme instance, we might have the birdcage in Redza Piyadasa and Sulaiman Esa's (1974) *Towards a Mystical Reality* (§ 4.5), which is (more or less) perceptually indistinguishable for all practical purposes from several other store-bought birdcages.[1] If objects that are perceptually indistinguishable must be aesthetically indistinguishable, then if one is beautiful, then the other has to be beautiful too. After all, they look alike.

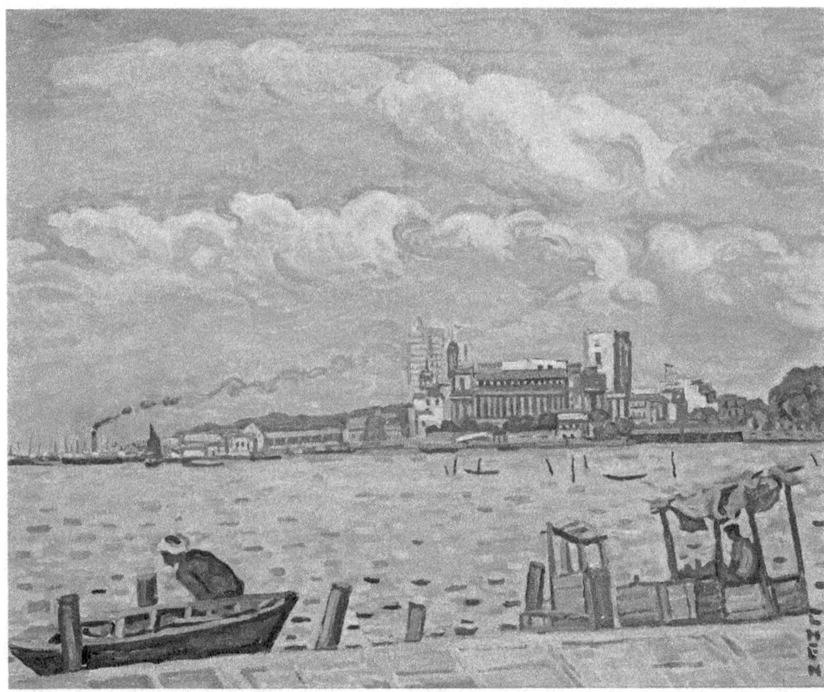

Figure 9.1 Georgette Chen's (*c.* 1963) *Singapore Waterfront*. Oil on canvas, 50 × 61 cm. Gift of Lee Foundation. Collection of National Gallery Singapore. Image courtesy of National Heritage Board, Singapore.

However, Redza Piyadasa and Sulaiman Esa's empty birdcage, one of several found objects on display at the *Towards a Mystical Reality* exhibition, has a certain aesthetic value that ordinary store-bought birdcages do not. Where B_1 denotes Redza Piyadasa and Sulaiman Esa's empty birdcage and B_2 denotes generic store-bought birdcages:

P1: B_1 and B_2 are perceptually indistinguishable.
P2: B_1 is beautiful.
P3: B_2 is not beautiful.
C1/P4: ∴ B_1 and B_2 are not aesthetically indistinguishable. – from P2–P3.
C2: ∴ Perceptual indistinguishability is distinct from aesthetic
    indistinguishability. – from P1–P4

Next, consider the statue of St Francis Xavier at St Joseph's Church in Singapore, before its restoration under the capable hands of Filipa

Machado.[2] One might overlook certain properties of the original statue of St Francis Xavier (viz. cracks, abrasions and holes on the surface of the statue, jaundiced skin tone, crude plaster substitutes for missing fingers, etc.) in the same way that one might overlook certain properties of the statue of the Venus de Milo at the Louvre (viz. two missing arms, a dark stain on the nose, rough spots, cavities and holes in the breast (probably a result of corrosion by water), etc.) (Ingarden, 1961). In the case of the statues of St Francis Xavier and Venus de Milo, on what grounds do we select some perceptible features over others in our aesthetic appreciation of the same artwork? All these considerations suggest that aesthetic appreciation of works of art is not exhausted by their perceptible features. As we shall see, things will only get even more complicated when we have to consider works of conceptual art.

9.2 Conceptual art

What is conceptual art? At a first pass, the idea or concept is the most important aspect of a work of conceptual art. Conceptual art is good only when the idea or concept is good. Cheo Chai Hiang's (1972, remade 2015) *5′ × 5′ (Inched Deep)* consists of lines etched on the wall and floor, collectively forming the outline of a 5-ft-by-5-ft square. The original submission in 1972, entitled *5′ × 5′ (Singapore River)*, was a set of mailed instructions to draw a square measuring 5 ft by 5 ft, straddling the floor and the wall, as a representation of the iconic Singapore River for the annual exhibition of the Modern Art Society (see Figure 9.2). The fact that Cheo chose to write the instructions, as opposed to actually producing at least some artwork by hand, underscores the conceptual nature of *5′ × 5′ (Singapore River)*.

Cheo's conceptual artwork takes aim at the formulaic representations of the iconic Singapore River, familiar to local Singaporeans, adored by tourists, and an indelible part of the history and iconography of modern Singapore. It stands opposed to both Georgette Chen's *Singapore Waterfront* and Lim Cheng Hoe's *Singapore River*; these idyllic river landscape paintings, though pleasing to look at, lack any proper and critical engagement with the more complex reality of Singapore.[3] Deliberately emptied of representational content, Cheo's original submission for the 1972 annual exhibition of the Modern Art Society was rejected for its iconoclastic nature.[4] Cheo's *5′ × 5′ (Singapore River)*, with its emphasis on the concept or idea over the perceptible features of the artwork, is now widely (and rightfully) recognized

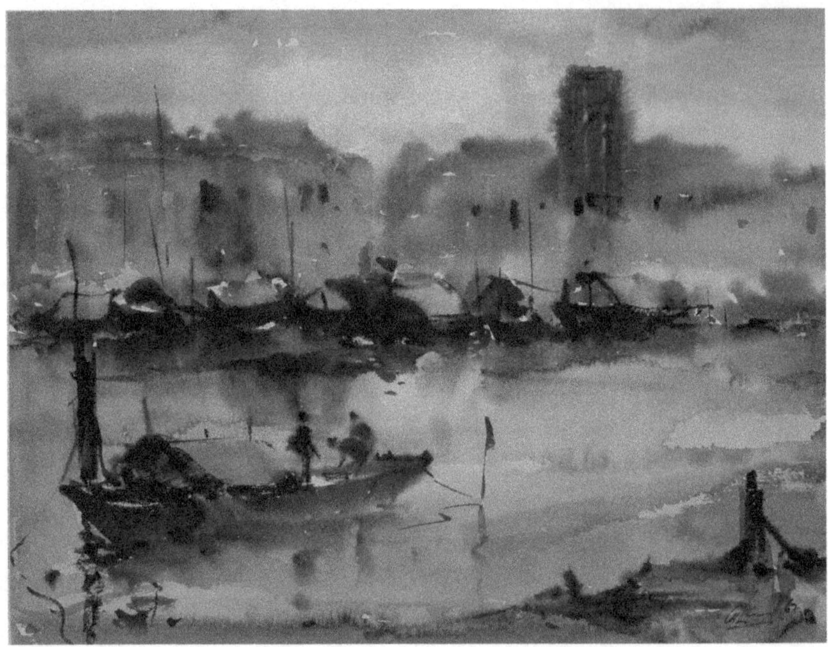

Figure 9.2 Lim Cheng Hoe's (1962) *Singapore River*. Watercolour on paper, 37.8 × 50.5 cm. Collection of National Gallery Singapore. Image courtesy of National Heritage Board, Singapore.

as a watershed moment in the history of Singaporean art, heralding both conceptual art and a sense of contemporaneity in the Singaporean context.

Redza Piyadasa's (1972) *The Great Malaysian Landscape* is another example of conceptual art. Whereas Cheo's original *5' × 5' (Singapore River)* relied on pure text (viz. written instructions) to convey the idea or concept, Piyadasa often integrated text into his artworks to emphasize the ideational value of his art. Given the focus on the idea or concept, we have good reason not to expect the aesthetic appreciation of works of conceptual art to be exhausted by their perceptible features. *The Great Malaysian Landscape* comprises both a landscape scene of a Malay peasant ploughing a paddy field and stencilled text indicating the various components of an artwork (viz. 'image', 'frame', 'title', 'signature', 'surface', 'gravity', etc.). Given the popularity of landscape paintings among Malaysian artists in the early decades of modern art, it has been argued that Piyadasa's *The Great Malaysian Landscape* raises important questions about the sacredness of landscape art as the only acceptable form of art (Abdullah, 2012).

More generally, *The Great Malaysian Landscape* is a wonderful example of Piyadasa fulfilling what he envisaged as his role as a conceptual artist: questioning the basis of modern art and the discourse of nation in Malaysia and reconceiving the form of art. *The Great Malaysian Landscape*, as Piyadasa (1981) observes in the role of an art historian, is a parody of a painting-within-a-painting situation in which stencilled text draws attention to the rhetoric governing modern painting. Furthermore, an attempt has been made to focus on the eye/mind conflict in modern painting through the use of visual (landscape scene) and verbal (stencilled text) components.

Yet another example of conceptual art is Phaptawan Suwannakudt's (1995) *Akojorn (No-Go Zone)*, in which Suwannakudt hung her used *pahtung*, a tube-shaped cloth worn by women, on the washing line between two poles over the gallery entrance in Bangkok, as part of the *Tradisexion* exhibition co-organized by five Thai women writers and artists in 1995.

In a Thai context, the *pahtung* is associated with the menstrual blood of women and cannot therefore be hung above a man's head, traditionally deemed the most sacred part of the body in Thai culture.[5] Suwannakudt's installation may be regarded as an act of defiance against Thai tradition: her *pahtung* was hoisted across the gallery entrance and every viewer, regardless

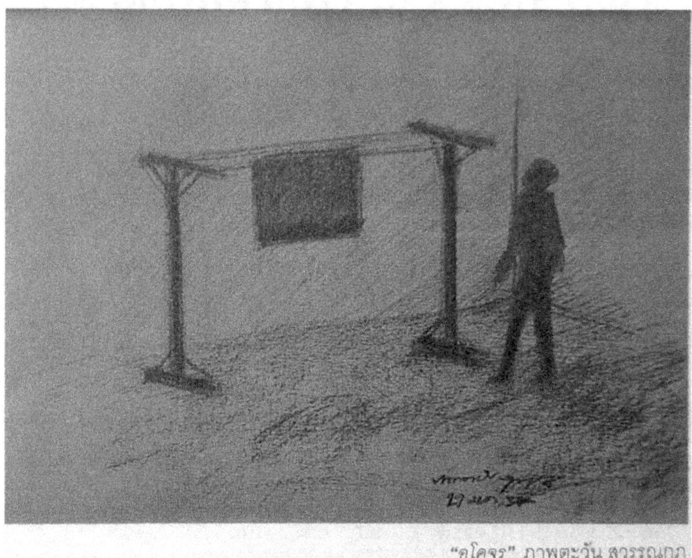

Figure 9.3 Phaptawan Suwannakudt's (1995) sketch of the *Akojorn (No-Go Zone)* installation. Pencil on postcard-sized paper. Image source: Low (2021, p. 229).

of gender, had to walk under the *pahtung* in order to enter. The taboo nature of Suwannakudt's *Akojorn (No-Go Zone)* is reflected in how several male viewers avoided this work, with many preferring to use the back entrance (presumably to avoid having to lower their heads below the *pahtung*) instead (Clark, 2010, p. 137).

According to Yvonne Low (2021), there is unfortunately no formal documentation of Suwannakudt's site-specific installation. No video of the work exists and there is only one sketch of *Akojorn (No-Go Zone)*, made by the artist herself (Figure 9.3). However, the power of the iconoclastic and feminist idea or concept undergirding Suwannakudt's *Akojorn (No-Go Zone)* is demonstrated by its effect on Southeast Asian art and art history: *Tradisexion* (the exhibition in which *Akojorn* featured) became the catalyst for similar exhibitions conceived and executed on women's terms; the roots were laid for Womanifesto, a biannual artist-initiated and Thailand-based event focusing on the work of women artists from around the world; and *Akojorn* inspired Flaudette May Datuin, a feminist art historian from the Philippines, to embark on her research on gender in Southeast Asian art history.[6]

9.3 Two views of conceptual art

There are at least two possible views of conceptual art: the art-historical view (View 1) and the broad church view (View 2). According to View 1, conceptual art refers to an artistic movement that reached its peak between 1966–1972. The conceptual art of the 1960s and 1970s aimed to overcome the tendency of art having for its principal goal the production of something beautiful or aesthetically pleasing.[7]

According to View 2, conceptual art is a vision and an approach to art, art making and society as opposed to a term that is historically restricted in usage. We may therefore denote by the term 'conceptual art' not only the artistic movement that reached its peak between 1966–1972 but also the spirit in which this artistic movement developed. While Cheo Chai Hiang's (1972) *5′ × 5′ (Singapore River)* and Redza Piyadasa's (1972) *The Great Malaysian Landscape* fit easily under View 1, the broad church View 2 offers more latitude and makes it plausible for us to identify Phaptawan Suwannakudt's (1995) *Akojorn (No-Go Zone)* as a conceptual work of art. Unlike Cheo and Piyadasa, for whom conceptual art involves novel and historically groundbreaking ways of imagining how contemporary art might take place, Suwannakudt is more interested in using conceptual art to raise important societal questions related to gender identity and gender politics. In the final analysis, it is not at all clear where the boundaries of conceptual art are to be drawn if we accept View 2. The elusive and slippery nature of conceptual art has been compared to Lewis Carroll's Cheshire cat, 'dissolving until nothing is left but a grin' (Wood, 2002, p. 6).

9.4 Weak and strong conceptual art

We may further distinguish between perceptual art, weak conceptual art and strong conceptual art in a manner that is consistent with View 2. We mean by perceptual art all and only those artworks the aesthetic appreciation of which is exhausted by their perceptible features. We mean by weak conceptual art those artworks the aesthetic appreciation of which is not exhausted by their perceptible features. Piyadasa's (1972) *The Great Malaysian Landscape* is weak conceptual art: it still requires the mediation of Piyadasa's integration of a landscape scene with stencilled text to function.

Last but not least, strong conceptual art comprises artworks the aesthetic appreciation of which is not determined by their perceptible features (Costello, 2013). Cheo's (1972) *5′ × 5′ (Singapore River)* has a good claim to counting as strong conceptual art: in its original form, it consists of a set of instructions to draw a square measuring 5 ft by 5 ft to represent the iconic Singapore River. Cheo's work of strong conceptual art is the same work, whether the square is projected, etched on the wall and floor, represented by tape, or merely entertained as an idea. The idea is the locus of the work and not the means by which the idea is conveyed.

According to philosophers such as Peter Goldie and Elizabeth Schellekens, the medium of strong conceptual art is ideas. The material vehicle of these ideas of strong conceptual art is a mere means to make these ideas available. Lucy Lippard has described conceptual art in terms of the dematerialization of the art object. Analogously, Sol LeWitt (1967) advises that the form of the artwork is not important and the greatest economy of means should be observed: any idea that is better stated in two dimensions should not be stated in three dimensions.

9.5 Mathematical proofs and literary works

We have a long history of according logical and mathematical proofs of theorems aesthetic status. Consider the following geometric theorem:

Theorem 1: The sum of interior angles in a triangle is 180°.

Relative to the diagram of △ ABC (Figure 9.4), the following Proof 1 of Theorem 1 may be constructed:

1. BD ∥ AC
2. ∴∠ACB = ∠CBD – congruence of alternate interior angles (2 parallel lines cut by a transversal)
3. ∴∠BAC = ∠FBD – congruence of corresponding angles (2 parallel lines cut by a transversal)
4. ∴∠ACB + ∠CBA + ∠BAC = ∠CBD + ∠FBD + ∠CBA = 180°– angles on a straight line (QED)

We might say of Proof 1 that it is beautiful or elegant. In other words, we are willing to attribute at least some degree of aesthetic merit to Proof 1. The beauty of a logical or mathematical proof is something we appreciate, even though we might not perceive it in a narrow sense. There are some similarities here to our aesthetic appreciation of Cheo's work of strong conceptual art. Likewise, even though we might not perceive it in a narrow sense, the aesthetic merit of literary works is also something we appreciate. Insofar as

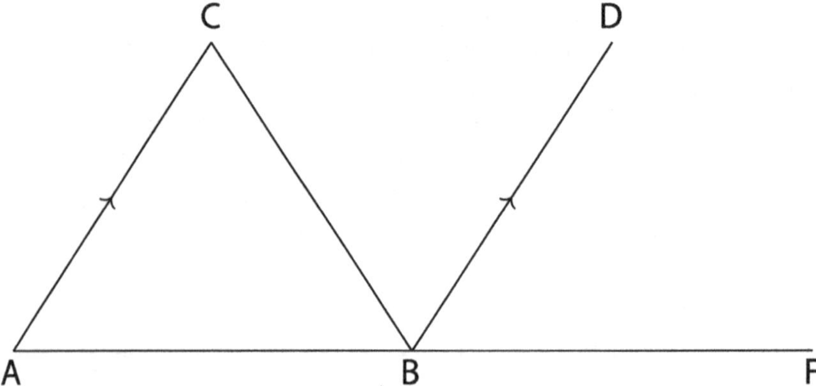

Figure 9.4 Diagram of △ ABC. © Melvin Chen (L^ATEX)

we are interested in the concepts or ideas in proofs and literary works, there is a case to be made in favour of our considering them as instantiations of strong conceptual art rather than perceptual art.

9.6 Shelley's trilemma

The problem of conceptual art may be cast in the form of a trilemma. Shelley (2003) invites us to consider the following trio of propositions:

(R) Artworks necessarily have aesthetic properties that are relevant to their appreciation as artworks.
(S) Aesthetic properties necessarily depend (at least in part) on properties perceived by means of the five senses.
(X) There exist artworks that need not be perceived by means of the five senses to be appreciated as artworks.

Each of these propositions R, S and X is independently plausible. However, these three propositions appear to be jointly inconsistent: $\neg(R \wedge S \wedge X)$. Response 1 to the trilemma involves asserting R and S and denying X: $(R \wedge S \wedge \neg X)$. This is the standard formalist response associated with Susanne Langer, Clive Bell, Clement Greenberg and Monroe Beardsley.[8] Response 1 denies that there exist artworks that need not be perceived by means of the five senses to be appreciated as artworks.

Some objections may be raised against Response 1 or the standard formalist response. According to the first objection (*reductio ad absurdum*), we could appreciate weak conceptual art (e.g. Duchamp's *Fountain*) for its perceptual properties. However, do we then have to appreciate something about the beauty of the landscape scene of a Malay peasant ploughing a paddy field and the elegance of the stencilled letters that Piyadasa employed in *The Great Malaysian Landscape*? Worse yet, must we go out of our way to look for perceptible features in strong conceptual artworks? According to the second objection (*petitio principii*), the formalists are committing the fallacy of question-begging with respect to the definition of art. They cannot define away anti-aesthetic art, which has been a fact of the artworld for some time. To assert that $\neg X$, as Response 1 has done, is however precisely to deny anti-aesthetic art. According to the third objection, our caring about artworks is more than merely caring about their appearances or sensuous forms.

Response 2 to the trilemma involves denying R and asserting S and X: (¬R ∧ S ∧ X). Response 2 was offered as a response under the pressure of Duchamp's legacy and the rise of conceptual art. Response 2, associated with Arthur C. Danto and Timothy Binkley, denies that artworks necessarily have aesthetic properties that are relevant to their appreciation as artworks and allows for the possibility of non-aesthetic art (whatever that might entail).

Unlike Response 1, Response 2 allows us to accept anti-aesthetic art, which has been a fact of the artworld for some time. However, Response 2 asks us to pretend that our engagement with thought is not affecting us in ways we know it is in the case of conceptual art. When defenders of Response 2 maintain that ¬R, they are claiming that it is false that artworks necessarily have aesthetic properties that are relevant to their appreciation as artworks. According to the first objection to Response 2 (*petitio principii*), if the appreciation of non-aesthetic art does not depend on the perception of aesthetic properties, on what does its appreciation depend? Thoughts move us and strike us with daring and wit (in the case of Cheo's *5' × 5' (Singapore River)* and Suwannakudt's *Akojorn (No-Go Zone)*) and with power and beauty (in the case of theorems and proofs). What are daring, wit, power and beauty if they are not aesthetic properties? Response 2 therefore commits the fallacy of question-begging with respect to the grounds for appreciating non-aesthetic art. The second objection (arbitrariness) is related to the first. Defenders of Response 2 (e.g. Danto) might attribute daring, impudence, irreverence, wit and cleverness to *5' × 5' (Singapore River)* and *Akojorn (No-Go Zone)*. On what grounds do we deny such properties as daring, impudence, irreverence, wit and cleverness aesthetic status?

Response 3 to the trilemma involves asserting R and X and denying S: (R ∧ ¬S ∧ X). Following Sibley, Shelley (2003) defines aesthetic properties as what might strike us.[9] We can further distinguish between perceptual aesthetic properties (which strike us and are perceived through the five senses) and non-perceptual aesthetic properties (which strike us and are perceived directly). This alternative definition of aesthetic properties allows us to discard the traditional definition of aesthetic properties in terms of a necessarily dependence (at least in part) on properties perceived by means of the five senses. Defenders of Response 3 (including Shelley himself) are therefore able to maintain that ¬S. The daring, wit and iconoclastic boldness of Cheo Chai Hiang's instructions to draw a square to represent the Singapore River and Phaptawan Suwannakudt's decision to hoist the *pahtung* across the gallery entrance are non-perceptual aesthetic properties that might strike us just as much as other perceptual aesthetic properties (e.g. the grace and beauty of Georgette Chen's (1963) soft-pastel and pointillist *Singapore Waterfront* in Figure 9.1). What do you think? Relative to the problem of conceptual art, are the propositions R, S and X independently plausible though jointly inconsistent? If so, then which of the possible responses to Shelley's trilemma ought we to prefer: Response 1, Response 2, or Response 3?

10

Art and Creativity

10.1 Creativity

As we have already discovered in Chapter 9, one possible response (viz. Response 3) to Shelley's trilemma concerning the problem of conceptual art involves asserting jointly that artworks necessarily have aesthetic properties that are relevant to their appreciation as artworks (R) and at least some artworks exist that need not be perceived by means of the five senses to be appreciated as artworks (X), while denying that aesthetic properties necessarily depend (at least in part) on properties perceived by means of the

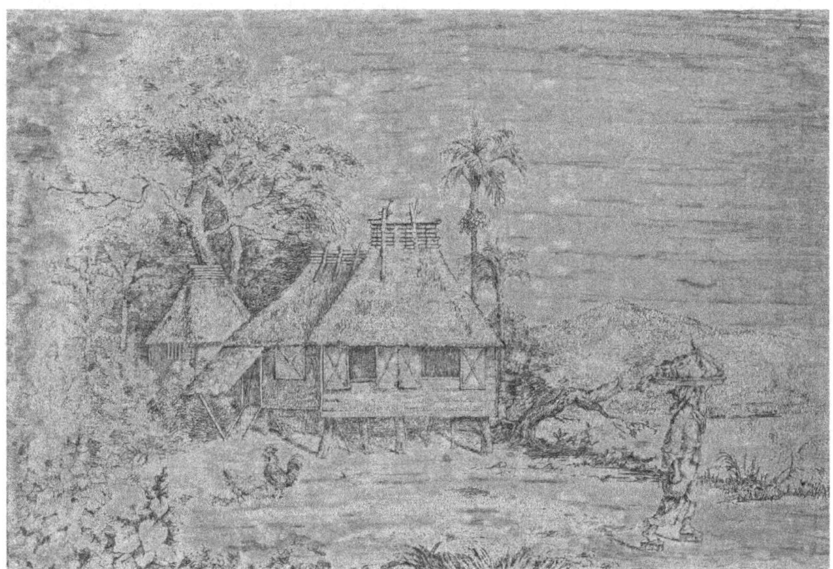

Figure 10.1 Adelaida Paterno's (*c.* 1880s) *Country Scene*. Human hair on silk fabric. Reproduced with permission of Bangko Sentral ng Pilipinas.

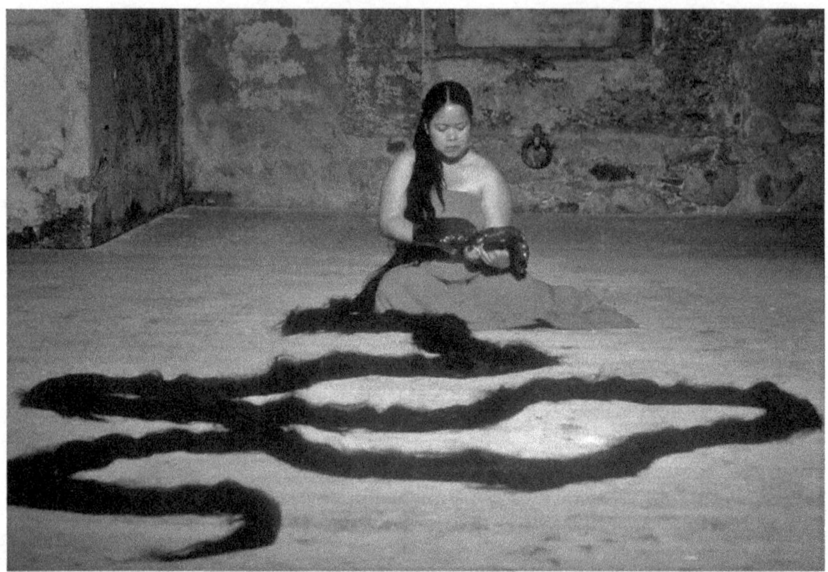

Figure 10.2 Melati Suryodarmo's (2002) *The Promise*. 3-hour performance. Image source: Oliver Blomeier. Reproduced with permission of the artist.

five senses ($\neg S$). Response 3, as constituted by ($R \wedge \neg S \wedge X$), defines aesthetic properties in terms of what might strike us.

Adelaida Paterno is known for having used human hair to make weaves of Chinese silk, satin, or jusi (a Philippine-made fabric). Paterno's adaptation of embroidery, a traditionally female craft, for the purposes of art is evident in her intricate hair paintings such as *Rural Scene with Child* (*c.* 1890s), *Country Scene* (1897) (Figure 10.1) and *Vista de Mariquina* (1897). Melati Suryodarmo is an Indonesian conceptual performance artist who is known for her physically demanding performances that make use of repetitive motions and often last for several hours. Suryodarmo's (2002) *The Promise* (Figure 10.2) is a three-hour performance work that draws on the Indonesian saying 'makan hati' (to swallow your own pain), alludes to Durga (the Hindu goddess associated with strength, motherhood, protection and destruction) and communicates a sense of pain and loss associated with Suryodarmo's mother's long-term battle with cancer. Suryodarmo spends three hours in a red dress and long hair extensions that wind out across the floor, while cradling a fresh cow's liver.

Paterno's famous rendering of the rural scene in human hair may strike us as creative, just as Suryodarmo's use of hair extensions to represent her personal state of mind in her exploration of pain, loss and the female experience may strike us as creative. It may be claimed that some particular aspect of the thought or action (i.e. process) of Paterno and Suryodarmo in the execution of their respective hair-relevant artworks warrants our concluding in favour of their artworks striking us as creative, notwithstanding that the former is a work of perceptual art (Figure 10.1) whereas the latter is a work of conceptual performance art (Figure 10.2).

More generally, creativity of thought or action is an important phenomenon in a number of different contexts, including artistic, theoretical, practical and scientific contexts (Claim 1). In addition, creativity of thought or action has been responsible for some of the most valuable advances of human civilization in the arts, natural sciences, social sciences, engineering, technology and business (Claim 2). Several philosophers have made assertions after the manner of Claim 1 and Claim 2 and these claims seem highly plausible at face value (Kieran, 2014; Stokes, 2011).

10.2 Creativity as an understudied phenomenon

At the same time and notwithstanding the high degree of plausibility of Claims 1 and 2, it is readily conceded we still do not know our way around with creativity. This gives rise to an additional claim, according to which creativity has been a relatively neglected field of study (Claim 3). Creativity has received comparatively little attention in philosophy. Even in psychology, where more work has been done on creativity, the psychological study of creativity pales in comparison with other phenomena such as concepts, imagination and folk mind-reading abilities. According to Sellars (1962) and as discussed in § 1.1, the central aim of philosophy is (arguably) to understand how things in the broadest possible sense of the term hang together in the broadest possible sense of the term. If that is the case, then much philosophical work remains to be done with respect to creativity in the context of aesthetics and the philosophy of art.

Even if we make the concession that philosophy has witnessed some important work on creativity in the last few decades, some caveats will remain in order. Among these caveats are the following:

Caveat 1: Although the creation of art ought to be a central topic for aesthetics, it has been relatively neglected in the philosophy of art (Gaut & Livingston, 2003);

Caveat 2: Few philosophers have devoted attention to the distinction between creativity and imagination (Stokes, 2014);

Caveat 3: Philosophers have tended to ignore the scientific literature on creativity (Paul & Kaufman, 2014).[1]

10.3 Creativity and originality

Part of the work that remains to be done (philosophically speaking) is conceptual analysis and the disambiguation between creativity and related though distinct concepts. Conceptual ideation, analysis and clarification constitute a key component of the philosophical method and may help us to make sense of the nature of the distinction between creativity and originality. Table 10.1 shows Nanay's (2014) argument in favour of the distinction.

It may be claimed that creativity is neither necessary nor sufficient for originality. Let us call this claim Claim 4. Claim 4 is a composite of two claims: creativity is not sufficient for originality (Claim 4A) and creativity is not necessary for originality (Claim 4B). Where C stands for creativity and O stands for originality, Claim 4A may be formally represented as $\neg(C \rightarrow O)$ or (alternatively) $(C \wedge \neg O)$. One could be creative and unoriginal (or derivative) After all and according to one line of thinking, creativity is a banal phenomenon and not the sole preserve of an artistic elite (e.g. Raden Saleh, Redza Piyadasa, Georgette Chen, Chua Mia Tee, etc.).

Claim 4B – the other half of Claim 4 – may be formally represented as $\neg(O \rightarrow C)$ or (alternatively) $(O \wedge \neg C)$. One could be original and uncreative (or mechanical). After all, a discovery, though original, could be the result of purely mechanical (i.e. thoughtless or uncreative) mental processes. High-throughput

Table 10.1 Distinction between creativity and originality. Data from Nanay (2014)

	Creativity	Originality
Nature of attribution	An attribute of mental processes	An attribute of the product of mental processes
Degree of public observability	Not normally publicly observable	A property of normally publicly observable entities
Antonym	Being mechanical	Being derivative

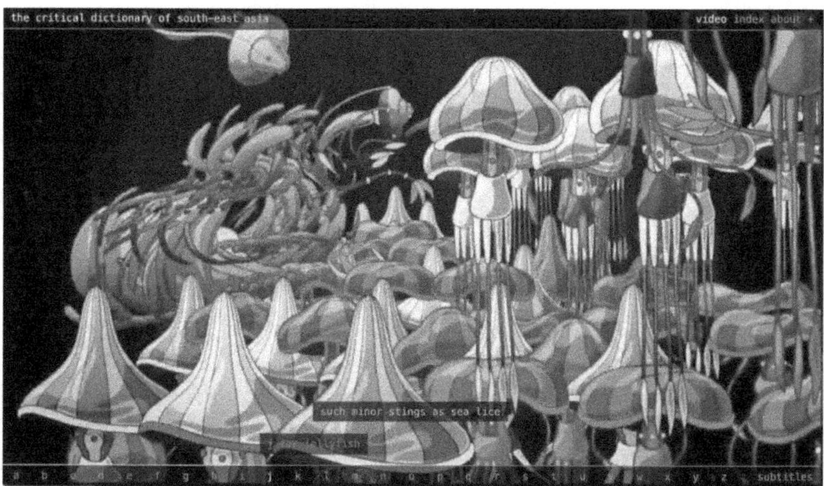

Figure 10.3 Ho Tzu Nyen's (2017) *The Critical Dictionary of Southeast Asia (CDOSEA)*. Synchronized 2-channel HD video, 6-channel sound, LED lights, 2 PCs, with English subtitles. Reproduced with permission of the artist and Kiang Malingue.

screening is a method that allows for the automated testing of large numbers of chemical compounds against a biological target for drug discovery purposes. While new candidate medications that emerge as a result of this method will count as original scientific discoveries, the high-throughput screening process itself is rather mechanical. Vulcanization is a chemical process that involves cross-linking rubber molecules chemically with organic or inorganic substance through the action of heat and pressure to improve the strength, elasticity and durability of rubber (natural or synthetic) (Bin Samsuri, 2010, p. 2417). A random method might involve dropping random substances into liquid rubber to determine whether any of these substances is capable of vulcanizing rubber. While the method, if successful, will lead to a chemical discovery with industrial applications, it is yet another example of a decidedly mechanical procedure.[2]

Ho Tzu Nyen, a Singaporean contemporary artist and filmmaker, relies on an algorithm to compose the image and select the soundtrack in his multimedia project entitled *The Critical Dictionary of Southeast Asia (CDOSEA)* (Figure 10.3).[3] The algorithm selects from an archive of images derived from online sources (YouTube, Vimeo, illegal torrent websites, etc.) and ten different versions of voice-overs that are performed in ten different ways, before matching the selected image and voice with a background soundtrack. While this ensures that the film never truly repeats itself, the algorithm itself represents a finite, step-by-step and mechanical procedure.

Tzu Nyen's reliance on a chance-based, aleatory procedure when generating original multimedia art bears striking similarities with the reliance on the method of high-throughout screening for drug discovery and the reliance on the method of dropping random substances into liquid rubber for chemical discovery in vulcanization.[4]

10.4 Different types of creativity

We may venture further on the conceptual front and distinguish between various types of creativity. One might deny Nanay's distinction between creativity and originality outright and reinstate talk about subjective creativity (i.e. creativity) – an attribute of persons, their minds and related mental processes – and objective creativity (i.e. originality) – an attribute of created works – after the manner of Jarvie (1981).

One might, with equal boldness, follow Boden (2004) in her distinction between H-creativity and P-creativity. H-creativity stands for historical creativity, whereas P-creativity stands for psychological creativity. An idea is P-creative if it is new to its originator. An idea is H-creative iff it is P-creative and it has never occurred before. It follows from this account of H-creativity and P-creativity that P-creativity is necessary but insufficient for H-creativity. We may use Boden's account to distinguish between artworks that are the result of everyday forms of creativity (e.g. the crayon drawings of pre-schoolers at a kindergarten) and artworks that are part of the artistic canon and the history of art.

10.5 Criteria for creativity

Andy Warhol's patent (patent number: D322,227) for a wristwatch with five faces, filed in 1989, is an example of a patent for an ornamental design for a watch. According to US patent law, any output is patentable on creative grounds iff it is statutory, novel, non-obvious and valuable. In a related vein, researchers on creativity have attempted to furnish criteria for creativity. While it is true that there are certain categories of discoveries that cannot be patented, art does not automatically fall into any of those categories. Design patent is most often associated with and used to protect art: it protect the physical appearance but not the underlying structure or use. Warhol's design patent only covers the look of the watch, not the underlying technology used to make it or the movement that allows the watch tell time. A better philosophical understanding of what constitutes creativity and creative grounds will facilitate a stronger legal understanding of what ought to be protected by patents.[5]

More generally, it has been argued that an output is creative iff it is original (novel and surprising) and valuable (Runco & Jaeger, 2012). While an absolute and indisputable criterion for creativity is not readily available, a number of constraints are typically associated with creativity: novelty; value, usefulness, appropriateness, or effectiveness; surprise or non-obviousness; flair and the use of a non-mechanical procedure; and something's being the nonaccidental result of agency. We may also think about a richer sense of creativity: Matthew Kieran (2014) asks what it is to be a creative person and whether it involves a kind of virtue or excellence of character.

Any attempt to furnish objective criteria for creativity will have to reckon with the value-ladenness and relativity of artistic value judgements. These value judgements are time-dependent, subjective, culturally relative and potentially unreliable. As the first Burmese artist to attend the prestigious Royal College of Art in London in 1921 before returning to Yangon in 1930, U Ba Nyan has been widely credited with introducing Western painting techniques to artists in Myanmar through both the rigorous apprenticeship of young artists and the episodic instruction to mature painters. These techniques have been inherited in Myanmar from Ba Nyan's students, passed down from one generation to the next, and provided the foundations of a realist and impressionist school of painting in Myanmar.

Despite his obvious significance in the art history of Myanmar, it has been argued that Ba Nyan, at least until recently, never got the full artistic recognition that he deserved. After all, several of Ba Nyan's paintings were lost during the Second World War and only a few of his paintings survive. At the same time, it cannot be denied that Ba Nyan's art is H-creative in both the sense intended by Boden and Myanmar's art-historical context. For instance, Ba Nyan's *Self-Portrait* demonstrates his excellent command of chiaroscuro (an effect first described in § 3.2) and impasto techniques.[6]

Conversely, although Raden Saleh is widely considered to be Indonesia's first modern painter, his reception in Indonesia is decidedly mixed (Kraus & Vogelsang, 2012). While Saleh was widely praised and acknowledged in Europe, where he spent more than 20 years living in the cities of Amsterdam, Paris and Dresden, his artworks have rarely been exhibited in his country of birth, Indonesia. Saleh, described by Syed Muhamad Hafiz as an opportunistic man who did all he could to make a successful career in Europe, was given a

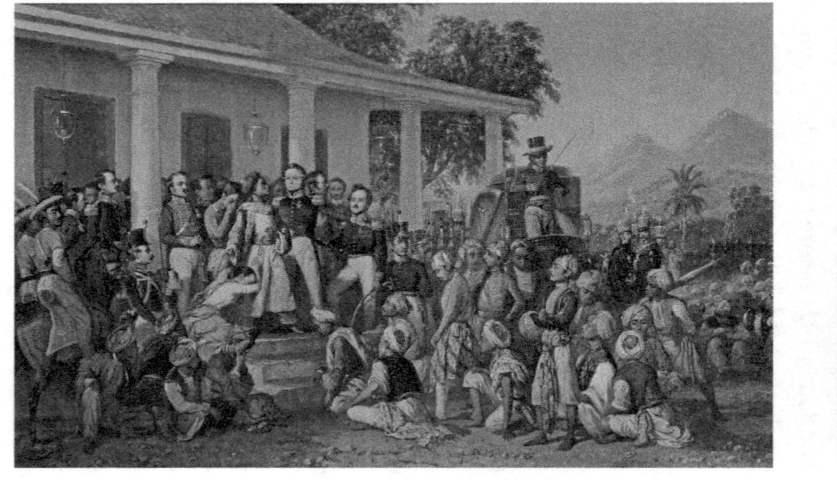

(a) Raden Saleh's (1857) *The Arrest of Pangeran Diponegoro*. Oil on canvas. Public Domain via Wikimedia Commons

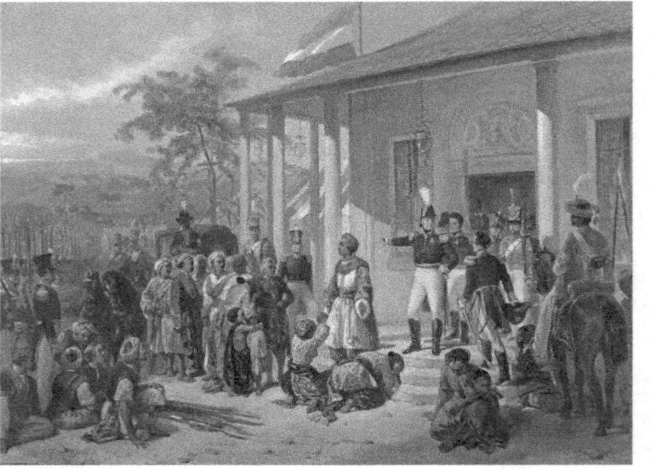

(b) Nicolaas Pieneman's (1830–5) *The Submission of Prince Diponegoro to General De Kock*. Oil on canvas. Wikimedia Commons

Figure 10.4 Two paintings of the arrest of Prince Diponegoro by Lieutenant General Hendrik Merkus de Kock on 28 March 1830.

regular allowance by the Dutch when living in luxury in Europe and controversy remains about the extent to which Saleh might count as a protopatriot. As illustrated by Figure 10.4a, Saleh's (1857) *The Arrest of Pangeran Diponegoro* depicts the harrowing scene of a green-turbaned Prince Diponegoro standing defiant after having been tricked by the Dutch to surrender during a peace negotiation to end the five-year Java War (1825–30).[7]

At the same time, Saleh's gesture of gifting this painting to King Willem III has been described as un-nationalistic, though entirely in keeping with the relationship of a courtier and his king (Bachtiar, 1976). Saleh's apologists (including Werner Kraus) will point out that Saleh's painting is a veiled critique of Nicolaas Pieneman's earlier painting on the same theme (Figure 10.4b). Whereas Pieneman's Diponegoro is submissive and subjugated on a lower step before de Kock, Saleh's Diponegoro, a victim of Dutch treachery, is angry, defiant, and standing on the same level as de Kock. The hotly debated nature of the extent to which Saleh was either a proto-patriot or a social climber in the pay of the Dutch has added a degree of cultural relativity to value judgements concerning the art-historical significance of Saleh.

Given the observed value-ladenness and relativity of artistic value judgements, we might try to push in the other direction. It has been argued that we ought to come up with an alternative definition of creativity, based on the criteria of intentional novelty and excluding value in any form (Weisberg, 1993, 2015). According to Weisberg, any output is creative iff it is novel and was produced intentionally. It remains however highly doubtful whether we can plausibly maintain Weisberg's value-free definition of creativity. We may well do better (philosophically speaking) by finding some way to accommodate or make room for the time-dependence, subjectivity, cultural relativity and unreliability of value judgements.

10.6 Philosophical accounts of creativity

Our conceptual ideation, analysis and clarification may lead us toward a philosophical account of creativity. According to eliminativist accounts of creativity, no ultimate distinction can be made between creative and non-creative mental processes (Feyerabend, 1987; Jarvie, 1981). The stronger argument in favour of this view may run as follows: the idea that culture needs individual creativity is not only absurd but also dangerous. The conceited view that some human beings, bearing the divine gift of creativity, can rebuild the world without asking the rest of us, has led to significant problems. There is no need for miracles. Therefore, there is no need for dangerous myths such as the myth of creativity. The weaker argument in favour of this view may run as follows: creativity is a one-off phenomenon in which every token of creativity is distinct. Therefore, the difference between creative and non-creative mental processes cannot ultimately be explained.

According to experiential accounts of creativity (Nanay, 2014), what is distinctive about a creative mental process is the way in which it is experienced. It is a necessary feature of creative mental processes that we experience the outcome of that mental process as something we have not taken to be possible before. The paradigm here is the eureka moment of discovery, inspiration, or insight popularly attributed to Archimedes.[8] Certain implications follow from this experiential account of creativity: creativity must be an experiential kind if it is a natural kind and there is no privileged recipe for creativity. There are many ways of being creative. While creativity may be taught and learnt, there is no royal road to creativity: you must experience it for yourself.

Apart from the eliminativist and experiential accounts of creativity, there is also the functionalist or computationalist account of creativity. According to the latter account, what is distinctive about creative mental processes is the functional or computational mechanism that leads to the emergence of a creative idea (Boden, 2004). In principle, it does not matter to the functionalist whether this mechanism is instantiated in human beings (carbon-based) or computers (silicon-based). The functionalist or computationalist account of creativity therefore makes possible the building of creative computers.

10.7 Are machines capable of creative art?

Computationalists may characterize creativity in terms of combination, exploration and transformation relative to a conceptual space. Combinatorial creativity involves the unfamiliar juxtaposition of familiar ideas. For example, consider José Garcia Villa's (2008, p. 12) 'Lyric 17'. In what has been described as one of the most metaphorical poems ever written, Villa attempts to convey what he believes are the characteristics of a poem. Language is used by Villa in both a literal and metaphorical sense to advance his case for the art of poetry. The adjectives 'magical' and 'musical' explicitly identify certain desired traits of a poem. Analogies such as a bird's flowering, something's being slender as a bell, and its being able to kneel like a rose suggest a certain reliance on associational processes and evoke a sense of combinatorial creativity at work. Exploratory creativity involves some familiar style/space being explored by generative processes that construct novel structures. Since 'Lyric 17' contains fourteen lines comprising seven rhymed couplets, it may be regarded as a (non-traditional) sonnet and some degree of exploratory creativity may also be imputed to Villa.

Here is a poem by Mookie Katigbak-Lacuesta:

WE, WON'T, BE, TENDING, GARDENS

Watch, scant, grow, lush, won't, turn, the, earth
for bulb, or root, I've, longed, to, say,
peppermint, and, thyme, juice, a, tomato, with,
my, teeth,

No, we, won't, be, tending, gardens, kiss,
A, wet, deep, for, what, might, grow, under,
   Dark, And,
    succulent,
  As, long, promises, the, orchids,

we, overlove, are, deep, in, water, do, not, aspire,
they, are, trying, to, tell, us, something,
   Trust,
   Says, the, sprig,
   And, *Trust*, says, the, spray,
  and, I, fear,

the, long, gather, I, nestle, my, palm, on,
a, groove, I've, no, time, for, or, roots, to,
spare,
    I, mark, my, air, with,
   dark, matter, kiss,

what won't, be, sown, or, held, to, light,

I'll, hate, my, scorn, and, swear, a, tender, year,
There, now, you, say, there, there, toeing, dirt,
over, the, groove, Tending, other, far, gardens.

After José Garcia Villa

Mookie Katigbak-Lacuesta (b. 1980)

Each word is separated from other words by commas in Katigbak-Lacuesta's 'WE, WON'T, BE, TENDING, GARDENS', a practice that recalls José Garcia Villa's poetic innovation of the comma poem, which used commas after every word in a poem. If the idea of tending gardens is associated with order, stability and the status quo, then Katigbak-Lacuesta's poem may be interpreted as a rejection of this status quo. The novel and non-traditional structure of the poem represents Katigbak-Lacuesta's attempt to break away from poetic norms and established conventions and may be regarded as another instance of exploratory creativity. Last but not least, transformational creativity (more radical) involves the generation of a novel structure that does not fit into any known style. where a comma is included after each word in the poem. Villa's innovative use of comma poems, supported by the idea that commas help to regulate the verbal density and time movement of a poem and referenced in Katigbak-Lacuesta's work, may be regarded as a prime instance of transformational creativity.

As aforementioned, the computationalist account of creativity makes possible the building of creative computers. We are now in a better position to ask the question: are machines capable of creative artistic output? Lovelace's objection (let us call it Objection 1) is a response in the negative and it runs as follows:

> The Analytical Engine has no pretensions whatever to originate anything. It can do [only] whatever we know how to order it to perform
>
> Lovelace (1953, p. 398)

Variations of Objection 1 might assert that machines can never really do anything new or that machines can never take us by surprise. Rather, machines merely do what we order them, via programs, to do. One possible response to Objection 1 involves the identification of a *non sequitur* fallacy in the objection. One might urge that it does not follow from the fact that computers can only do what their programs enable them to do that there cannot be interesting relations between creativity and computers (Boden, 1994). The computationalist account of creativity accommodates the possibility that machines might be capable of creative artistic output. One implication of this response to Objection 1 is that machines could provide us with working (if ultimately inaccurate) models for creative cognition. Another possible response to Objection 1 may appeal to the limited sample size relative to which Ada Lovelace had drawn her inferences. The evidence available to Lady Lovelace did not encourage her to believe that machines had the property of originating anything (Turing, 1950). However, once we look beyond Babbage's Analytical Engine and Lovelace's limited sample size, a larger body of evidence may lead us to conclude that machines can in fact do something novel and take us by surprise.

10.8 Examples of machine art

This larger body of evidence to which we might appeal could include the work of Vincent Leong. Leong's (2008) *Socketron* is a Lego-and-Transformer inspired robotic figure constructed from everyday objects such as plug sockets, bulbs and wires. Even as experience is pared down to a modest set of systems, structures and processes, Leong invites us to consider how even robots, everyday objects and robots made of everyday objects could be constitutive of a creative enterprise.

The work of Agan Harahap, an Indonesian photographer known for both digitally manipulating images and spinning fantastical stories to accompany these digitally manipulated images, would be even more relevant. At the 2013 Jakarta Biennale, Harahap exhibited a series of photos entitled *Sejarah X*, taken by a fictitious palace photographer named Amrizal Chaniago. These undocumented though supposedly official photos were ultimately nothing more than historically manipulated images, featuring Indonesian historical figures alongside pop culture figures from the same era. Agan Harahap's digitally manipulated image of Sukarno, Indonesia's first president, with Marilyn Monroe, Elizabeth Taylor and Jacqueline Kennedy Onassis is part of Harahap's *Sejarah X* series of photos. Harahap used Adobe Photoshop and other related digital technologies to create the fake photo, before attributing it to an equally fictitious Amrizal Chaniago. Harahap's artistic intention was to foreground the problems of untrustworthy though viral Internet content, an unhealthy contemporary obsession with celebrity, paparazzi culture, and the woefully inadequate levels of digital literacy in Indonesia.

On a separate occasion and when granted 8 GB of colonial-era images to play with, Harahap created a fictional studio, Mardijker Photo Studio, where members of the Mardijker community ostensibly had their photos taken.

Mardijkers were descendants of freed slaves found in major cities in the Dutch East Indies, comprising both indigenous people from conquered Portuguese territories and people of Portuguese ancestry. Harahap's reworking of archival images to present a fictive portrait of the Mardijkers raises interesting questions about the role of colonial-era photography, the exoticization of colonial subjects, truth in photographic images, and identity in flux in a globalized world. The sense of artifice in both art and artificial intelligence is present in abundance in the artwork of Harahap.

We may however question how much poetic licence we might be willing to grant Harahap. Recall how the poetic licence argument in § 3.6 allows us to conclude in favour of a poet having *pro tanto* reasons to deviate from fact in at least some instances. Harahap has produced faux-paparazzi images of Hollywood celebrities such as Angelina Jolie and Rihanna being detained by the Indonesian police. While it might be argued that Harahap's faux-paparazzi images raise legitimate concerns about fake news, we may question whether there is in fact any conceptual basis for us to distinguish between Harahap's use of faux-paparazzi images for artistic purposes and the malicious use of deepfake technologies to falsely implicate, compromise, or disgrace individuals. If no conceptual distinction can be made between the former and the latter and the latter is regarded as impermissible, then the former must be regarded as impermissible too. The *pro tanto* reasons that have been identified in the poetic licence argument are by definition limited in their strength and it is plausible to maintain that not everything will be permitted in the name of art.

Another example of machine art may be located in the digital poetry of Eileen R. Tabios, a Filipino-American poet. In 2013, when she became weary of her twenty-seven poetry collections that had been published up to that point, she decided to find another way to generate poetry. Tabios created a database made up of 1,167 lines of her own poetry, selected from her twenty-seven poetry collections. This repository of poetic lines eventually constituted an algorithm that Tabios termed the MDR Poetry Generator. The central conceit of this MDR Poetry Generator is that any combination of the 1,167 lines of the database succeeds in creating a poem. Whether or not the conceit is ultimately merited, the five-year-long MDR project, relying on the use of this MDR Poetry Generator, has yielded six published books and four chapbooks (Tabios, 2014, 2015a, 2015b, 2016a, 2016b, 2016c, 2016d, 2017, 2018a, 2018b). Tabios's (2016a) *AMNESIA: Somebody's Memoir* and Tabios's (2018b) *MURDER DEATH RESURRECTION: A Poetry Generator* both utilize all 1,167 lines of the database, although these lines are ordered differently in each book-length poem. According to Tabios, when this database remains unused or lies fallows, the lines are dead. However, if the lines are lifted out of the database and used to generate poetry, they are resurrected into new poems.[9]

All things considered, Agan Harahap's digitally manipulated photographic art and Eileen R. Tabios's reliance on the MDR Poetry Generator in her digital poetry constitute examples that appear to weaken the force of Objection 1 (or Lovelace's Objection) and may be supported by a computationalist account of creativity. The Neukom Institute (Dartmouth College) for Computational Science runs annual Turing Tests in the creative arts, including DigitLit (for short stories), PoetiX (for sonnets) and Musical Style (for musical improvisation). These examples of machine art lead to interesting philosophical issues about what constitutes real creativity, which in turn have implications for our understanding of the nature of art, artworks and the artistic process. The idea of machine art, rather unsurprisingly, also appears to be catching on in tech-savvy Singapore. At the 2019 Singapore Writers Festival, a panel entitled 'The Poem as Machine', moderated by Joses Ho and featuring Qamar Firdaus Saini, Debbie Ding, and Jacob Sam-La Rose, discussed how software tools might allow poems to be generated through algorithmic means, the prospects of computer-generated poetry, and how both writers and programmers might be able to wield these software tools for their creative practices.

If computers are capable of generating poetry, what is it in virtue of which poetry counts as poetry? In the final analysis, must we simply bow to the poem-as-machine metaphor – as it appears William Carlos Williams and Matthew Zapruder have already done – and welcome our new AI overlords in poetry in particular and art in general? While computationalists are inclined to answer in the affirmative, something about their response seems too facile. Might it not be urged that Harahap's digitally manipulated photographic art and Tabios's digital poetry both rely on human-machine interfaces rather than fully automated computational processes, with machines lacking the relevant intentionality and human beings remaining the ultimate sources of creativity? It is clear that philosophical work remains to be done in both the research on creativity and the burgeoning domain of machine art.

11

Ambiguity, Interpretation and Meaning

11.1 Verbal ambiguity

If our aim is to understand a work of art and avoid getting misled about its meaning, then any possible sources of confusion will need to be properly addressed from the outset. Ambiguity is a common source of confusion in artworks: different, coherent and (possibly) mutually exclusive interpretations of the same work may arise if it contains at least some ambiguity. Ambiguity in language is associated with the presence of two or more possible meanings. Consider the opening two stanzas of the following poem by Edwin Thumboo (1993, p. 138):

After the leaving

There are two countries here:
One securely meets the eye;
The other binds your heart.

This is Perth, and yet Malacca.
Outside, suddenly spring arrives
In many wild, surprising flowers.
But no chempaka, no melor
Show that beauty of the heart.
You have lost more hair, though
Your spectacles perch as usual,
Looking quizzical, slightly anxious.

Edwin Thumboo (b. 1933)

The subject of Thumboo's poem is his friend Ee Tiang Hong, a Malaysian artist who has moved to Australia. According to Thumboo's poem, where does Ee feel most at home? His motherland Malaysia (Interpretation 1)? His adopted country Australia (Interpretation 2)? Both Malaysia and Australia (Interpretation 3)? Neither Malaysia nor Australia (Interpretation 4)? Interpretation 1 is both plausible and consistent with the poem's affirmation of the ties that bind individuals to their motherland even in a state of exile. It is telling that the flowers identified in the second stanza (viz. chempaka, melor) hail from Ee's motherland of Malaysia rather than his adopted country of Australia. Interpretation 2 is plausible to a certain extent: in the tug-of-war between the heart and the eye, it could well be the sensible reality of Ee's Australian environs that wins out. Interpretation 3 is also plausible to a certain extent: perhaps Ee, despite the conflict, is able to emerge as a cosmopolitan or citizen of the world. Interpretation 4 finds much in its favour. After all, the opening two stanzas foreground a sense of divided loyalties between Malaysia (Malacca) and Australia (Perth), possibly leaving the migrant subject stranded in a no man's land. Furthermore, Interpretation 4 will find a sympathetic audience in Singh (1998), for whom the travellers in Thumboo's poems are in a state of flux and possibility and between places of fixed abode.

11.2 Visual ambiguity

It is relatively uncontroversial to claim that ambiguity can exist in literary works of art. After all, the words and phrases employed by these works may be polysemous. Can ambiguity exist in non-verbal works of art? While the topic of ambiguity in music has been explored by at least some philosophers, I will not pursue the matter further here.[1] Instead, I will focus on visual ambiguity and defend the claim that visual ambiguity exists, insofar as ambiguity in visual works of art is associated with the presence of multiple possible perceptual readings.[2]

The parang rusak (or broken sword) pattern happens to be one of the larangan (or forbidden) patterns traditionally restricted to the royalty and aristocracy. Furthermore, certain older pieces of parang rusak batik give the impression that they were crudely drawn, almost as if the waxing needle was moved by the hands of an infant playing with a crayon. Farish Noor (2010) argues that batik, more than just pieces of hand-waxed and painted cloth, must be understood in the original Javanese context (viz. its complex web of social relations and social hierarchies). The parang rusak motif – a simple pattern in a series of broken waves – may seem crude when held in our hands and examined up close, but the same batik will have a far more arresting effect when viewed from a distance (of at least 10 metres). This implies that the parang rusak, as worn by the aristocracy, is intended to be viewed from afar. With respect to the part-whole ambiguity, we have either a crude representation of a series of broken waves when viewed up close (parts) or an entire batik motif whose effect is regal and striking when viewed from a respectable distance (whole). Once we have the requisite level of understanding of batik-relevant norms and expectations, we should be able to resolve the part-whole ambiguity in favour of the latter rather than the former.

There is also figure-ground ambiguity to be considered. Figure-ground ambiguity could arise when there is an immense quantity and complexity of figures and shapes, such that it becomes difficult or impossible to determine where a figure stops and the ground begins (and vice versa). The semi-abstract

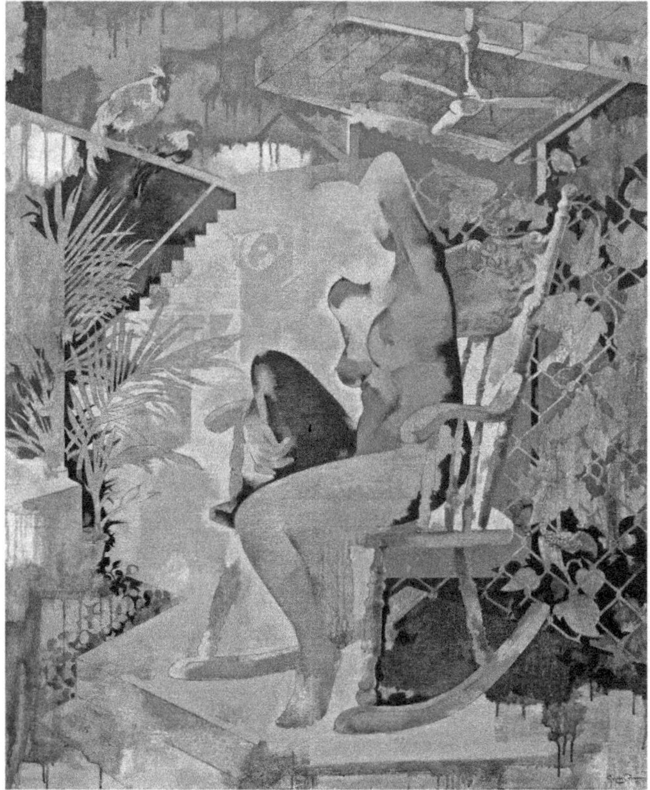

Figure 11.1 Yeo Siak Goon's (2012) *The Rocking Chair*. Acrylic on canvas. Reproduced with permission of the artist.

paintings of Yeo Siak Goon, for whom artistic inspiration is associated with the transformation of time, space and objects into one, often exhibit a certain figure-ground ambiguity.

As illustrated in Figure 11.1, Yeo's *The Rocking Chair* relies on atypical colour juxtapositions and combines the female form (figure) with tropical settings (ground), while leaving the form unfinished, allowing the head to disappear into the canvas. Given Yeo's commitment to playing on the relationship between space and time and letting both figure and ground blend into a single painting, it may be plausible for us to maintain that the artist does not wish for the figure-ground ambiguity to be resolved.

11.3 Caveats about visual ambiguity

As the concept of ambiguity is itself prone to ambiguous representations, it must first be disambiguated. Anamorphosis is a distorted projection, requiring the viewer to occupy a specific vantage point, use special devices, or both to view a recognizable image. It should be declared from the outset that an anamorphic image is not truly ambiguous. After all, the anamorphic visual puzzle resolves itself to an accurate representation when the viewer occupies a specific vantage point. Consider Hee Suhui's (2022) *Body, Door* at the Jurong Lake Gardens in Singapore (see Figure 11.2).

Another caveat is that impossible objects are not truly ambiguous. Take for instance Ella Zheng's (2017) *Internet Explorer*. *Internet Explorer* was an Internet-themed poster for *Eyeyah!*, a new children's magazine.[3] Right at the heart of this poster by the Singaporean illustrator and graphic designer is an impossible object. An impossible object is a type of optical illusion that can be unsettling, because of our natural desire to interpret two-dimensional drawings as three-dimensional objects. In most cases, the impossibility becomes apparent after viewing the figure for a few seconds. The basic idea behind Ella's design is that the Internet is a land you can access with a connection (WiFi), a computer and an open mind. Two ladies (one dressed in white and the other in a red sweater) are making a connection in the vicinity of this impossible object. An impossible object is paradoxical rather than ambiguous. The paradoxical nature of impossible objects defeats any attempt to achieve even a single coherent perceptual reading and may be contrasted with any visual ambiguity that can sustain multiple possible perceptual readings.

In addition, ambiguity is not immediately perceived but inferred. When a work of art is ambiguous, we have different, coherent and (possibly) mutually

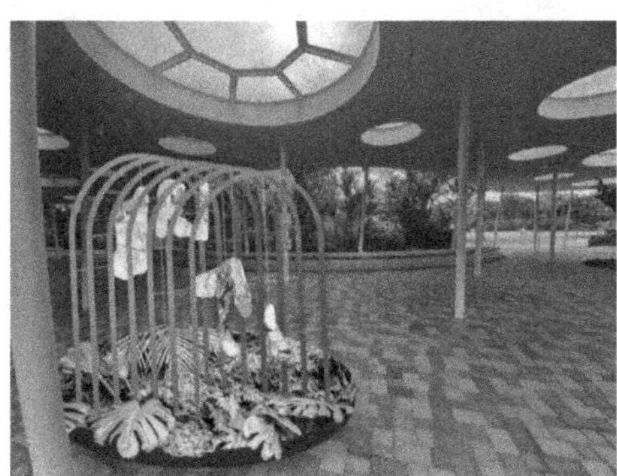

(a) Hee Suhui's (2022) *Body, Door.* Installation with hand-drawn and painted parts of a silhouette suspended across 7 arches. Reproduced with permission of the artist.

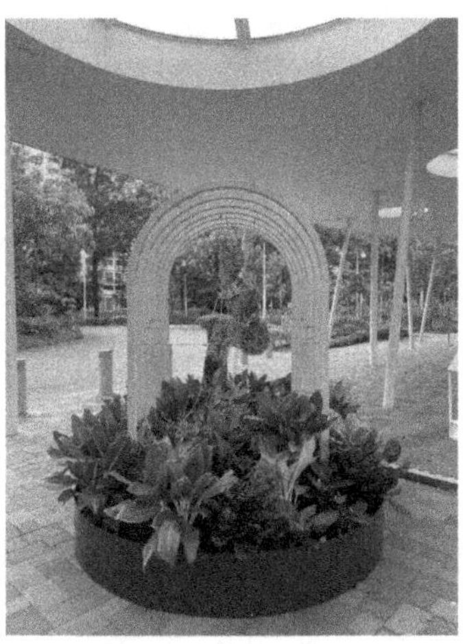

(b) Hee Suhui's (2022) *Body, Door.* Resolution of the anamorphic visual puzzle. Reproduced with permission of the artist.

Figure 11.2 Hee Suhui's anamorphic art installation This anamorphic art installation is composed of hand-drawn and painted parts of a silhouette suspended across seven arches. The illustrations are of flora and fauna found in Jurong Lake Gardens, the site of this installation. At a specific vantage point, the different parts of the silhouette resolve themselves to an accurate representation of a whole silhouette of a figure in a foetal position.

exclusive interpretations of the same work. I may get an interpretation of an artwork at t_i and another interpretation of the same work at t_j. Since both interpretations are mutually exclusive, we may conclude that $ti \neq t_j$. Gombrich (1961) arrives at a similar conclusion that ambiguity is inferred rather than perceived, since ambiguous works of art cannot be perceived immediately. It should also be noted in passing that ambiguous works of art may generate significant ontological problems: how might we identify an ambiguous work of art as the same work of art if the different interpretations are mutually exclusive?

Furthermore, not all ambiguity needs to be resolved. It may even be urged in several instances that works of art may refuse to permit easy categorization and interpretation. The continued existence of different, coherent and (possibly) mutually exclusive interpretations may add to the interest in and aesthetic value of a work of art. However, where not all possible interpretations are equally admissible, the resolution of ambiguity may be needed.

Consider one of the most famous demonstrative pronouns in the history of art, René Magritte's 'Ceci' (or 'This'). The English translation of 'Ceci n'est pas une pipe' – the text in Magritte's (1929) *Treachery of Images* oil painting – is 'This is not a pipe'. 'This' is a demonstrative pronoun. Demonstrative pronouns are typically deictic: their meaning depends on a particular frame of reference. Does the demonstrative pronoun refer to the pipe (Interpretation 1), the image of a pipe (Interpretation 2), the canvas used by Magritte (Interpretation 3), or even the entire sentence 'Ceci n'est pas une pipe' (Interpretation 4)? Interpretation 1 is less feasible, since an entity cannot both be and not be a pipe at the same time.

The following remark by Magritte could well help us to resolve the ambiguity (Torczyner, 1977, p. 71):

> The famous pipe. How people reproached me for it! And yet, could you stuff my pipe? No, it's just a representation, is it not? So if I had written on my picture 'This is a pipe,' I'd have been lying!

If the meaning of Magritte's painting is identical to the intention of Magritte the artist (as declared in his utterance), then a further resolution of ambiguity with the demonstrative pronoun 'This' may be effected in favour of Interpretation 2: Magritte was simply referring to the image of a pipe. Given the role that might be played by Magritte's remarks in the resolution of ambiguity in this instance, it is sensible for us to consider the following question: where the resolution of ambiguity is needed, do the intentions of the artist matter?

11.4 Absolute actual intentionalism

Actual intentionalism is the view that the intentions of the artist are relevant to interpretation. According to absolute actual intentionalism, the meaning of a work of art is wholly determined by the intentions of the artist (Irwin, 1999). Absolute actual intentionalism is also known (rather unflatteringly) as Humpty-Dumpty-ism. Humpty Dumpty is a literary figure in Lewis Carroll's (1872) *Through the Looking-Glass*, a sequel to *Alice's Adventures in Wonderland* (1865). In this sequel, Humpty Dumpty tells Alice that he can make a word mean whatever he intends it to mean:

> Humpty Dumpty: There's glory for you.
> Alice: I do not understand what you mean because I do not understand what you mean by 'glory'.

Humpty Dumpty: 'There's glory for you' means 'There's a nice knockdown argument for you' because I intend 'glory' to mean 'a nice knockdown argument'.

The intentions of the artist are necessary and sufficient for us to determine the meaning of a work of art in absolute actual intentionalism. Irwin has explicitly stated that if Humpty had the intention to mean 'There's a nice knockdown argument for you' with 'There's glory for you', the utterance truly meant that.[4] Analogously, works of art mean whatever it is that their artists intend them to mean and understanding works of art becomes a matter of tracking the declarations of intentions of artists. However, most philosophers would ordinarily concede a certain gap between what is intended by the artist and what the text ends up meaning.

11.5 Moderate actual intentionalism

According to moderate actual intentionalism, the success conditions of intentions are parsed in terms of compatibility (Carroll, 2001; Livingston, 2005). More generally, the intentions of the artist may or may not be successful. When they succeed, these intentions determine the meaning of the artwork. An intention is successful just in case the intended meaning is compatible with the work of art. An intention is compatible with the work in the sense that it meshes well with the work: this is known as the meshing condition. Otherwise, when these intentions fail, meaning is determined by convention and context. Context refers to the contextual factors at the time of production of the work of art. Convention refers to artistic conventions that provide constraints on meaning (e.g. institutions such as the artworld; art-historical relations, etc.).

11.6 Objections to actual intentionalism

There are several possible objections to actual intentionalism (absolute or moderate). According to the epistemic objection, can we ever be said to know anyone's intentions? According to the problem of other minds, we only have direct and unmediated access to our own minds. Indeed, we are necessarily epistemically handicapped with respect to the mental states of others (including artists and their intentions). According to the argumentative objection, actual intentionalists regularly rely on the conversation argument (Carroll, 2001; Jannotta, 2014). The conversation argument is an argument by analogy to the following effect:

P1: The analogy between understanding others in conversation (source) and understanding a work of art (target) is sufficiently strong.
P2: Relative to the source, the standard goal in a conversation is to grasp what the speaker intends to say.
C1: ∴ Relative to the target, the standard goal in art should be to grasp the intention of the artist.
C2: ∴ Actual intentionalism is correct.

While P2 is widely accepted, P1 may be false. After all, there is a certain disanalogy between conversation (source) and art (target): art is closer to a monologue delivered by the artist than a dialogic interchange of ideas.[5]

11.7 Anti-intentionalism

Given the objections to actual intentionalism (absolute or moderate), we may have reasons to believe that the artist's intentions at best underdetermine meaning even when they operate relatively successfully. We may even have reasons to turn to anti-intentionalism, the view according to which artistic conventions are necessary and sufficient for determining the meaning of a work of art. For the anti-intentionalist, the intentions of the artist are irrelevant to interpretation. Anti-intentionalism is associated with New Criticism, a movement in literary theory that represented a reaction against biographical criticism. According to biographical criticism, we need to study the life of the author to understand the meaning of the work. However, this resulted in literary criticism becoming a criticism of biography rather than a criticism of a literary work.

New Criticism distinguishes between three types of evidence: internal evidence, intermediate evidence and external evidence. Internal evidence is public and it includes the semantics and syntax of a work of literature and our linguistic conventions. Intermediate evidence, on the other hand, is semi-private: it concerns the meanings attached to words or topics by an author. External evidence is private or idiosyncratic: it consists of revelations about how or why an author may have written a work of literature. External evidence includes such sources as the letters or diaries of the author. While biographical criticism privileges external evidence, the New Critic prioritizes internal evidence and – in certain instances – intermediate evidence. This prioritization reflects a belief that the reader should aim to understand the work of literature by focusing solely on the inherent properties of the text.

Anti-intentionalism is supported by the following argument (Wimsatt & Beardsley, 1946):

P1: Either the artist's intention is successfully realized in the work of art or it fails.

P2: If the artist's intention is successfully realized in the work, then appeal to external evidence of the artist's intention is not necessary (i.e. we should be able to detect the intention from the work).

P3: If the artist's intention fails, then appeal to external evidence of the artist's intention is not sufficient (i.e. the intention will be extraneous to the work).

C: ∴ An appeal to external evidence of the artist's intention is either unnecessary or insufficient.

This argument supports the claim that anyone who regards evidence of the artist's intention as relevant to understanding the meaning of a artwork will be committing the intentional fallacy. Indeed, convention alone ought to do the trick: artistic convention alone will be necessary and sufficient for determining the meaning of the work of art.

11.8 Objections to anti-intentionalism

We can still formulate objections to anti-intentionalism. In the first instance, artistic conventions are not sufficient for determining the meaning of a work of art. People still debate about interpretation because certain artworks might not offer sufficient internal evidence to resolve ambiguity. When a work of art can sustain multiple possible meanings, an appeal to external evidence of the artist's intention could help people to deal with this problem of choice. We have already seen this in the case of the use of Magritte's remarks to resolve the ambiguity surrounding the multiple possible interpretations of 'Ceci' (or 'This'). In the second instance, there is a certain arbitrariness in how anti-intentionalists and New Critics might distinguish between internal evidence, intermediate evidence and external evidence. Even Wimsatt and Beardsley (1946, p. 478) must finally concede that the different types of evidence shade into one another so subtly that it is not always easy to draw a line between these types of evidence. More generally, anti-intentionalism has trouble making a clear distinction between what is part of the autonomous aesthetic object and what lies outside the aesthetic object.

11.9 Hypothetical intentionalism

The various concerns raised about both anti-intentionalism and actual intentionalism may lead us to hunt for some golden mean between the former and the latter. Hypothetical intentionalism is often regarded as precisely this golden mean: it is the view according to which the correct meaning of an artwork is determined by the best hypothesis about the artist's intentions made by a contextually informed audience (Levinson, 1996, 2016; Tolhurst, 1979). Hypothetical intentionalists recommend that we should hypothesize about what the artist intended when creating a work of art, relative to the perspective of a qualified audience. Hypothetical intentionalists might first distinguish between semantic intention and categorical intention: the former refers to the intention by which an artist conveys their message in the work of art, whereas the latter refers to the artist's intention to categorize their work of art (e.g. as a work of art, a particular artform such as postmodernism, or a particular genre such as slam poetry). Categorical intention is treated as among the contextual factors relevant to the identity of the artwork. In addition, hypothetical intentionalists could introduce aesthetic considerations as tie-breakers. For example, in certain cases where competing interpretations or hypotheses H_1 and H_2 are equally good, aesthetic considerations could function as a tie-breaker. We should pick the hypothesis H_1 that makes the artwork artistically better.

11.10 Objections to hypothetical intentionalism

At the same time, hypothetical intentionalism is not without issues. If the intended and contextually informed audience is an extremely small group possessing esoteric knowledge of the artist, meaning becomes a private matter and we might end up uncomfortably close to the much-maligned Humpty Dumpty-ism of absolute actual intentionalism. In addition, hypothetical intentionalism may have to grapple with certain factual errors that artists clearly did not intend. Recall a claim made in § 3.5 about how Coppola's *Apocalypse Now* is rife with mistakes and inaccuracies, including historical errors (viz. the misidentification of the colour of tracer bullets). If the Viet Congs used tracer bullets of a single colour, then these bullets cannot be both green (historically accurate) and red (historically inaccurate). An informed audience would be justified in believing that Coppola did not intend to make it true that both green and red tracer bullets were used by the Viet Congs. Furthermore, hypothetical intentionalism is committed to the view that the work does not mean what it fictionally asserts. Let $p \wedge q$ denote the conjunctive statement that at least some Viet Cong tracer bullets were green (p) and at least some other Viet Cong tracer bullets were red (q). While the audience is justified in believing that q was not intended, Coppola's *Apocalypse Now* does *ex hypothesi* imply that $p \wedge q$ in virtue of both its having fictionally asserted that q and our background knowledge that p.

Visual continuity errors pose further problems for the hypothetical intentionalist in the domain of film (Stecker & Davies, 2010). A visual continuity error is a lapse in the self-consistency of the scene or story being portrayed.[6] In the film *Crazy Rich Asians*, after a character Nick proposes on the plane to another character Rachel and puts the ring on her finger, both characters kiss. In the next shot, however, we do not see this ring on any of Rachel's fingers. In another scene, Rachel initially has the bamboo mahjong tile in her left hand, before switching it to her right hand. However, this tile is in her left hand again in the next shot. The audience of *Crazy Rich Asians* is justified in believing that these visual continuity errors are not intended. At the same time, we would not conclude – as the hypothetical intentionalist might – that visual continuity errors are not part of the meaning of the film.

11.11 Concluding remarks

All things considered, although there is a strong tradition in favour of deferring to the intentions of the artist when resolving ambiguity and determining the meaning of an artwork, it by no means follows that this tradition is ultimately correct. Relative to the central question of whether the intentions of the artist are relevant to understanding an artwork, a range of positions may be identified: absolute actual intentionalism, moderate actual intentionalism, anti-intentionalism and hypothetical intentionalism.[7] As there remains a lack of consensus about which of these positions is the best one to adopt, we must proceed with care and diligence whenever our interests incline toward the interpretation and meaning of works of art.

12

Art and Morality

12.1 Four theses

Chapter 3 identified the Platonic grounds on which my work of historical fiction about the ang ku kueh seller would count as dangerous rather than valuable and provide reasons for the banishment of poets from the ideal and just city-state. Chapter 4 outlined Argument 1 in favour of art being dangerous, demonstrated its proof-theoretic validity, and proposed various strategies for nonetheless resisting Argument 1 (in virtue of the falsity of at least one of is premises). The denial of P1 of Argument 1 was associated with an appeal to non-propositional modes of aesthetic knowledge. Argument 2, an argument in support of aesthetic anti-cognitivism, was also introduced. Chapter 5 foregrounded the century of taste and its influential use of taste as a metaphor for judgements of aesthetic merit or aesthetic value. It also engaged with Hume's position on the established norms, practices of evaluation, or standards of aesthetic taste relative to which my tale of the ang ku kueh seller may have aesthetic merit.

Chapter 6 outlined Kant's response to Hume's position, including Kant's denial of the existence of standards of taste and his alternative characterization of aesthetic judgement in terms of its four moments. Chapter 7 engaged with various metaphysical concerns about the work of art, including its identity conditions and ontological status. Chapter 8 addressed the challenges posed by forgeries to the identity conditions of works of art, the epistemic threats and risks carried by forgeries (especially undetected ones), and how we might go about dealing with the perfect fake. Chapter 9 delineated the problem of conceptual art and cast it in the form of a trilemma and its horns R, S and X (independently plausible though jointly inconsistent). It also introduced a variety of responses (viz. Response 1 or $(R \wedge S \wedge \neg X)$, Response 2 or $(\neg R \wedge S \wedge X)$, Response 3 or $(R \wedge \neg S \wedge X)$). Chapter 10 addressed creativity as an understudied phenomenon, the role of conceptual ideation, analysis and clarification in helping us to understand creativity in the context of art, and the possibility of machines being capable of creative artistic output. Chapter 11 identified the need to resolve ambiguity in the context of interpreting, understanding, and making sense of artworks and foregrounded the vexed status of the intentions of the artist (including the role these intentions ought to have) in this meaning-making enterprise.

The current chapter will be devoted to a discussion about the nature of the relationship (or lack thereof) between art and morality. It should be noted from the outset that the task of determining the boundaries of goodness and badness with respect to art is by no means an easy one. Sam Lo, a contemporary artist in Singapore, famously pasted stickers with Singlish phrases such as 'Press until shiok' and 'Anyhow paste kena fine' at traffic junctions, only to be arrested by the police for vandalism. This in turn sparked a debate about how we might go about distinguishing between a work of art and a work of vandalism (with its attendant moral implications).

Furthermore and throughout human history, the human form has been one of the principal subjects for artistic representation. At least some

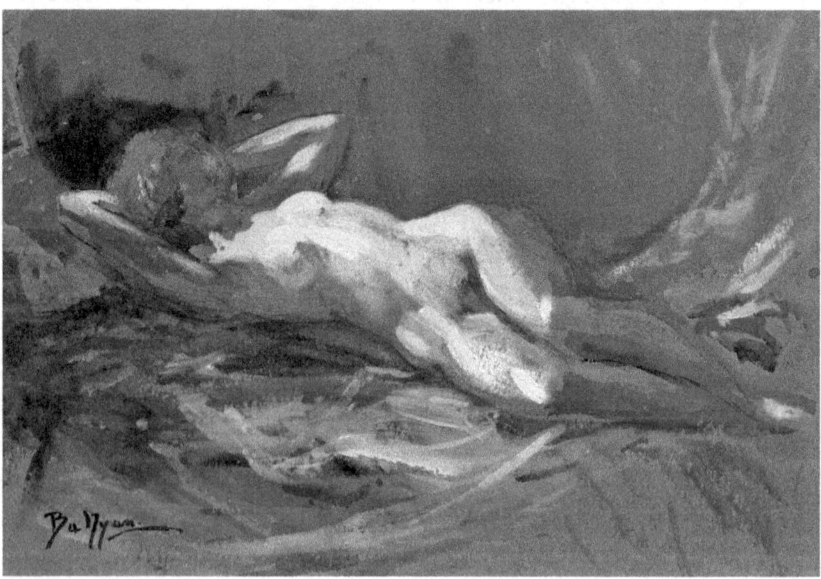

Figure 12.1 U Ba Nyan's (*c.* 1925–1930s) *Before*. Gouache on paper, 18 × 26 cm. Collection of National Gallery Singapore. This acquisition was made possible with donations to the Art Adoption & Acquisition Programme. Image courtesy of National Heritage Board, Singapore.

individuals tend to equate all depictions of nudity with sexuality and therefore consider representations of the nude human form to be obscene or morally offensive. U Ba Nyan's *Before* is widely considered to be the first nude in Myanmar (Figure 12.1). While it may be admired for its expressive brushstrokes and impasto technique and Ba Nyan's excellent command of human anatomy, the taboo nature of nudity in a Southeast Asian context cannot be ignored.[1]

Last but not least, recall our discussion in § 10.8 about how it may not be easy to make a conceptual distinction between Harahap's faux-paparazzi images and images that rely on the malicious use of deepfake technologies to falsely implicate, compromise, or disgrace individuals. If the latter is morally impermissible, then it is at least plausible that the former will be morally impermissible as well. All things considered, we shall ultimately need a non-question-begging account of moral value, the nature of the relationship between moral value and artistic value, and how this relationship might be considered separately from other sorts of axiological concerns (e.g. religious, social, economic, legal, etc.).

A second point to consider would be whether or to what extent a distinction should be made between the artist and the artwork. Consider Juan Luna, whose historical painting *Spoliarium* was awarded the gold medal at the prestigious *Exposicion de Bellas Artes* or Madrid Art Exposition (May 1884).[2] At a gathering of Filipino expatriates in Madrid, the Filipino nationalist José Rizal praised the achievement of both Luna and Félix Hidalgo (the latter had won a silver medal at the same exhibition) and described *Spoliarium* as an embodiment of social, moral and political life in the Philippines and the struggle with prejudice, fanaticism and injustice (Maria Guerrero, 1974, p. 114).[3] If Rizal's claims are correct, then we have good reason to believe that *Spoliarium* counts as a source of moral value.

At the same time, there is a certain detectable streak of violence in *Spoliarium* that eventually betrayed itself in real life, when Luna murdered both his wife, Maria Paz Pardo de Tavera, and her mother, Juliana Gorricho, in a fit of jealous rage in 1892. To what extent (if any) should knowledge of this biographical fact alter our aesthetic evaluations of Luna? How might Luna's subsequent portrayals of women, including his paintings of his own relatives (Figure 12.2), after 1892 be interpreted in the light of this biographical fact (Nelson, 2019, p. 26)?

At least some approaches to art criticism make it possible for us to analyse artworks without making reference to an artist's biography: recall how both anti-intentionalism and its associated movement of New Criticism

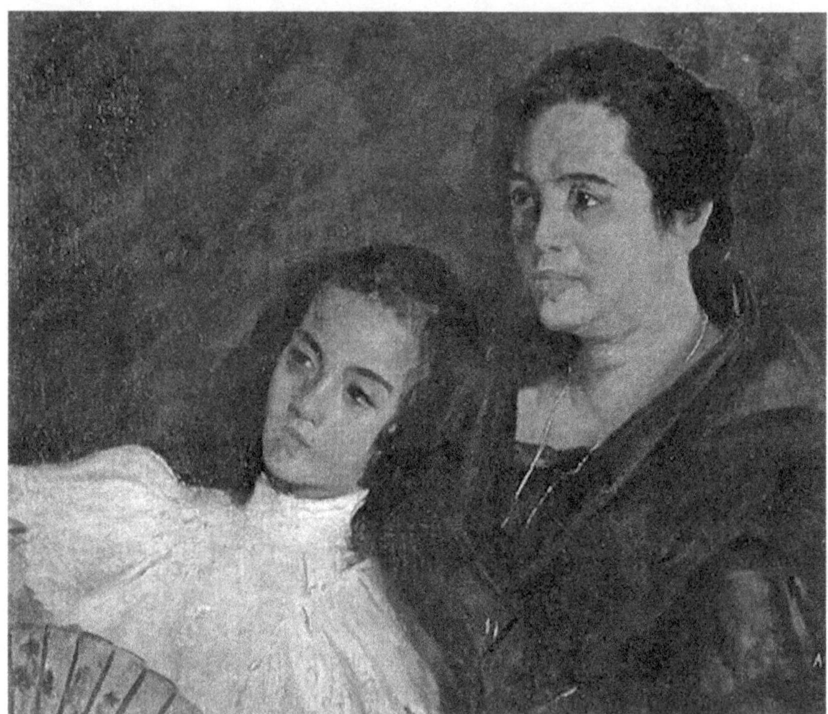

Figure 12.2 Juan Luna's (1897) *Nena y Tinita*. Oil on canvasboard. Public Domain. The Picture Art Collection / Alamy Stock Photo

encourage a sole focus on the inherent properties of each artwork and the underlying artistic conventions that allow us to determine the meaning of that artwork (§ 11.7). Other critical approaches (e.g. biographical criticism) that regard the artist's biography as relevant to understanding the meaning of the work may not let Luna off the hook as easily. How are the conceptual boundaries to be drawn between the artist and the artwork? To what extent are biographical facts relevant to the relationship (or lack thereof) between art and morality? There are no straightforward answers here.

In sum, here are a few caveats we have to consider:

Caveat 1: We need a non-question-begging account of how we distinguish between the morally good, the morally bad, and neither the good nor the bad (i.e. the morally indifferent);

Caveat 2: Ideally, this account should have an interface between art and morality, allowing us to determine the nature of the relationship between moral value and artistic value;

Caveat 3: This account should be designed to allow us to consider the nature of the relationship between moral value and artistic value separately from other axiological concerns;

Caveat 4: This account should provide guidance on whether or to what extent a distinction should be made between the artist and the artwork.

With Caveats 1–4 out of the way, here are some plausible theses of the relationship between art and morality:

Thesis 1: Bad art corrupts and has a negative moral effect on its audience;

Thesis 2: Bad art always corrupts its audience;

Thesis 3: Good art edifies and has a positive moral effect on its audience;

Thesis 4: Good art always brings about moral improvement in its audience.

A few initial observations are in order. Thesis 1 may be termed the negative causal thesis, whereas Thesis 3 may be termed the positive causal thesis. Theses 2 and 4 – (respectively) the strong versions of the negative and positive causal theses – are implausible and more difficult to prove. Thesis 1 leads to the worry that artworks deemed bad or dangerous may be subject to censorship, whereas Thesis 3 suggests that good art may have an important role to play in moral education.

12.2 Traditional varieties of moralism

By 'moralism' is meant the view that the aesthetic value of an artwork should be determined by its moral value. We have already distinguished between Platonic moralism and Humean moralism: Platonic moralism is supported by Argument 1, which favours the banishment of the poets (see Chapter 3), whereas Humean moralism emerges from the denial of P3 (i.e. that art is powerful) of Argument 1 (see Chapter 4). Plato's version of Platonic moralism is bleak and pessimistic. Thesis 2 (the strong negative causal thesis) is defended: Bad art always corrupts its audience. In certain instances, we can only guard against the moral dangers of poetry by its banishment or evisceration. This is why Plato sees fit to banish the poets from his ideal city-state. Tolstoy's version of Platonic moralism, on the other hand, is more optimistic. Tolstoy embraces a humanism in which good art joins us together in bonds of fellow feeling and demands of art that it communicates a morally good message to its audience, even as he inveighs against the ills and dangers of decadent art. There is Tolstoyan support for both Thesis 2 (the strong negative causal thesis) and Thesis 4 (the strong positive causal thesis).

Central to Hume's moralism is the claim that all moral defects count as aesthetic defects. When an artwork deviates from our moral standards, this must be allowed to disfigure the artwork and be a real deformity. Indeed, if an artwork is immoral, then the artwork's beauty must be significantly diminished by its moral defects. Humean moralism, more generally, defends the weaker claim that whenever an artwork's moral defects are relevant to its aesthetic evaluation, they figure as aesthetic defects or blemishes.[4] Both Platonic and Humean moralism locate the appeal and significance of art in its ability to move us emotionally. Furthermore, both Platonic and Humean moralism warn that immoral art can have only corrupting effects.

Nonetheless, there are important differences between these two varieties of moralism. Plato associates aesthetic strength with moral dangers: he fears that immoral art is capable of moving even virtuous people and therefore agitates in favour of the banishment of the poets. Conversely, Hume is confident that a virtuous audience will be immune to the seductions of immoral art: if the artwork is immoral, then it will have too little power to move us. Humean moralism defends Thesis 1 (the negative causal thesis): bad art corrupts and has a negative moral effect on its audience. However, a virtuous audience will demonstrate its immunity to the corrupting influence of bad art and exhibit imaginative resistance (§§ 4.2–4.3).

12.3 Objections to moralism and possible responses

Certain objections may be raised against such traditional varieties of moralism as the Platonic and Humean strands:

Objection 1: Moralism is reductive. The more extreme versions of moralism (e.g. Platonic moralism) tend to reduce all aesthetic considerations to moral ones;

Objection 2: Moralism tends to ignore certain fundamental aspects
    having to do with aesthetic value (e.g. formal features, beauty, etc.);
Objection 3: Moralism has trouble distinguishing between art and other
    cultural products (e.g. propaganda).

Consider my work of historical fiction about the ang ku kueh seller, first introduced in § 3.1. Suppose that I have made this ang ku kueh seller my heroic protagonist. According to genre conventions, a folk hero in a work of historical fiction is characteristically celebrated and admired for their rise or transformation from humble origins, sense of community, and ability to imprint their name and deeds into popular consciousness. Suppose further and for argumentative purposes that the ang ku kueh seller in my tale happens to be a serial killer. Insofar as we refuse to celebrate or admire anyone who happens to be a serial killer, whatever other traits they might possess, my work of historical fiction may not be successful in achieving its aesthetic purpose.

My example is analogous to the Hitler-as-a-tragic-protagonist example in Carroll (1996). Consider a tragedy with Hitler as the central figure. A tragedy achieve its aesthetic purposes by securing the response of pity for its central tragic figure. However, it will fail to do so in this instance, insofar as we refuse to share the defective moral perspective of Hitler (i.e. Nazism and anti-Semitism). Both the ang-ku-kueh-selling-serial-killer-as-folk-hero work of historical fiction and Hitler-as-a-tragic-protagonist tragedy, in their failure to secure their aesthetic aims, motivate a version of Humean moralism known as moderate moralism. The aesthetic failures of my work of historical fiction and Carroll's hypothetical tragedy are an upshot of their moral character. We may infer therefrom that moral judgements are sometimes aesthetically relevant.

Amanda Lee Koe deliberately treads a moral tightrope in her groundbreaking debut novel in 2019, *Delayed Rays of a Star*. Koe's novel features Anna May Wong (the first Chinese American film star), Marlene Dietrich (a German actress) and Leni Riefenstahl (a German actress and film director).[5] Riefenstahl would later become known for her Nazi propaganda film *Triumph of the Will*. Instead of Hitler as a tragic protagonist, we have Leni Riefenstahl as a woman-victim. Koe wishes to make Riefenstahl's motivations more intelligible to us: after all, there is nothing unusual about artists like Riefenstahl using state resources to make state-commissioned work. There is also a sense in which Riefenstahl might be regarded as a scapegoat: it is easier to blame a woman than the system. At the same time, Koe makes it clear that Riefenstahl is unreliable and morally compromised and refuses to deny or downplay her complicity in the Nazi regime. Koe's artistic decisions may be motivated (at least in part) by the moralist concerns we have already raised, although her treatment of Riefenstahl suggests that nuanced and careful approaches still leave room for some artistic freedom and flexibility.[6]

Moderate moralism is supported by the Common Reasons Argument (or Argument 3):

P1: It is sometimes the case that a moral defect in an artwork is an aesthetic defect because it prevents us from fully engaging with the artwork.

C: ∴ Sometimes the reason an artwork is morally flawed is the same reason that the artwork is aesthetically flawed.

The moral features of my hypothetical work of historical fiction and Carroll's hypothetical tragedy prevent us from fully engaging with the artworks: they can secure neither admiration for the ang ku kueh-selling serial killer (the epic hero) nor pity for Hitler (the tragic protagonist). Here, admiration and pity are the emotional responses from the audience that each artwork needs to elicit in order to successfully achieve its aesthetic purposes. However, these requisite emotional responses are not forthcoming, owing to certain moral features of the work.

A version of Humean moralism that is stronger than moderate moralism is ethicism (Gaut, 1998). According to ethicism, there is a plurality of aesthetic values and the ethical values of an artwork are but a single kind. Ethicism is supported by an ethicist principle, according to which an artwork is aesthetically meritorious (or defective) insofar as it manifests ethically admirable (or reprehensible) attitudes. As a *pro tanto* principle, the ethicist principle allows for good and even great artworks that are ethically flawed and below-average artworks that manifest admirable ethical attitudes. However good and even great artworks in both the mooi indie genre (§ 4.4), against which Sudjojono inveighed, and the bucolic genre paintings of the Philippines (§ 5.4), against which Edades stood opposed, might be, their Orientalist tropes suggest a static and undeveloped Oriental culture and would count as a flaw.[7] Lacquerware made in Myanmar, functioning as anti-colonial propaganda, has been used to promote the struggle for independence from British colonial rule (Nelson, 2019, p. 168). Although this lacquerware is middling or below-average (artistically speaking), it serves as a powerful testament to the uplifting and inspirational qualities of art.[8] We may note in passing that ethicism does not automatically entail either Thesis 1 (the negative causal thesis) or Thesis 3 (the positive causal thesis). Instead, we need to make an all-things-considered judgement when called upon to determine the value of an artwork.

Ethicism is supported by the Merited Response Argument (or Argument 4):

P1: Although an artwork may prescribe a particular response (e.g. that we pity Hitler as a tragic protagonist or admire the ang ku kueh-selling serial killer as a folk hero), it does not follow that it succeeds in making this response merited.

C: ∴ Prescribed responses are subject to evaluative criteria.

Argument 4 is accompanied by the following philosophical implications: the fact that we have a reason not to respond in a prescribed manner is an aesthetic defect or failure of the artwork and a work's manifestation of ethically bad attitudes may count as an aesthetic defect in it.

Moderate moralism is supported by Argument 3 (Carroll, 1996). Ethicism, on the other hand, is supported by the ethicist principle and Argument 4 (Gaut, 1998). While both moderate moralism and ethicism are versions of Humean moralism, the former does not have to appeal to aesthetic cognitivism in the manner that the latter does.[9] For the moderate moralist, all that matters is whether the audience can get sufficiently absorbed by an artwork for it to realize its aesthetic aims. Ethicism, on the other hand, embraces aesthetic cognitivism. It may therefore be easier for aesthetic anti-cognitivists to accept moderate moralism (a weaker version of Humean moralism) than ethicism.

12.4 Most moderate moralism

If neither moderate moralism nor ethicism is your cup of tea, then there is still most moderate moralism to consider (Kieran, 2001). The most moderate moralist is intimately concerned with questions of intelligibility. Do we have a coherence and consistency of imagery, description, thoughts and affective responses? In addition, how plausible, psychologically probable, informative, explanatory or insightful might the understanding afforded through imaginative experience be? According to most moderate moralism, the moral features implicit in and central to the imaginative experience afforded by an artwork are relevant to a narrative's value as art, to the extent that they undermine or promote the intelligibility, with respect to appropriately sensitive audiences, of the characters, events and states of affairs.

12.5 Alternatives to moralism

Moralists of various stripes all agree that the aesthetic value of an artwork should be determined by its moral value. Platonic moralism and Humean moralism constitute its two chief and traditional strands. Less traditional strands include such versions of Humean moralism as moderate moralism, ethicism and most moderate moralism. One alternative to moralism is autonomism, the view that the aesthetic value of art should be autonomous from other kinds of value (including moral value). Aestheticism, the view that the aesthetic value of art is the highest of all values, is another alternative to moralism. It follows from aestheticism that the aesthetic value of an artwork will trump its immorality. Formalism is the view that the aesthetic value of an artwork is determined solely by its formal features. While formalists tend to be autonomists, at least some formalists (e.g. David Pole) have argued that it is possible to consider the immorality of an artwork as a formal defect.[10] Autonomism, aestheticism and formalism may be regarded as broadly interchangeable positions.

12.6 Immoralism

Besides autonomism, aestheticism and formalism, there is also immoralism as a possible alternative to moralism. Jacobson (1997) invites us to consider Emily Dickinson's (1858–1865) 'Tell all the truth but tell it slant –':

> Tell all the truth but tell it slant –
>
> Tell all the truth but tell it slant –
>   Success in Circuit lies
> Too bright for our infirm Delight
>   The Truth's superb surprise
> As Lightning to the Children eased
>   With explanation kind
> The Truth must dazzle gradually
>   Or every man be blind –
>
> Emily Dickinson (1830–86)

The central trope of Dickinson's poem is one of truth as a source of overwhelming electric power or a sun too bright to be viewed straight on. The insight of Emily Dickinson's poem has aesthetic merit. On the other hand, readers who question the propriety of its ethical perspective may see the poem as an apologia for deception. Are we therefore compelled to either recommend the banishment of poets (Plato) or imaginatively resist the poem (Hume)?

Not necessarily, according to the immoralist. The moral defects of this poem's ethical perspective can sensibly be deemed an aesthetic flaw only if the poem can be improved aesthetically by its alteration. However, this is impossible. It would be utterly absurd to suppose that we can always sanitize an artwork's ethical perspective, while keeping its aesthetically valuable qualities intact. An immoral artwork can be incorrigible: it cannot be sanitized, only expurgated.[11] It may be impossible to conceive of any adequate notion of an artwork's formal beauty as divorced from its content. The immoralist is prepared to extend the notion of incorrigibility from the Dickinson poem to Leni Riefenstahl's (1935) *Triumph of the Will*, a Nazi propaganda film. Both Dickinson's poem and Riefenstahl's film possess aesthetic merit, yet are incorrigible. Where no sanitization of their ethical perspective is possible, they can only be expurgated.

12.7 Case study: Khoo's *In the Room*

Eric Khoo's (2015) *In the Room* is an erotic drama film set in room 27 of the Hotel Singapura, weaving together six stories of love, lust, longing and loss.[12] Damien, a 1970s musician, meets a hotel maid, Imrah, and promises to write a song for her, shortly before dying of of a heroin overdose on New Year's Eve. The ghost of Damien sticks around to haunt the sexual exchanges in room 27, even as Imrah continues to be employed at the hotel. The story of foiled love between Damien and Imrah, interspersed between the other vignettes, threads together the entire narrative. A British colonist and a foreign-educated Chinese rubber tree plantation owner form a gay couple that has to part ways as a result of the Japanese invasion in the 1940s. In the surreal and comedic interlude of the 1950s, Madame Orchid instructs her students how to exert sexual dominance over men. A Singaporean man has a tryst with a married Japanese woman, although the latter is as cynical as the former is hopeful of a shared future for them. A Thai man is in love with a transgender Thai woman who is preparing for sex reassignment surgery.

Last but not least, a lusty Korean woman shares a room with her virginal male school buddy.

In the Room is widely regarded as Singapore's first erotic film, in itself a feat given the general conservatism, strict censorship laws, and moral guidelines prevalent in Singapore. After some initial controversy involving the Media Development Authority (MDA), the film was eventually allowed to screen in Singapore with an R21 rating. The film has been screened as part of the official selection at the Toronto International Film Festival, San Sebastián International Film Festival, Busan International Film Festival and Singapore International Film Festival. The traditional liberal defence of the softcore pornographic aspects of Khoo's film may appeal to the freedom of expression (i.e. the right that Khoo has not to be stopped from making, publishing, exhibiting and distributing his film), the right to privacy (i.e. the right that individuals who consume the film have to explore and indulge their own personal tastes and convictions) and the comparative harmlessness of the film (West, 2021).

However, anti-pornography feminists may object to the central role that pornography is thought to play in the exploitation and oppression of women (Itzin, 1992; MacKinnon, 1993). There may be some moral justification for feminist concerns in the final story involving the Korean woman and her male school buddy. Although the interaction between the sexually promiscuous and emotionally unsettled Korean woman (played by Kim Kkobbi) – who laments her inability to achieve an orgasm and even brings a stranger to the hotel room for a sexual encounter while her hotel roommate is in the same room – and her virginal school buddy (played by Choi Woo-Shik) is played for laughs, things take a disturbing turn when the latter takes advantage of his female friend while she is inebriated. At least one reviewer, Raymond Tan, has objected to the trivialization of the rape scene in this film. Is the harm that may be caused to women sufficiently great to justify censoring or prohibiting the film on both liberal and feminist grounds, notwithstanding any potential artistic value that may be found in the film? These are legitimate concerns and make Khoo's *In the Room* a useful case study for our discussion of the nature of the relationship (or lack thereof) between art and morality. Given the response that you might offer to the question of how we ought to approach Khoo's *In the Room*, how might you classify your own position: moralism, autonomism, aestheticism, formalism, or immoralism? What are some reasons that you might provide in support of your position?

Conclusion

We opened our proceedings with Chapters 1 and 2, which helped to lay the important foundations for our foray into philosophical aesthetics. Chapter 1 offered both a primer on the standard philosophical method (including the use of precise arguments) and a response to scepticism about the possibility of Southeast Asian philosophy, while Chapter 2 attempted to provide an adequate response to scepticism about the possibility of Southeast Asian art. Chapter 3 invited us to consider a hypothetical tale about an ang ku kueh seller in 1980s Singapore, fashioned in the form of a work of historical fiction. We discussed whether this tale of the ang ku kueh seller would count as valuable, in virtue of its satisfying all the artistic constraints that are satisfied by works of historical fiction. Our discussion about the value of art intertwined with our discussion about truth and knowledge in art. Insofar as art produces appearances alone and not the truth of things, its mimetic nature will open up a gap between truth and appearance and give rise to certain epistemic dangers. In addition, as a poet lacks the relevant expertise relative to what they describe, it may be argued that they cannot be relied on (epistemically speaking). Things fare little better when we rely on the art as inspiration account: a divinely inspired poet cannot be said to be any more epistemically reliable than a poet who lacks the relevant expertise relative to what they describe.

In pursuit of various desired artistic effects, a poet may also be said to have *pro tanto* reasons to include incorrect information in literary artworks. To compound matters, the institutional argument allows one to conclude in favour of literature as a whole being indifferent to the truth or falsity of claims advanced by literary works (§ 3.7). Platonists will maintain that art does not necessarily involve knowledge (Claim 1) and art does not necessarily involve truth (Claim 2). In addition, given the powerful nature of art (Claim 3), we have Platonic grounds to conclude in favour of art being dangerous. The dangerous nature of art lends motivation to the banishment of the poets from the ideal and just city-state.

In Chapter 4, we discovered how the denial of Claim 3 may lead us toward a Humean view about art, according to which it will have too little power to arouse, appeal to and engage with a suitably virtuous audience in precisely those instances when it might pose certain moral dangers. The denial of Claim 1 may lead us toward aesthetic cognitivism, according to which art gives its audience knowledge and the knowledge-conferring capacity of art enhances its aesthetic value. A denial of Claim 1 may involve an appeal to various modes of aesthetic knowledge, including (but not limited to) propositional knowledge, practical knowledge, conceptual knowledge, moral knowledge and phenomenal knowledge.

Denying Claim 3 allows us to invoke the phenomenon of imaginative resistance and point out how art has too little power to move us in certain instances: as art is not as dangerous as it seems, there may not be any need to banish the poets. Denying Claim 1 allows us to recognize the opportunity cost of banishing the poets: we may lose vital sources of propositional knowledge, practical knowledge, conceptual knowledge, moral knowledge and phenomenal knowledge.

In Chapter 5, we engaged critically with the concept of aesthetic merit, how might it be distinguished conceptually from other concepts, and whether there might be any criteria according to which we will be able to determine the degree of aesthetic merit of an object. According to the Ogilby-Milton phenomenon, we have good reasons for maintaining that tastes are better or worse. The Humean position allows for this view to be maintained by indexing our aesthetic preferences to certain established norms and practices of evaluation: the rules of art, the rules of composition, and the laws of criticism (s_1), a decision that comprises the joint verdict of true judges or ideal critics (s_2), and a canon (s_3).

In Chapter 6, we examined Kant's response to Hume and the Kantian account of aesthetic judgement in terms of its moments: universality (Moment 1 or Quantity), disinterestedness (Moment 2 or Quality), purposiveness (Moment 3 or Relation) and necessity (Moment 4 or Modality). We also motivated Kant's denial of the existence of standards of taste, established norms and practices of evaluation and traced the association between Kantian aesthetics – especially with respect to its assertion that the beautiful is a symbol of the morally good – and autonomism (or the view that art and ethics are autonomous and independent realms of value).

In Chapter 7, we attempted to determine that in virtue of which certain entities get grouped into the category reserved for works of art. We also identified certain ontological distinctions that ought to be observed within the category of artworks. After elaborating on and critically evaluating a range of hypotheses about the identity conditions and ontological status of artworks (viz. the simple physical object hypothesis, the imaginary entity hypothesis, the abstract entity hypothesis), we devoted much critical attention to Goodman's more sophisticated ontology of artworks and its account of the symptoms of the aesthetic and the allographic–autographic distinction.

Chapter 8 provided us with an opportunity to develop and engage with a case study of Chen Wen Hsi in the context of forgery. We introduced several caveats about forgery, before trying to provide an account of the universal condemnation of forgery and the consensus on the epistemic risks posed by forgery (viz. the undermining of our bootstrapping strategy, the misdirection of our trust, the creation of spurious associations, the contamination of our aesthetic understanding). Last but not least, we addressed the question of how we might go about dealing with the perfect fake.

In Chapter 9, we engaged critically with the phenomenon of conceptual art and its implications for aesthetics and the philosophy of art. Two possible views of conceptual art were suggested: the art-historical view (View 1) and the broad church view (View 2). We identified a clear parallel between our aesthetic appreciation of concepts or ideas in conceptual art and our appreciation of the beauty or elegance of concepts or ideas, as they might be instantiated in logical or mathematical proofs and literary works. In addition, we engaged with Shelley's trilemma, a trilemma in which the problem of conceptual art might be cast. Responses to this trilemma include the standard formalist response (Response 1), the response of Arthur C. Danto and Timothy Binkley (Response 2) and James Shelley's own response (Response 3), although each response is not without its issues.

In Chapter 10, we devoted philosophical attention to the understudied phenomenon of creativity, were introduced to various classificatory schemata and criteria for creativity, and encountered several philosophical accounts of creativity: the eliminativist account, the experiential account, and the functionalist or computationalist account. Last but not least, we gave serious and due consideration to the following question: are machines capable of creative art?

In Chapter 11, we distinguished between verbal and visual ambiguity and provided some sense of how ambiguity might be resolved when interpreting and making sense of works of art. We identified and engaged critically with a range of positions relative to the question of whether the intentions of the artist might be relevant to understanding and interpreting an artwork: absolute actual intentionalism, moderate actual intentionalism, anti-intentionalism and hypothetical intentionalism.

In Chapter 12, we addressed the nature of the relationship (or lack thereof) between art and morality. Four plausible theses were outlined: bad art corrupts and has a negative moral effect on its audience (or Thesis 1), bad art always corrupts its audience (or Thesis 2), good art edifies and has a positive moral effect on its audience (or Thesis 3) and good art always brings about moral improvement in its audience (or Thesis 4). We further distinguished between varieties of moralism (viz. Platonic moralism, Humean moralism, ethicism, moderate moralism, most moderate moralism) and alternatives to moralism (viz. autonomism, aestheticism, formalism, immoralism). Where an artwork possesses both aesthetic merit and certain moral defects in terms of its ethical perspective, one need not recommend either the banishment of the poet (Plato) or imaginative resistance (Hume). According to the immoralist, the immoral artwork may plausibly be characterized as incorrigible.

We have covered quite some distance since the opening chapter. Our philosophical investigations have led us to reflect on such diverse topics as the nature of truth, knowledge, taste, aesthetic merit, aesthetic judgement, the role of both perception and conception in art, creativity, the possibility of machine art and morality in the context of art. I have taken the liberty of peppering our philosophical investigations with examples from the Southeast Asian artistic canon and ideas from philosophers connected to the Southeast Asian region. As aforementioned in the Introduction, it is my ardent hope that my textbook will help to address at least two areas of intellectual concern: the criminally understudied nature of aesthetics and the philosophy of art in the Western tradition and the relative dearth of examples and references from Southeast Asian art to counteract the prevailing Eurocentric tendency to defer to the Western artistic canon.

It would be remiss of me to end this textbook without any reference to a highly influential claim made by Weitz (1956) to the effect that the concept of art is an open one. According to Weitz, if the necessary and sufficient conditions for the application of a concept can be stated, then the concept is closed. Otherwise, if the range of uses for a concept cannot be arbitrarily stipulated in advance, then the concept is an open one. In other words, a concept is open if the conditions for its application are emendable and corrigible. Art, an endeavour that is often characterized in terms of its own protean nature, a sense of adventure, boldness, creativity, and a transgression of boundaries, is a concept whose uses are regularly extended to cover either this or that new candidate work. If Weitz is correct and art is an open concept, then this textbook cannot be the final word on aesthetics and the philosophy of art. It is my ardent hope that any lacunae in the current edition of this textbook will continue to be served – whether by my hand or someone else's – in the Southeast Asian idiom in the future. *Sikit-sikit, lama-lama jadi bukit.*[1]

Appendices

A Philosophical Argumentation

As the use of precise arguments is part of the stable of philosophical methods and will be regularly employed in this textbook, this appendix should help you to get more acquainted with the use of formal language and notation. Each system of logic L_i comprises an alphabet, a syntax, a proof theory and a semantics.[1] Propositional logic L_0 is an example of a system of logic and various formulae may be generated from its alphabet of symbols. Extensions of propositional logic rely on L_0 as their base, while introducing additional quantifiers and operators. These extensions include first-order predicate logic (with the universal and existential quantifiers $\forall$ and $\exists$), alethic modal logic (with the necessity and possibility operators $\Box$ and $\Diamond$) and epistemic logic (with the epistemic modalities for belief and knowledge B_S and K_S relative to agent S).

Consider the claims 'Art confers knowledge to its audience' and 'The knowledge-conferring capacity of art enhances its aesthetic value'. As discussed in Chapters 4 and 5, these claims are hotly contested in the debate between aesthetic cognitivism and aesthetic anti-cognitivism. The first claim 'Art confers knowledge to its audience' is an atomic proposition: it cannot be further broken down into simpler or more ultimate propositions. The lowercase letters p, q, etc. (known as propositional variables) may be assigned to atomic propositions. As the first and second claims are distinct, we may assign p to the former and q to the latter. The claim 'Art confers knowledge to its audience and the knowledge-conferring capacity of art enhances its aesthetic value' is a compound proposition that can be expressed using the atomic propositions p and q and the logical connective $\wedge$ (for 'and'). The formal-language equivalent for the natural-language claim 'Art confers knowledge to its audience and the knowledge-conferring capacity of art enhances its aesthetic value' would be $p \wedge q$.

Table A.1 represents the formal notation for atomic propositions, logical connectives and truth-values.

Table A.1 Formal notation or symbols in the alphabet of propositional logic. © Melvin Chen

Symbol		Description
p, q	**Propositional variables**	
¬	not	
∧	and	
∨	or	
→	if . . . then	
↔	iff	
⊥	falsity	
⊤	truth	

In accordance with certain rules in linguistics, '*Art its audience to confers knowledge' is grammatically ill-formed, whereas 'Art confers knowledge to its audience' is grammatically well-formed. There are also rules in logic that govern the ways in which symbols from the alphabet of propositional logic combine to form formulae. If a formula satisfies these syntactic rules, then it is well-formed. Well-formed formulae are referred to as wffs. Otherwise, the formula is syntactically ill-formed.

Table A.2 lists the syntactic rules of propositional logic. According to the syntax of propositional logic L_0, the compound proposition $p \wedge q$ is a wff: it may be obtained from an application of Rules 1 and 3. Last but not least, we need to make precise how reasoning in a particular system of logic will proceed through the manipulation of formulae in accordance with certain axioms or rules of inference. Proof theory helps us to do this. According to a famous rule of inference known as *modus ponens* (R_1), if $p \rightarrow q$ and q are true, then we may infer that q likewise is true. This may be formally represented as $p \rightarrow q, p \vdash q$, where $\vdash$ denotes syntactic entailment or consequence. Furthermore, each logical connective ('not', 'and', 'or', 'if . . . then', etc.) is associated with introduction (*I*) and elimination (*E*) rules. As the

Table A.2 Syntactic rules of propositional logic. © Melvin Chen

Rule 1	All atomic propositions are wffs.
Rule 2	If ϕ is a wff, then $\neg\phi$ is a wff.
Rule 3	If ϕ and ψ are wffs, then $\phi \wedge \psi$, $\phi \vee \psi$, $\phi \rightarrow \psi$, and $\phi \leftrightarrow \psi$ are wffs.
Rule 4	If ϕ is a wff, then (ϕ) is a wff.
Rule 5	A formula is a wff iff it can be obtained from a finite and recursive application of Rules 1–4.

modus ponens rule allows us to infer q from a premise set containing $p \to q$ and q, it may be classified as an elimination rule for $\to$.

Here is a list of valid rules of inference:

$[R_1]\ p \to q, p \vdash q - \to_{E1}$ (i.e. elimination rule for $\to$)

$[R_2]\ \neg(p \to q) \vdash p, \neg q - \to_{E2}$

$[R_3]$ ass.: $p, \cdots, q \vdash p \to q$, where 'ass.' stands for 'assume' $- \to_I$

$[R_4]\ (p \vee q), p \to r, q \to r \vdash r - \vee_E$

$[R_5]\ p \vdash (p \vee q) - \vee_I$

$[R_6]\ (p \wedge q) \vdash p, q - \wedge_E$

$[R_7]\ p, q \vdash (p \wedge q) - \wedge_I$

$[R_8]\ \neg p \vdash p \to \bot - \neg_E$

$[R_9]\ p \to \bot \vdash \neg p - \neg_I$

$[R_{10}]\ \vdash$ ass.: p – Assumption

$[R_{11}]$ ass.: $\neg p, \cdots, \bot \vdash p$ – *Reductio ad absurdum*

$[R_{12}]\ \neg(p \vee q) \leftrightarrow (\neg p) \wedge (\neg q)$ – De Morgan's law

$[R_{13}]\ \neg(p \wedge q) \leftrightarrow (\neg p) \vee (\neg q)$ – De Morgan's law

$[R_{14}]\ p \leftrightarrow q \vdash p \to q, q \to p - \leftrightarrow_E$

Other rules of inference may be derived from R_1–R_{14}. For instance:

1. $p \to q$
2. $\neg q$
3. ass.: p – R_{10}
4. $\therefore q$ – R_1 or $\to_{E1}$ (from 1 & 3)
5. $q \wedge \neg q$ – R_7 or $\wedge_I$ (from 2 & 4)
6. $\therefore \neg p$ – R_{11} (from 3 & 5)
7. $\therefore \neg q \to \neg p$ – R_3 or $\to_I$ (from 2 & 6)

This yields the *modus tollens* rule of inference:

$[R_{15}]\ p \to q \vdash \neg q \to \neg p$ – *modus tollens*

While not all of these rules of inference will be used in this textbook, at least some of them will be employed in the construction of arguments that are intended as reasoned defences of certain claims. Chapter 1 may be referred to whenever a reminder is needed about the role and nature of philosophical argumentation in the toolkit of the standard philosophical method.

Notes

Chapter 1

1. The standard method, with its emphasis on conceptual analysis (discovery-oriented), may be contrasted with the non-standard method of Haslanger (2006, 2012), with its emphasis on ameliorative analysis (engineering-oriented). More information about the nature of this distinction and how it is wielded in the context of this textbook may be found in the Introduction.
2. A *kōan* is a question, statement, dialogue, or story that is employed in Zen practice to provoke doubt.
3. Pigliucci draws our attention in the latter instance to the origins of science in natural philosophy.
4. Validation refers broadly to all processes aimed at establishing the soundness of some belief, process, or practice (Dotson, 2012). Like legitimation, validation is an evaluative concept, although it is happily not confined to evaluation according to accepted patterns and standards.
5. Given that Van Norden's response was recorded in a 2016 interview and he later went on to serve as the Kwan Im Thong Hood Cho Temple Professor of Humanities and Head of Studies in Philosophy at Yale-NUS College in Singapore from 2017–20, his views about the status of Southeast Asian philosophy might since have altered. Despite being an American citizen, Van Norden can still be regarded as a philosopher connected to the Southeast Asian region in virtue of his Yale-NUS stint.
6. Emerita Quito (1990) draws a contrast between academic or formal philosophy (universal) and popular or grassroots philosophy (grounded in a sense of national or cultural awareness) and appears to favour the latter, since one seeks the spirit of the Filipino people in Filipino philosophy. Elsewhere, Quito (1983) reflects that 'pilosopo' (the Filipino word for 'philosopher') is used pejoratively for someone who argues lengthily, whether rightly or wrongly. Pilósopo Tasyo (or Tasyo the Philosopher), a character in *Noli Me Tángere*, one of the novels of the Filipino nationalist and writer José Rizal, is depicted with the pejorative sense of 'pilosopo' in mind. We shall encounter Rizal again in § 12.1. Meanwhile and according

to Quito, the pejorative sense of 'pilosopo' provides a reason why philosophy does not enjoy as much prestige in the Philippines. Her arguments support the second approach (anthropological or cultural).

Chapter 2

1. It should be obvious that quite a lot of our discussion in this chapter may equally be applied to our take on Southeast Asian philosophy in Chapter 1, since '*Southeast Asian* philosophy' and '*Southeast Asian* art' (italics for emphasis) share the same adjectival modifier.

2. As Patke (2012) has pointed out, the account of imperialism in the Philippines is more complex: more than 350 years of Spanish rule ended in 1898, only to be followed by the Philippine–American war of 1898–1901, almost half a century of American rule that ended in 1946, and a further period of American neo-colonial influence that only ended with the closure of the American military bases in the Philippines in 1991.

3. This mirrors the lazy move of subsuming Southeast Asian thought under Chinese, Indian and Islamic philosophy. Recall Pham's (2013) second view of Vietnamese thought, first described in § 1.4.

4. This mirrors similar questions raised in Chapter 1 about the philosophical status of Asian thought in general and Southeast Asian thought in particular.

5. It might be argued that whether or not Southeast Asian art is a unified phenomenon is ultimately a moot issue, at least for the purposes of this textbook. After all, neither Western art, European art, nor even North American art appear to be unified phenomena, yet this fact has not stopped people from writing textbooks with almost exclusively Western, European, or North American examples. We are simply returning the favour here and choosing examples from whichever region (including the Southeast Asian region) we might wish. I am grateful to an anonymous reviewer for having raised this point for my consideration. In the context of the ameliorative approach, whether or not Southeast Asian art is ultimately a unified phenomenon, we have a normative commitment to making the concept of art what we want it to be (i.e. inclusive, non-Eurocentric, capable of accommodating works from the Southeast Asian artistic canon).

6. The boundaries of the concept of art have been collectively negotiated and decided on in the past and may be collectively renegotiated in a reflective equilibrium in the future. Why should we expect matters to be any different with the concept of Southeast Asian art?

7. As discussed in § 1.5, a comparable development in Southeast Asian philosophy can be traced to the tireless efforts and organizational nous of George F. McLean.

8.   This rejection of scepticism on behalf of Southeast Asian art echoes our earlier rejection of scepticism on behalf of Asian philosophy and Southeast Asian philosophy in §§ 1.3–1.5.

Chapter 3

1.   Hokkien is a Chinese dialect widely spoken in Fujian province in southeastern mainland China.
2.   Other ang ku kueh fillings include peanut, bean, salted bean, coconut, durian, yam, sweet potato, sweet corn, coffee, green tea. The different colours indicate the different fillings used for the ang ku kueh.
3.   In a related vein, Liao describes the past-directed imaginings across generations evoked by sweet potato congee, a dish associated with the pre-economic-development era in Taiwan's history.
4.   The debate on whether food is art raises further philosophical questions about what art is, how a distinction is made between the major arts (e.g. the fine arts of music, sculpture and painting and the applied arts of design, architecture and crafts) and the minor arts, and whether such a distinction is a principled one. We may even consider whether further aesthetic distinctions should be made between food-based art (e.g. *Untitled (Free)* (1992), Rirkrit Tiravanija's first solo exhibition which involved converting the gallery into a kitchen space where the artist served Thai vegetable curry and rice to the audience), artified food and the food of everyday life (e.g. ang ku kueh) (Liao & Meskin, 2018).
5.   This implies that food, even if it counts as art (major or minor), would not be valuable in virtue of its counting as art.
6.   See R_{15} and the discussion about epistemic logic as an extension of propositional logic in Appendix A.
7.   A rhapsode is a classical Greek performer of epic poetry.
8.   Emma is fond of romances, has a tendency for confusing fiction with reality, and makes the frequent mistake of deriving her opinions on love from these romances. Other fictional characters who demonstrate a tendency toward bovarysme and are subject to ironic treatment in virtue of this tendency include Don Quixote (from Miguel de Cervantes's *Don Quixote*) and Catherine Morland (from Jane Austen's *Northanger Abbey*). Emma Bovary has memorably been described as a female Don Quixote in skirts (by Gasset, 2000).
9.   Credit is due to Mara Miller for having pointed out the relevance of the Lady Sarashina example in the context of bovarysme.
10. In the Platonic dialogue *Ion*, Socrates compels Ion to make an analogous concession in a critical appraisal of Homer.

11. This argument is valid. See R_1 or the *modus ponens* rule of inference in Appendix A. It also relies on another rule of inference from quantificational logic:
    $[R_{15}]$ $\forall x\phi \vdash \text{Subst}(\{x/a\}, \phi) - \forall_E$

12. For empirical work on the effects of incorrect information in narratives, see Green and Donahue (2011), Prentice et al. (1997) and Wheeler et al. (1999). For a discussion of Dickens's anachronism in *Barnaby Rudge*, see Ricks (1996) and Rowe (1997).

13. The 1987 Marxist Conspiracy led to the arrest and detention without trial of several individuals under the Internal Security Act (ISA), on the grounds of their alleged involvement in a Marxist conspiracy against the state of Singapore.

14. The Eisner Awards are often described as the comics industry's equivalent of the Academy Awards for the film industry.

15. In its official statement explaining the withdrawal of the grant, the NAC cited the sensitive content of the work. There are certainly fascinating parallels here between the NAC's withdrawal of a government grant for Liew's artwork and the Socratic recommendation in favour of the banishment of the poets.

16. It has been reported that at least some early readers and reviewers mistook Liew's graphic novel, a fictional biography of a fictional cartoonist, for an actual biography of a real cartoonist. This attests to the power of illusion in art, especially when art produces or imitates appearances (recall our account of art as *mimësis* or imitation in § 3.2). This power of illusion may equally be invoked in the *trompe l'œil* effect in painting (the illusion of depth and life-likeness on a two-dimensional painted surface) and the rumoured panic and terror of the audience when watching a train moving directly toward the camera in film (as reported at a screening of the Lumière brothers' (1896) *Arrival of a Train* and attributable to the illusion of depth and movement in a two-dimensional medium).

17. Nonetheless, there is one passage in Book 4 of Plato's *Laws* (Plato, 1926) where Plato calls poetry both *mimêsis* (imitation or representation) and the product of *enthousiasmos* (inspiration or possession) (Pappas, 2012).

18. The exclusive disjunction relation ($\veebar$) may be defined as follows: $p \veebar q \overset{\text{def}}{=} (p \vee q) \wedge \neg(p \wedge q)$
    Furthermore, this argument is valid in virtue of R_4 or $\vee_E$.

Chapter 4

1. To wit, imaginative resistance is also a problem in the philosophy of fiction, especially with respect to those accounts of fiction that highlight

the role of the imagination (Currie, 2020; Walton, 1990). How we might approach any question concerning the cognitive value of art may differ between (say) a fictional work of art that invites us to imagine a fictional scenario and a photographic work of art that attempts to faithfully represent reality. Nonetheless, given how the Humean move of denying P3 of Argument 1 (viz. the powerful nature of art) can be directly related to the puzzle of imaginative resistance, I consider the next section (§ 4.3) an opportune one in which to identify and expound on the latter notion. I am grateful to an anonymous reviewer for comments offered in this regard.

2. There is an interesting parallel here with Piero Manzoni's (1961) *Artist's Shit*, consisting of ninety tin cans allegedly filled with faeces.

3. Given the similarity between the latter newspaper article title and the title of Dotson's (2012) article (viz. 'How is this paper philosophy?'), we may infer that the culture of justification, privileging legitimation as a vetting process, is equally present in philosophy and art. Questions of the form 'Is X really Y?' or 'How is X Y?' will standardly be fielded by X (non-canonical) in a domain (Y) where there are expectations of conformity to accepted standards and patterns (i.e. justifying norms).

4. For more on aesthetic cognitivism, see Goodman (1968), Kivy (1997) and Walsh (1969).

5. For more on how we might stand to attain practical knowledge from works of art, see Currie (1998), Diamond (1993), Nussbaum (1990), Putnam (1976) and Robinson (1995).

6. John (1998) has argued that Virginia Woolf allows us to gain knowledge of the concept of sympathy, Kazuo Ishiguro offers conceptual knowledge of dignity, Marcel Proust provides us with insight into the concept of desire, and conceptual knowledge of beauty may be gleaned from Toni Morrison.

7. It may also be argued that the horrors are sometimes so unspeakable that art can fail and artists might find themselves unwilling or unable to confront the traumatic experiences directly.

8. According to Article II of the 1948 Convention on the Prevention & Punishment of the Crime of Genocide by the United Nations, genocide refers to any of the following acts committed with intent to destroy, in whole or in part, a national, ethnical, racial or religious group, as such:

    1 Killing members of the group;
    2 Causing serious bodily or mental harm to members of the group;
    3 Deliberately inflicting on the group conditions of life calculated to bring about its physical destruction in whole or in part;
    4 Imposing measures intended to prevent births within the group;
    5 Forcibly transferring children of the group to another group. (UN, 1948)

Besides the Khmer Rouge genocide, the state-sponsored and large-scale killings of Communists and suspected Communists (many of whom were from ethnically Chinese families) by the Suharto regime in Indonesia led to the deaths of 500,000–1 million people between 1965–6. More recently, the persecution and killings of the Rohingya Muslim people by the Burmese army since 2016 have been described as a genocide or an ethnic cleansing and over 1 million Rohingya have been forced to flee to other countries.

9. Kelantan is a state in the north-east of Peninsular Malaysia. Kota Bharu is its state capital and royal seat and Kelantan is bordered by Narathiwat Province of Thailand to the north. Given its geographical location, Kelantanese culture is inflected with a variety of influences from Indian, Thai, Islamic and even Cham culture. These cultural influences and the rural nature of Kelantan ensure that Kelantanese culture is rich and distinct from the cultures of other Malay sub-ethnic groups. Besides the *dikir barat*, other Kelantanese cultural practices include *wau bulan* (kite-flying) and *gasing* (top-spinning).

10. Recall from our discussion of Argument 1 in § 4.1 how an argument is valid iff, assuming the truth of all its premises, the truth of its conclusion follows by logical necessity. Furthermore, an argument may be valid though unsound: while all its premises offer logical support for its conclusion, at least one of its premises could be false. An argument is sound iff it is valid and all its premises are true.

11. To be precise, Argument 2 relies chiefly on R_4. It also relies on another rule of inference known as the hypothetical syllogism:

$$[R_{16}]\ p \to q, q \to r \vdash p \to r$$

Here is how R_{16} might be derived:

1. $p \to q$
2. $q \to r$
3. ass. $p - R_{10}$
4. $\therefore q - R_1$ (from 1 & 3)
5. $\therefore r - R_1$ (from 2 & 4)
6. $\therefore p \to r - R_3$ (from 3 & 5)

Chapter 5

1. The translation for the Japanese saying is 'there are even bugs that eat knotweed'. It should also be noted in passing that 蓼食う虫 is the title of a 1929 novel by Jun'ichirō Tanizaki. The English translation of Tanizaki's

Japanese title is *Some Prefer Nettles*. Again, Mara Miller must be acknowledged for having generously offered this piece of information.
2. See also Rowe (1999).
3. See the Introduction and § 1.3 respectively for more information about the ameliorative approach and the culture of praxis.

Chapter 6

1. For instance, Hume identifies strong and sound sense among the characteristics possessed by true judges or ideal critics.
2. For more on the full nature of the fascinating disagreement between Hume and Kant, see Kulenkampff (1990).
3. See the discussion about alethic modal logic in Appendix A.
4. For more information about the stone materials used to build the Angkor Wat (including sandstone, laterite and brick), see Uchida et al. (1998).
5. Imagination is the cognitive faculty for the gathering together of the manifold of parts.
6. Understanding is the cognitive faculty for the integration of these manifold parts into a whole. Furthermore, understanding is at the service of imagination and not vice versa.
7. You may recall that Platonic moralism is supported by Argument 1, which favours the banishment of the poets. Humean moralism, in turn, emerges from denying P3 (i.e. that art is powerful) of Argument 1, as we have already seen in Chapter 4.

Chapter 7

1. 'Visayan' is a term that refers to the people, language, culture, products, etc. of Visayas, a group of islands in the central part of the Philippine Archipelago: Panay, Samar, Negros, Leyte, Cebu and Bohol. This term may also be extended to include some sections in Mindanao settled by Cebuano emigrants. The balitaw is widely considered to be a truly native form of folk art, having been practised in the Visayas long before the arrival of the Spaniards (Gutierrez, 1961).
2. 'Dead Stars' was written by Márquez-Benítez in the wake of Anglo-American prose and poetry models being brought to the attention of Filipino students in the 1920s.
3. Furthermore, a string of characters may have multiple extensions. While the string of characters 'bank' in the English language is syntactically

unique, it has multiple extensions: an establishment for the custody, loan, exchange, or issue of money, the extension of credit, etc.; the land alongside or sloping down to a river or lake.

4. In the first edition of *Languages of Art*, Goodman fails to specify the ordering in question, although this omission is rectified in the second edition.

5. An image of Haribhitak's painting may be accessed with the following link: https: //www.nationalgallery.sg/gallerykids/pdf/explore/Awesome-Art-Face.pdf

6. Certain diagrams (e.g. diagrams capable of illustrating both the overlap and size of sets) are more relatively replete than other diagrams (e.g. diagrams capable of illustrating only the overlap of sets). Similar distinctions can be made between drawings and photographs: a black-and-white photograph is replete relative to a line drawing, whereas a colour photograph is replete relative to a black-and-white photograph (Blumson, 2011).

7. For further information about Harvard Project Zero, see Howard (1971).

8. By a notational scheme is meant a score, a script, a choreography, etc.

9. Given the challenges posed by forgeries to the identity conditions of works of art, there is little doubt that forgeries constitute an important object of philosophical investigation. They will be covered in more detail in the next chapter.

Chapter 8

1. For an art-historical perspective, see Sabapathy (1979).

2. See Lessing (1965) for a similar position.

3. Mark Landis is an American who forged and donated a large number of paintings to American art museums, sometimes even dressed as a Jesuit priest. Landis did not gain economically from his actions: he refrained from taking a tax deduction on his donations and went around the United States at his own expense, giving away free though forged paintings to museums. The exploits of Landis have been chronicled in the 2014 documentary *Art & Craft*.

4. This led to an eight-year legal battle between Gunarsa and several defendants, including the gallery owner Sinyo. Sinyo was accused of selling counterfeit paintings as Gunarsa's paintings in his gallery. Sinyo's defence attorneys argued that either the counterfeit paintings might have been authentic or Sinyo in any case thought that the counterfeit paintings were authentic when he first offered them for sale. When later called upon as a witness in the trial, Indrawati was able to deflect the defence's various attempts to discredit her as an expert on her husband Gunarsa's art. We must remember that Indrawati had spent several decades assisting her husband with his painting.

5. At a juncture of the trial, Gunarsa left the witness stand, where he had
    hitherto been providing purely verbal testimony, to offer a physical
    demonstration of Balinese dance. Through Gunarsa's demonstration, one
    would be able to infer the impossibility of the Balinese dancers' positions
    in the counterfeit paintings. Although the Indonesian judges eventually
    reached the verdict that the paintings were demonstrably counterfeit, they
    declined to hold anyone – including the art forgers, distributors and
    gallery owner Sinyo – responsible (Jenkins, 2010).
6. In a related context, Goodman (1968) furnishes the example of
    Rembrandt's original *Lucretia* and its perfect fake.

Chapter 9

1. The Western analogy here would be Andy Warhol's (1964) *Brillo Boxes*,
    which are (more or less) perceptually indistinguishable for all practical
    purposes from the Brillo boxes that are delivered to supermarkets.
2. Images of the original and restored versions of the statue may be accessed
    with the following link: https://biblioasia.nlb.gov.sg/vol-17/issue-3/
    oct-dec-2021/stjosephchurch
3. There is an analogy here with Sudjojono's critique of the mooi indie genre,
    which failed to reflect the more complex reality of the colonial situation in
    the Dutch East Indies (§ 4.4).
4. Ho Ho Ying's commitment to the perceptual and aesthetic nature of art – as
    opposed to its conceptual or ideational aspects – was reflected in his 1972
    response to Cheo's proposal: 'Viewers will not get any satisfaction even if
    they look at [*5′ × 5′ (Singapore River)*] for a whole day' (Nelson, 2019, p. 36).
5. As pointed out by Suwannakudt (2007) herself, the significance of the Thai
    site and context cannot be underestimated: putting up the same washing
    line in a gallery in Sydney would be irrelevant and even ridiculous.
6. Womanifesto has grown in leaps and bounds: from its humble beginnings
    as a Thailand-based event funded by organizations such as the Japan
    Foundation and Bangkok Metropolitan Authority in 1997 and 1999, it has
    expanded in recent years into Sydney (the 2019 'Archiving Womanifesto'
    exhibition), Hong Kong (the 2020 'Crafting Communities' exhibition at
    Asia Art Archive), Baroda, Sydney, London, Basel and Berlin (the 2020
    Womanifesto gatherings) and the United Kingdom (the 2021 Womanifesto
    exhibitions at Cooper Gallery and Hatton Gallery). I must thank
    Phaptawan Suwannakudt for having kindly informed me about these
    Womanifesto-relevant developments in a private correspondence.
7. Its influences would have included the following: Dadaism, Surrealism,
    Suprematism, the Fluxus Group and Abstract Expressionism (Lippard, 1973).

8. Recall our previous discussion about aesthetic formalism in Chapter 8.
9. Response 3 is not without its issues, as Shelley himself readily concedes. For example, how might we draw the line between properties that just cause feeling and bona fide aesthetic properties? Furthermore, might there not be properties that strike us, yet are not aesthetic properties? All things considered, although Response 3 is a promising alternative, more philosophical work remains to be done.

Chapter 10

1. In certain extreme instances, some philosophers have gone as far as to claim that creativity is by its very nature unpredictable and beyond the scope of science.
2. Charles Goodyear apparently dropped random substances (including cream cheese) into liquid rubber until he stumbled upon sulphur, which is capable of vulcanizing rubber. According to Nanay (2014), if Goodyear put all the substances found in his lab, including cream cheese and sulphur, in a row and then dropped them into liquid rubber one after another to see what happens, then we have good grounds to accept the mainstream view that Goodyear's scientific discovery of vulcanization, though original, was not creative. See also Gaut (2003b) and Novitz (2003) for a further discussion of Goodyear's scientific discovery of vulcanization in the context of the philosophy of creativity.
3. It may be noted in passing that Tzu Nyen was interested in the question of what makes Southeast Asia a region and constitutes its unity, given that the different Southeast Asian countries share neither a common language nor a common religion. According to the artist, no higher-resolution images of *CDOSEA* are available, since the video relies on found footage from YouTube. The pixelated quality of the footage may therefore be regarded as part of the work.
4. An aleatory procedure is one that is characterized by luck, randomness, chance, or contingency. Aleatory art may involve the use of random or statistical processes (e.g. coin-tossing, dice-throwing) during its composition, production, or performance.
5. It should be noted that copyright law is also invoked to protect creative works. Recall our discussion of Gunarsa's legal battle in § 8.6 and Gunarsa's vain hope for the protection of his original artworks under Indonesian copyright law.
6. An impasto technique is one in which paint may be laid on an area of the surface thickly or even mixed directly on the canvas.

7. Around 200,000 Javanese and 15,000 Dutch soldiers had been killed during the Java War (Protschky, 2011, p. 74).
8. Archimedes is the scientist who reportedly ran naked through the streets of Syracuse shouting 'Eureka!' (or 'I have it!' in Greek), after having stumbled upon the solution – the Archimedes principle – to the problem of demonstrating that the new crown of Hieron (the King of Syracuse) was not made of pure gold.
9. Tabios's computational approach is equally informed by the Filipino indigenous value of *kapwa* (for togetherness).

Chapter 11

1. Meyer (1956) constitutes an excellent resource for an investigation of ambiguity in music.
2. Much of this defence has been adapted from Tormey and Tormey (1983), although the examples from Southeast Asian art are my contribution to the philosophical discussion.
3. An image of this poster may be accessed with the following link: https://eyeyah.com/product/internet-explorer-by-ella-zheng/
4. *X* is a knockdown argument iff all experts accept *X*'s conclusion on the basis of *X*'s premises. This argument is powerful enough to overwhelm or knock down all its opponents.
5. For a detailed criticism of the conversation argument, see Huddleston (2012).
6. On a related note, AI researchers at Oxford are interested in the automatic detection of visual continuity errors in films, with a view to promoting higher standards of continuity among filmmakers (Pickup & Zisserman, 2009).
7. For a bird's-eye perspective on this debate, see Lin (2018).

Chapter 12

1. Recall our related discussion about the taboo trade-off phenomenon in § 4.3.
2. The title refers to the basement of the Roman Colosseum where the fallen and dying gladiators were dumped.
3. *Spoliarium* is often regarded as a metaphor for the treatment endured by the Philippines during the Spanish colonial period.
4. Humean moralism is a family of views whose influence may be traced back to Hume.

5. Alfred Eisenstaedt's (1928, printed 1980) *Marlene Dietrich, Anna May Wong, Leni Riefenstahl, Berlin* photo of these three women served as the inspiration for Koe's novel.

6. Koe's novel was shortlisted for the 2020 Singapore Literature Prize and won the 2017 Henfield Prize. These accolades suggest that aesthetic flaws are at a minimum with respect to *Delayed Rays of a Star*.

7. See Said (1979) for a critical account of how these Orientalist tropes both reflect the essentializing tendency of the West and produce a fabricated view of Oriental culture that is fitted for the purposes of Western imperialism.

8. In Western discourse, the prevailing view is that propaganda should not count as art. In Southeast Asia, on the other hand, modern art has regularly been used to communicate political messages and for political purposes. Nonetheless, there is a general consensus that propaganda is of a lower artistic value.

9. Recall from Chapter 4 that aesthetic cognitivism is the position according to which art gives its audience knowledge and the capacity of art to give its audience knowledge enhances its aesthetic value.

10. According to Pole, ethicism is compatible with formalism, since the immorality of an artwork is a type of internal incoherence and therefore a formal defect.

11. To expurgate is to have the objectionable or unsuitable matter removed.

12. Hotel Singapura is based on the historic 7th Storey Hotel that was demolished to make way for Bugis MRT.

Chapter 13

1. This Malay proverb (literally: 'Bit by bit, a mountain is built') may be translated into English as 'Mighty oaks from little acorns grow'. The proverb is incidentally also the title of an anthology of poems, edited and translated by Annaliza Bakri, about specific places in Singapore and what they mean to poets and the people who built the nation of Singapore.

Appendices

1. For convenience, I will omit mention of semantics.

Bibliography

Abdullah, S. (2012). The environment as a theme in Malaysian art. *JATI-Journal of Southeast Asian Studies, 17,* 261–80.

Abdullah, S., & Chung, A. K. (2014). Re-examining the objects of Mystical Reality. *JATI – Journal of Southeast Asian Studies, 19,* 203–17.

Adamson, P. (2015). *Philosophy in the Islamic world: A Very Short Introduction* (Vol. 445). Oxford University Press, USA.

Adamson, P., & Taylor, R. C. (2004). *The Cambridge Companion to Arabic Philosophy.* Cambridge University Press.

Arntzen, S., Itoˉ, M., et al. (2014). *The Sarashina Diary: A Woman's Life in Eleventh-Century Japan.* Columbia University Press.

Audi, R. (1999). *The Cambridge Dictionary of Philosophy.* Cambridge University Press.

Bachtiar, H. W. (1976). Raden Saleh: Aristocrat, painter & scientist. *Majalah Ilmu-Ilmu Sastra Indonesia/Indonesian Journal of Cultural Studies,* 31–79.

Bhushan, N., & Garfield, J. L. (2011). *Indian Philosophy in English: From Renaissance to Independence.* Oxford University Press.

Bin Samsuri, A. (2010). Degradation of natural rubber & synthetic elastomers. *Shreir's Corrosion, 3,* 2407–38.

Blumson, B. (2011). Depictive structure? *Philosophical Papers, 40*(1), 1–25. https://doi.org/10.1080/05568641.2011.560026

Boccia, M., Nemmi, F., Tizzani, E., Guariglia, C., Ferlazzo, F., Galati, G., & Giannini, A. (2015). Do you like Arcimboldo's? Esthetic appreciation modulates brain activity in solving perceptual ambiguity. *Behavioural Brain Research, 278,* 147–54.

Boden, M. (1994). Pr´ecis of *The Creative Mind: Myths & Mechanisms. Behavioral & Brain Sciences, 17*(3), 519–31.

Boden, M. (2004). *The Creative Mind: Myths & Mechanisms.* Routledge.

Brennan, C. (2001). Religion, cultural identity, & Kelantan's *dikir barat. The Australian Journal of Anthropology, 12*(3), 302–11.

Candee, H. C. (1924). *Angkor the Magnificent.* Frederick A. Stokes Co.

Cao, M. (2021). Ang ku kueh – significance, traditions, & its relevance today. Roots.gov.sg.https://www.roots.gov.sg/en/stories-landing/stories/Ang-Ku-Kueh-Significance-Traditions-And-Its-Relevance-Today/Ang-Ku-Kueh-Significance-Traditions-And-Its-Relevance-Today

Carroll, N. (1996). Moderate moralism. *The British Journal of Aesthetics, 36*(3), 223–39.

Carroll, N. (2001). *Beyond Aesthetics: Philosophical Essays.* Cambridge University Press.

Carroll, N. (2007). Literary realism, recognition, & the communication of knowledge. In J. Gibson, W. Huemer, & L. Pocci (eds), *A Sense of the World* (pp. 24–42). Routledge.

Chin, S. F. (2022). Exhibition to mark 80th anniversary of Singapore's oldest surviving dragon kiln. *The Straits Times.* https://www.straitstimes. com/singapore/exhibition-to-celebrate-80th-anniversary-of-singaporesoldest-surviving-dragon-kiln

Clark, J. (2010). *Asian Modernities: Chinese & Thai Art Compared, 1980 to 1999.* Power Publications.

Cleary, S. (2016). Chinese philosophy in the English-speaking world: Interview with Bryan Van Norden. *APA Blog, May, 17,* 2016.

Coe, C. L. (2019). Angkor Wat at sunrise. *JAMA Internal Medicine, 179*(1), 8.

Cœd'es, G. (1920). A propos de la date d''edification d'angkor vat. *Journal Asiatique, 15,* 96–100.

Cœd'es, G. (1940). La destination fun'eraire des grands monuments khm'ers. *Bulletin de l'Ecole fran¸caise d'Extreme-Orient', 40,* 315–49.

Cohen, H. (1988). How to draw three people in a botanical garden. *AAAI, 89,* 846–55.

Collingwood, R. G. (1938). *The Principles of Art.* New York: Oxford University Press.

Conrad, J. (1912). *A Personal Record: Some Reminiscences.* Doubleday, Page.

Costello, D. (2013). Kant & the problem of strong non-perceptual art. *British Journal of Aesthetics, 53*(3), 277–98.

Coxeter, H. S. M. (1957). Crystal symmetry & its generalizations. *Royal Society of Canada, 51,* 1–13.

Currie, G. (1989). *An Ontology of Art.* St. Martin's Press.

Currie, G. (1998). Realism of character & the value of fiction. In J. Levinson (ed.), *Aesthetics & Ethics: Essays at the Intersection* (pp. 161–81). Cambridge University Press.

Currie, G. (2020). *Imagining & Knowing: The Shape of Fiction.* Oxford University Press.

Davies, S. (2003). Ontology of art. In J. Levinson (ed.), *The Oxford Handbook of Aesthetics* (pp. 155–80). Oxford University Press.

Diamond, C. (1993). Martha Nussbaum & the need for novels. *Philosophical Investigations, 16*(2), 128–53. https://doi.org/10.1111/j.1467-9205.1993. tb00456.x

Dickie, G. (1996). *The Century of Taste: The Philosophical Odyssey of Taste in the Eighteenth Century.* Oxford University Press.

Diffey, T. J. (1995). What can we learn from art? *Australasian Journal of Philosophy, 73*(2), 204–11. https://doi.org/10.1080/00048409512346541

Dorter, K. (1990). Conceptual truth & aesthetic truth. *Journal of Aesthetics & Art Criticism, 48*(1), 37–51. https://doi.org/10.2307/431198

Dotson, K. (2012). How is this paper philosophy? *Comparative Philosophy, 3*(1), 3–29.

Drissen, E., & Landell, O. (1983). *Vastgelegd voor Later: Indische Fotos (1917–1942) van Thilly Weissenborn.* Amsterdam: Sijthoff.

du Chattel, F. J. v. R. (1930). *Mooi Indie: Afbeeldingen in kleuren van twaalf aquarellen.* Nederlandsche Boekenclub.

Dutton, D. (1979). Artistic crimes: The problem of forgery in the arts. *British Journal of Aesthetics, 19*(4), 302–14. https://doi.org/10.1093/bjaesthetics/19.4.302

Ernst, G., Steinbrenner, J., & Scholz, O. R. (2009). *From Logic to Art: Themes From Nelson Goodman.* Frankfurt: Ontos.

Feyerabend, P. (1987). Creativity: A dangerous myth. *Critical Inquiry, 13*(4), 700–11.

Fiske, A. P., & Tetlock, P. E. (1997). Taboo trade-offs: Reactions to transactions that transgress the spheres of justice. *Political Psychology, 18*(2), 255–97.

Fletcher, R., Evans, D., Pottier, C., & Rachna, C. (2015). Angkor Wat: An introduction. *Antiquity, 89*(348), 1388–401.

Flores, P. D. (2017). Art history & the contemporary in Southeast Asia. *Citation Deja Vu, 6,* 23–31.

Ganeri, J. (2014). *The Lost Age of Reason: Philosophy in Early Modern India 1450–1700.* Oxford University Press.

Ganson, T. (2009). The rational/non-rational distinction in Plato's Republic. *Oxford Studies in Ancient Philosophy, 36,* 179–97.

Gaut, B. (1998). The ethical criticism of art. In J. Levinson (ed.), *Aesthetics & ethics: Essays at the intersection* (pp. 182–203). Cambridge University Press.

Gaut, B. (2003a). Art & knowledge. *The Oxford Handbook of Aesthetics,* 436–50.

Gaut, B. (2003b). Creativity & imagination. In B. Gaut & P. Livingston (eds), *The creation of art: New essays in philosophical aesthetics* (pp. 148–73). Cambridge University Press.

Gaut, B., & Livingston, P. (2003). *The Creation of Art: New Essays in Philosophical Aesthetics.* Cambridge University Press.

Gendler, T. S. (2000). The puzzle of imaginative resistance. *Journal of Philosophy, 97*(2), 55–81. https://doi.org/jphil200097238

Glaize, M. (1944). *Les Monuments du Groupe d'Angkor.* Saigon: Portail.

Gombrich, E. H. (1961). *Art & illusion: A study in the psychology of pictorial representation.* Pantheon.

Goodlander, J. (2012). Rua bineda in Bali: Counterfeit justice in the trial of Nyoman Gunarsa. *Asian Theatre Journal, 29*(1), 316–19.

Goodman, N. (1968). *Languages of Art: An Approach to a Theory of Symbols*. Bobbs-Merrill.

Green, M. C., & Donahue, J. K. (2011). Persistence of belief change in the face of deception: The effect of factual stories revealed to be false. *Media Psychology, 14*(3), 312–31.

Gripaldo, R. M. (2000). *Filipino Philosophy: A Critical Bibliography*. Manila: De La Salle University Press.

Gripaldo, R. M. (2003). Is there a Filipino philosophy? *21st World Congress of Philosophy Proceedings*.

Guczalski, K. (2021). Nelson Goodman's Aesthetics – A Critique. *Arts, 10*(4), 84.

Guczalski, K. (2022). The density of symbol systems – A critique of Nelson Goodman's notion. *Philosophia, 50*(3), 1131–52. https://doi.org/10.1007/s11406-021-00449-w

Gupta, B. (2021). *An Introduction to Indian Philosophy: Perspectives on Reality, Knowledge, & Freedom*. Routledge.

Gutierrez, M. C. (1961). The Cebuano Balitao & how it mirrors Visayan culture & folklife. *Folklore Studies, 20*, 15–135.

Hampson, R. (1992). Two prototypes of betrayal: Almayer's folly. In *Joseph Conrad: Betrayal & Identity* (pp. 11–31). Springer.

Haslanger, S. (2006). What good are our intuitions: Philosophical analysis & social kinds. *Aristotelian Society Supplementary Volume, 80*(1), 89–118. https://doi.org/10.1111/j.1467-8349.2006.00139.x

Haslanger, S. (2012). *Resisting Reality: Social Construction & Social Critique*. New York, US: Oxford University Press.

Hidayat, F. (2015). On the struggle for recognition of Southeast Asian and regional philosophy.

Hintikka, J. (1962). *Knowledge & Belief: An Introduction to the Logic of the Two Notions*. Ithaca: Cornell University Press.

Holden, P. (2016). 'Is it manipulative? Sure. But that's how you tell stories': The graphic novel, metahistory & the artist in *The Art of Charlie Chan Hock Chye. Journal of Postcolonial Writing, 52*(4), 510–23.

Hongladarom, S. (1996). How is Thai philosophy possible? *The 6th International Conference on Thai Studies*.

Howard, V. (1971). *Harvard Project Zero: A Fresh Look at Art Education. Technical Report No. 1.* (tech. rep.). ERIC.

Huddleston, A. (2012). The conversation argument for actual intentionalism. *British Journal of Aesthetics, 52*(3), 241–56. https://doi.org/10.1093/aesthj/ays020

Hume, D. (1739). *A Treatise of Human Nature: Being an Attempt to Introduce the Experimental Method of Reasoning into Moral Subjects & Dialogues Concerning Natural Religion*. London, England: Printed for John Noon, at the White-Hart, Near Mercer's Chapel, in Cheapside.

Hume, D. (1757). Of the standard of taste. In *Four Dissertations* (pp. 203–40). A. Millar.

Igloria, L. (2007). The American period. In *World & Its Peoples: Eastern & Southern Asia (Malaysia, Singapore, Brunei & the Philippines)*. Marshall Cavendish.

Ingarden, R. (1961). Aesthetic experience & aesthetic object. *Philosophy & Phenomenological Research, 21*(3), 289–313.

Ingarden, R. (1986). *The Work of Music & the Problem of its Identity*. University of California Press.

Irvin, S. (2007). Forgery & the corruption of aesthetic understanding. *Canadian Journal of Philosophy, 37*(2), 283–304. https://doi.org/10.1353/cjp.2007.0016

Irwin, W. (1999). *Intentionalist Interpretation: A Philosophical Explanation & Defense*. Greenwood Press.

Itzin, C. (ed.). (1992). *Pornography: Women, Violence & Civil Liberties*. Oxford University Press.

Jacobson, D. (1997). In praise of immoral art. *Philosophical Topics, 25*(1), 155–99. https://doi.org/10.5840/philtopics199725123

Jannotta, A. (2014). Interpretation & conversation: A response to Huddleston. *British Journal of Aesthetics, 54*(3), 371–80. https://doi.org/10.1093/aesthj/ayu002

Jarvie, I. C. (1981). The rationality of creativity. In *The Concept of Creativity in Science & Art* (pp. 109–28). Springer.

Jenkins, K. (2016). Amelioration & inclusion: Gender identity & the concept of woman. *Ethics, 126*(2), 394–421. https://doi.org/10.1086/683535

Jenkins, R. (2010). *Rua Bineda in Bali: Counterfeit Justice in the Trial of Nyoman Gunarsa*. Indonesia Institute of the Arts.

John, E. (1998). Reading fiction & conceptual knowledge: Philosophical thought in literary context. *Journal of Aesthetics & Art Criticism, 56*(4), 331–48. https://doi.org/10.2307/432124

Kant, I. (1783). *Prolegomena to Any Future Metaphysics That Will Be Able to Present Itself as a Science*. Manchester University Press.

Kant, I. (1952). *Kant's Critique of Judgment* (J. C. Meredith, Trans.). Clarendon Press.

Kee, J. (2011). Introduction contemporary Southeast Asian art: The right kind of trouble. *Third Text, 25*(4), 371–81.

Kieran, M. (2001). In defence of the ethical evaluation of narrative art. *British Journal of Aesthetics, 41*(1), 26–38. https://doi.org/10.1093/bjaesthetics/41.1.26

Kieran, M. (2014). Creativity as a virtue of character. In E. S. Paul & S. B. Kaufman (eds), *The Philosophy of Creativity: New Essays* (pp. 125–44). Oxford University Press.

Kivy, P. (1997). *Philosophies of Arts: An Essay in Differences*. Cambridge University Press.

Korsmeyer, C. (1999). *Making Sense of Taste: Food & Philosophy*. Ithaca, NY: Cornell University Press.

Kraus, W., & Vogelsang, I. (2012). *Raden Saleh: The Beginning of Modern Indonesian Painting*. Goethe Institut.

Kulenkampff, J. (1990). The objectivity of taste: Hume & Kant. *Nouˆs*, 93–110.

Kulvicki, J. V. (2006). *On Images: Their Structure & Content*. Oxford University Press.

Lamarque, P., & Olsen, S. H. (1994). *Truth, Fiction, & Literature: A Philosophical Perspective*. Oxford University Press.

Leoˊn, E. D. (2020). Descriptive vs. ameliorative projects. In *Conceptual Engineering & Conceptual Ethics* (pp. 170–86). Oxford University Press.

Lessing, A. (1965). What is wrong with a forgery? *Journal of Aesthetics & Art Criticism, 23*(4), 461–71. https://doi.org/10.2307/427668

Levinson, J. (1996). *The Pleasures of Aesthetics: Philosophical Essays*. Cornell University Press.

Levinson, J. (2002). Hume's standard of taste: The real problem. *Journal of Aesthetics & Art Criticism, 60*(3), 227–38. https://doi.org/10.1111/1540-6245.00070

Levinson, J. (2016). *Aesthetic Pursuits: Essays in Philosophy of Art*. Oxford University Press.

Lewis, D. K. (1971). Analog & digital. *Nouˆs, 5*(3), 321–7. https://doi.org/10.2307/2214671

LeWitt, S. (1967). Paragraphs on conceptual art. *Artforum, 5*(10), 79–83.

Liao, S. (2021a). Bittersweet food. *Critica, 53*(157), 71–93. https://doi.org/10.22201/iifs.18704905e.2021.1246

Liao, S. (2021b). Diverse philosophies: (What) are they?: (What) do we want them to be? *The Philosophers' Magazine*, (93), 64–70.

Liao, S., & Meskin, A. (2018). Morality & aesthetics of food. In A. Barnhill, M. Budolfson, & T. Doggett (eds), *The Oxford Handbook on Food Ethics* (pp. 658–79). Oxford University Press.

Lim, C. (2015). The dragon kiln breathes. *Roots.gov.sg*. https://www.roots.gov.sg/stories-landing/stories/the-dragon-kiln-breathes-thowkwang-dragon-kiln/story

Lin, S. (2018). Art & interpretation. In B. J. & D. Fisher (eds), *The Internet Encyclopedia of Philosophy*.

Lippard, L. R. (1973). *Six Years: The Dematerialization of the Art Object from 1966 to 1972*. Praeger.

Livingston, P. (2005). *Art & Intention: A Philosophical Study*. Oxford University Press.

Lovelace, A. (1953). Notes on Menabrea's sketch of the analytical engine invented by Charles Babbage. In B. V. Bowden (ed.), *Faster Than Thought*. Pitman.

Low, Y. (2021). Phaptawan Suwannakudt's Akojorn (1995): Connecting Women. In *Iconic Works of Art by Feminists & Gender Activists* (pp. 223–35). Routledge.

MacKinnon, C. A. (1993). *Only Words*. Harvard University Press.

Maria Guerrero, L. (1974). *The First Filipino: A Biography of José Rizal*. Manila: National Historical Commission.

Matusky, P. (1985). An introduction to the major instruments & forms of traditional Malay music. *Asian Music, 16*(2), 121–82.

Maxwell, A. (2020). Thilly Weissenborn: Photographer of the Netherlands East Indies. *History of Photography, 44*(2-3), 128–50.

May Datuin, F. (2011). The grid & the nomadic line in the art of Phaptawan Suwannakudt. *Contemporary Aesthetics*, (3), 4.

McGinnis, J., & Reisman, D. C. (2007). *Classical Arabic Philosophy: An Anthology of Sources*. Hackett Publishing.

McKinnon Wood, R., & Masterman, M. (1968). Computer poetry from clru. *Cybernetic Serendipity: The Computer & the Arts*, 55–6.

Meskin, A. (2013). The art of food. *The Philosophers' Magazine, 61*(61), 81–6. https://doi.org/10.5840/tpm20136161

Meyer, L. B. (1956). *Emotion & Meaning in Music*. University of Chicago Press.

Moran, R. (1994). The expression of feeling in imagination. *Philosophical Review, 103*(1), 75–106. https://doi.org/10.2307/2185873

Mothersill, M. (1989). Hume & the paradox of taste. In G. Dickie (ed.), *Aesthetics: A Critical Anthology*. St. Martin's.

Nanay, B. (2014). An Experiential Account of Creativity. In E. Paul & S. B. Kaufman (eds), *The philosophy of creativity* (pp. 17–35). Oxford University Press.

Nelson, R. (2019). *Modern Art of Southeast Asia: Introductions from A to Z*. National Gallery Singapore.

Noor, F. A. (2010). Everything in its place: Reading batik as a marker of social-spatial relations. *BeMuse, 3*(4), 36–43.

Novitz, D. (2003). Explanations of creativity. In B. Gaut & P. Livingston (eds), *The Creation of Art: New Essays in Philosophical Aesthetics* (pp. 174–91). Cambridge University Press.

Nussbaum, M. C. (1990). *Love's Knowledge: Essays on Philosophy & Literature*. Oxford University Press.

Osman, S. M. b. S. (1998). Dikir barat *in Kelantan & Singapore: Looking beyond its superficiality* [Unpublished Honours thesis], National University of Singapore.

Pappas, N. (2012). Plato on poetry: Imitation or inspiration? *Philosophy Compass, 7*(10), 669–78.

Patke, R. (2012). Postcolonial literature in Southeast Asia. In A. Quayson (ed.), *The Cambridge History of Postcolonial Literature* (pp. 352–84). Cambridge University Press.

Paul, E. S., & Kaufman, S. B. (2014). *The Philosophy of Creativity*. Oxford University Press.

Perrett, R. W. (2016). *An Introduction to Indian Philosophy*. Cambridge University Press.

Pham, V. D. (2013). Some reflections on key orientations in philosophical research in Vietnam today. In W. Sweet, G. F. McLean, O. Blanchette, & W. Park (eds), *Philosophy Emerging from Culture*. Council for Research in Values; Philosophy.

Phillips, S. H. (1997). *Classical Indian Metaphysics: Refutations of Realism & the Emergence of New Logic*. Motilal Banarsidass Publ.

Phuong, T. K., & Lockhart, B. (2011). *The Cham of Vietnam: History, Society & Art*. NUS Press.

Pickup, L., & Zisserman, A. (2009). Automatic retrieval of visual continuity errors in movies. *Proceedings of the ACM International Conference on Image & Video Retrieval*, 1–8.

Pigliucci, M. (2006). On the pseudo-profundity of some Eastern philosophy. *Rationally Speaking*.

Pinder, M. (2022). Is Haslanger's ameliorative project a successful conceptual engineering project? *Synthese*, *200*(4), 1–22. https://doi.org/10.1007/s11229-022-03803-x

Piyadasa, R. (1981). The treatment of the local landscape in modern Malaysian art, 1930-1981. *Imagining Identities*, 26–51.

Piyadasa, R., & Esa, S. (1974). Towards a mystical reality: A documentation of jointly initiated experiences by Redza Piyadasa & Suleiman Esa.

Plato. (1914). *Phaedrus* (H. N. Fowler, Trans.). Loeb Classical Library.

Plato. (1925). *Ion* (W. R. M. Lamb, Trans.). Loeb Classical Library.

Plato. (1926). *Laws, Volume I Books 1-6* (R. G. Bury, Trans.). Loeb Classical Library.

Plato. (c. 375 B.C.E./1935). *The Republic Volume II Books 6-10* (P. Shorey, Trans.). Loeb Classical Library.

Prabhu, A. (2018). *The Sympathizer*: A Dialectical Reading. *PMLA*, *133*(2), 388–95.

Prabhu, J. (2001). Philosophy in an age of global encounter. *APA Newsletter on Asian & Asian American Philosophers & Philosophies*, *1*(1), 29–31.

Prentice, D. A., Gerrig, R. J., & Bailis, D. S. (1997). What readers bring to the processing of fictional texts. *Psychonomic Bulletin & Review*, *4*(3), 416–20.

Protschky, S. (2011). *Images of the Tropics: Environment & Visual Culture in Colonial Indonesia*. Brill.

Putnam, H. (1976). Literature, science, & reflection. *New Literary History*, *7*(3), 483–91.

Quito, E. (1983). *The State of Philosophy in the Philippines*. Manila: De La Salle University.

Quito, E. (1990). Volkgeist in vernacular literature. *A Life of Philosophy: Feschrift in Honor of Emerita Quito.*

Ricks, C. (1996). Literature & the matter of fact. *Essays in Appreciation*, 280–310.

Robinson, J. (1995). L'education sentimentale. *Australasian Journal of Philosophy, 73*(2), 212–26.

Robinson, J. (2000). Languages of art at the turn of the century. *Journal of Aesthetics & Art Criticism, 58*(3), 213–18. https://doi.org/10.2307/432102

Rohrbaugh, G. (2013). The ontology of art. In B. Gaut & D. Lopes (eds), *Routledge Companion to Aesthetics* (pp. 235–45). Routledge.

Rowe, M. W. (1997). Lamarque & Olsen on literature & truth. *The Philosophical Quarterly, 47*(188), 322–41.

Rowe, M. W. (1999). The objectivity of aesthetic judgements. *British Journal of Aesthetics, 39*(1), 40–52. https://doi.org/10.1093/bjaesthetics/39.1.40

Runco, M. A., & Jaeger, G. J. (2012). The standard definition of creativity. *Creativity Research Journal, 24*(1), 92–6.

Sabapathy, T. K. (1979). The Nanyang artists: Some general remarks. In *Intersections, innovations, institutions: A reader in Singapore modern art* (pp. 166–76). World Scientific.

Sabapathy, T. K. (ed.). (1994). *Vision & idea: Relooking modern Malaysian art.* National Art Gallery.

Sabapathy, T. K. (2018). *Writing the Modern: Selected Texts on Art & Art History in Singapore, Malaysia & Southeast Asia, 1973–2015.* NUS Press.

Said, E. W. (1979). *Orientalism.* Vintage.

Sartre, J.-P. (1966). *The Psychology of Imagination* (B. Frechtman, Trans.). New York: Washington Square Press.

Sellars, W. (1962). Philosophy & the scientific image of man. In R. Colodny (ed.), *Science, Perception, & Reality* (pp. 35–78). Humanities Press/Ridgeview.

Shelley, J. (1994). Hume's double standard of taste. *Journal of Aesthetics & Art Criticism, 52*(4), 437–45. https://doi.org/10.2307/432031

Shelley, J. (2003). The problem of non-perceptual art. *The British Journal of Aesthetics, 43*(4), 363–78.

Singh, K. (1998). *Interlogue: Studies in Singapore Literature* (Vol. 8). Ethos Books.

Sinhababu, N. (2017). Desire & aesthetic pleasure. *Australasian Philosophical Review, 1*(1), 95–9. https://doi.org/10.1080/24740500.2017.1296396

Stecker, R. (2006). Moderate actual intentionalism defended. *Journal of Aesthetics & Art Criticism, 64*(4), 429–38. https://doi.org/10.1111/j.1540-594x.2006.00221.x

Stecker, R., & Davies, S. (2010). The hypothetical intentionalist's dilemma: A reply to Levinson. *British Journal of Aesthetics, 50*(3), 307–12. https://doi.org/10.1093/aesthj/ayq022

Stokes, D. (2011). Minimally creative thought. *Metaphilosophy*, 42(5), 658–81.

Stokes, D. (2014). The role of imagination in creativity. In B. Gaut & P. Livingston (eds), *The Creation of Art: New Essays in Philosophical Aesthetics* (pp. 157–84). Oxford University Press.

Stolnitz, J. (1992). On the cognitive triviality of art. *British Journal of Aesthetics*, 32(3), 191–200. https://doi.org/10.1093/bjaesthetics/32.3. 191

Streitfeld, D. (2016). For Viet Thanh Nguyen, Author of 'The Sympathizer,' a Pulitzer but No Peace. *New York Times*.

Sudjojono, S. (1939). Kesenian meloekis di Indonesia: Sekarang and jang akan datang. *Keboedajaan dan Masjarakat*.

Suwannakudt, P. (2007). Merpeople in a man's land: The comfort zone of awkwardness in which we dwell. *Ctrl + Pdf Journal of Contemporary Art*, 6, 3–6.

Tabios, E. R. (2014). *44 RESURRECTIONS*. PostModernPoetry E-Ratio Editions.

Tabios, E. R. (2015a). *DUENDE IN THE ALLEYS*. Swirl Editions.

Tabios, E. R. (2015b). *I FORGOT LIGHT BURNS*. Moria Books.

Tabios, E. R. (2016a). *AMNESIA: Somebody's Memoir*. Black Radish Books.

Tabios, E. R. (2016b). *EXCAVATING THE FILIPINO IN ME*. Tinfish Press.

Tabios, E. R. (2016c). *THE CONNOISSEUR OF ALLEYS*. Marsh Hawk Press.

Tabios, E. R. (2016d). *THE OPPOSITE OF CLAUSTROPHOBIA: Prime's Anti-Autobiography*. Knives, Forks & Spoons Press.

Tabios, E. R. (2017). *WHAT SHIVERING MONKS COMPREHEND*. Locofo Chaps.

Tabios, E. R. (2018a). *HIRAETH: Tercets from the Last Archipelago*. Knives, Forks & Spoons Press.

Tabios, E. R. (2018b). *MURDER DEATH RESURRECTION: A Poetry Generator*. Dos Madres Press.

Taylor, N. (2000). *Studies in Southeast Asian Art: Essays in Honor of Stanley J. O'Connor* (Vol. 29). SEAP Publications.

Telfer, E. (1996). *Food for Thought: Philosophy & Food*. Routledge.

Tetlock, P. E., Kristel, O. V., Elson, S. B., Green, M. C., & Lerner, J. S. (2000). The psychology of the unthinkable: Taboo trade-offs, forbidden base rates, & heretical counterfactuals. *Journal of Personality & Social Psychology*, 78(5), 853.

Thomasson, A. L. (2004). The ontology of art. In P. Kivy (ed.), *The Blackwell Guide to Aesthetics* (pp. 78–92). Blackwell.

Thompson, A. (2022). 'She engages us with a steady, cool look': Creating the Field of Southeast Asian Art. *Art History*, 45(2), 394–404.

Thumboo, E. (1993). *A Third Map: New & Selected Poems*. UniPress, Centre for the Arts, National University of Singapore.

Tolhurst, W. E. (1979). On what a text is & how it means. *British Journal of Aesthetics*, 19(1), 3–14. https://doi.org/10.1093/bjaesthetics/19.1.3

Torczyner, H. (1977). *Magritte: Ideas & Images* (R. Miller, Trans.). H. N. Abrams.

Tormey, J. F., & Tormey, A. (1983). Art & ambiguity. *Leonardo*, 183–7.

Tran, V. D. (2008). Globalization & the emergence of philosophy in Southeast Asia. *Philosophy, Culture, & Traditions*, 5, 31–46.

Turing, A. M. (1950). Computing machinery & intelligence. *Mind*, 59(October), 433–60. https://doi.org/10.1093/mind/LIX.236.433

Uchida, E., Ogawa, Y., & Nakagawa, T. (1998). The stone materials of the Angkor monuments, Cambodia. The magnetic susceptibility & the orientation of the bedding plane of the sandstone. *Journal of Mineralogy, Petrology & Economic Geology*, 93(11), 411–26.

UN. (1948). Convention on the Prevention & Punishment of the Crime of Genocide. *United Nations, Treaty Series*, 78, 277. https://www. un.org/en/ genocideprevention/documents/atrocity-crimes/Doc. 1 Convention%20 on%20the%20Prevention%20and%20Punishment% 20of%20the%20 Crime%20of%20Genocide.pdf

Villa, J. G. (2008). *Doveglion: Collected Poems* (J. E. Cowen, ed.). Penguin.

Walsh, D. (1969). *Literature & Knowledge*. Middletown, Conn., Wesleyan University Press.

Walton, K. L. (1970). Categories of art. *Philosophical Review*, 79(3), 334–67. https://doi.org/10.2307/2183933

Walton, K. L. (1990). *Mimesis as Make-believe: On the Foundations of the Representational Arts*. Harvard University Press.

Walton, K. L. (1994). Morals in fiction & fictional morality (i). *Proceedings of the Aristotelian Society*, 68, 27–50. https://doi.org/10.2307/4107022

Waytz, A. (2010). The psychology of the taboo trade-off. *Scientific American*.

Wee, C. J. W.-l. (2010). 'We Asians?' Modernity, Visual Art Exhibitions, & East Asia. *boundary 2*, 37(1), 91–126.

Weisberg, R. (1993). *Creativity: Beyond the Myth of Genius*. WH Freeman.

Weisberg, R. (2015). On the usefulness of 'value' in the definition of creativity. *Creativity Research Journal*, 27(2), 111–24.

Weitz, M. (1956). The role of theory in aesthetics. *The Journal of Aesthetics & Art Criticism*, 15(1), 27–35.

West, C. (2021). Pornography & censorship (E. N. Zalta, ed.). *The Stanford Encyclopedia of Philosophy*.

Wheeler, C., Green, M. C., & Brock, T. C. (1999). Fictional narratives change beliefs: Replications of Prentice, Gerrig, and Bailis (1997) with mixed corroboration. *Psychonomic Bulletin & Review*, 6(1), 136–41.

Whiteman, S. H., Abdullah, S., Low, Y., & Scott, P. (2018). *Ambitious Alignments: New Histories of Southeast Asian Art, 1945–1990*. Power Publications.

Wiggins, G. A. (2008). Computer models of musical creativity: A review of computer models of musical creativity by David Cope. *Literary & Linguistic Computing*, 23(1), 109–16.

Wimsatt, W. K., & Beardsley, M. C. (1946). The intentional fallacy. *The Sewanee Review, 54*(3), 468–88.

Wollheim, R. (1980). *Art & Its Objects*. Cambridge University Press.

Wolterstorff, N. (1980). *Works & Worlds of Art*. Oxford University Press.

Wood, P. (2002). *Conceptual Art*. Tate.

y Gasset, J. O. (2000). *Meditations on Quixote*. University of Illinois Press.

Zeimbekis, J. (2012). Digital pictures, sampling, & vagueness: The ontology of digital pictures. *Journal of Aesthetics & Art Criticism, 70*(1), 43–53. https://doi.org/10.1111/j.1540-6245.2011.01497.x

Zeimbekis, J. (2015). Why digital pictures are not notational representations. *Journal of Aesthetics & Art Criticism, 73*(4), 449–53. https://doi.org/10.1111/jaac.12203

Index

References to footnotes are indicated by 'n.'